CAPTAIN FOR LIFE

CAPTAIN FOR LIFE

My Story as a Hall of Fame Linebacker

HARRY CARSON

ST. MARTIN'S PRESS ≈ NEW YORK

www.stmartins.com

Library of Congress Cataloging-in-Publication Data

Carson, Harry.
  Captain for life : my story as a Hall of Fame linebacker / Harry Carson.—1st ed.
    p. cm.
  ISBN 978-0-312-55062-2 (hardback)
1. Carson, Harry. 2. Football players—United States—Biography. 3. African American football players—Biography. I. Title.
  GV939.C375A3 2011
  796.332092—dc23
  [B]   2011019799

ISBN 978-0-312-55062-2

First Edition: September 2011

10 9 8 7 6 5 4 3 2 1

To

My wife, Maribel, for your unconditional love and support
Three of the best people I know, my children, Aja, Donald, and Lucky
My "Puddin," Jamison and my "Package," Kellen
And my "lifetime cheering section" (my family)
Momma and Daddy
Sonny, Ruth, Louise, Loretta & Ronnie

My other family . . .
All the coaches and players I played with at
The Florence Boys Club
Wilson and McClenaghan High Schools
South Carolina State University
The New York Football Giants
and
Every football player who has played the game and
carries the residual pain and effects of the game
but no longer has the voice to express himself
to others in that regard.

CONTENTS

PREFACE

This . . . is *my* living testimony! It is a testimony for the world but, more important a testimony for my family and loved ones to get a fuller and better understanding of who I am and who I was.

I genuinely feel as passionate about few things as my natural family, but if there is one thing, it is my extended football family. The passion I feel is not about the games per se but for those who take on the challenge of playing the sport on any level. I have respect for every player I took the field with, from my very first game to the final whistle of my last game. Every player I played with and every coach who coached me gave me a part of his life. My deep, abiding passion for them drives me to give back to them either as an advocate or a representative to enrich their lives in some way. I share a part of me with others I may never know because my mission now that I'm older is to provide "full disclosure" as I see it to those who wonder what sacrifices it takes to get to the top of the football profession and what might come later in their lives.

I played football on the highest level but I never considered myself to be "a football star." Football was what I did, it was never who I was. Playing on the highest level was never my goal; instead, it was something I fell into. My teammates always knew I stood shoulder to shoulder with them and never put myself above them. While I was trained by coaches to be a player, I never lost track that I was educated by great teachers to be an educator. The educator side of me has always felt a need to share my experiences not only as an athlete but as a living subject in a silent epidemic many other football players and athletes in other contact sports might deal with—the effects of traumatic brain injuries. As an active player, I sustained concussions on the field of play. Now as a former player, and far removed from the scene, I am in a unique position as I live my life with the physical aches and pains as well as neurological issues few people ever thought of until now.

With the increase in artificial-turf fields this may no longer be the case, but as I was growing up, almost every young boy who played or attempted to play football was familiar with the scent of freshly cut grass. This scent comes to my mind when I reflect on my football beginnings. Other things jog my memory, too, such as the intense heat and humidity of July and August practice days. Or the pungent scent of the men's locker room filled with discarded sweat-stained T-shirts, football jerseys, and jockstraps. But above all else, before the locker room, before actually stepping foot on the field, the smell of cut grass signals to me that it's time to strap on the pads, fasten the chin strap, and play football.

Every year hundreds of thousands of young boys decide to play football. Whether it's Pop Warner, grade school, junior high, or regular high school teams, they all decide to be football players. Regardless of what level in which they begin, the experiences of football are the same: the excitement of taking the field for the first time with their teammates, the screams and shouts of the coach with his whistle at the ready. For most, from a sports standpoint, it is the first time they are subjected to commands from anyone other than their own parents. And just as young boys strive to please their parents, they also strive to please their coaches. Unfortunately, the players and their parents may not fully understand the neurological risks they might be taking.

My story is just one of many millions of football players', but it is unique. Why? you ask. Because it is mine, and while similar experiences are shared by many, no two journeys are completely the same. This is my journey and my testimony from my very first steps on the football field, through my years of playing the game, to my life after the cheering stopped.

CAPTAIN FOR LIFE

CHAPTER 1

Mama's Boy

Every journey has to start somewhere, and mine begins at 404 South John Street, Florence, South Carolina. It is my foundation. It's etched in my mind as *my home,* even though I was not born there. I was actually born up the street in the next block but was too young when I left there to have any real memories of that house. No hospital for me; I was born at home, which was probably the case for most black children during that time, on November 26, 1953. Midwife Ola Jones delivered me, and since I weighed ten and a half pounds, it was a good bet that I would be the last of six children for my mother. My mama, Gladys Carson, was my rock! Yes, I was a mama's boy, but then again I was everybody's baby boy.

One of my first memories was the joy I got when Mama changed the linen on the beds. Whenever she and one of my three sisters made the beds, they would wrap me up in the sheets and swing me around and from side to side. I can clearly remember my laughter and excitement as I begged them, "Do it again, do it again," as they played with me in the bedroom. My sister Loretta, whom we affectionately called Rhettie, was my interpreter and my "gofer." I'm not embarrassed to say that I was on the bottle and seldom talked until I reached age four. Whenever I wanted something, I would simply point and mumble with the bottle in my mouth, and Rhettie would decipher what I was trying to say and get whatever I wanted. As I grew, I realized that she was the "family en-forcer," and I thought she was fearless. She was the shortest and smallest in the family, but if anyone bothered me or my brother Ronnie, she had no problem with beating up that person for us.

While 404 South John Street was the first home I knew, it and other homes like it in my neighborhood made up what others would call our "village." Many people refer to the old African proverb that "it takes a village to raise a child." My home was my entire neighborhood, where I felt safe. It was nothing for a kid like me to stray away from home and walk next door or down the street because my hood was a safe haven where everybody knew one another. While we may not have all gotten along or seen eye to eye all of the time, the neighbors were like my extended family. As people walked by our house, they would stop and spend a few moments talking to my mama. "Hey, Gladys, how you doin' today?" Usu-ally the conversation centered on their health or a program at the church, and then they'd say, "Girl, that boy of yours sho is gitten' big!" Or they would refer to the gray patch in my hair. I was born with a gray patch about the size of a silver dollar on the top right side of my head. Most people said that I was "born for good luck" because of that. It made me a little different from all the other kids. The point is, people stopped, talked, and took an interest in one another. We were poor, but like many people back then we didn't know we were poor. It simply was the way that it was!

Overall I was a happy kid, but I was devastated when I learned that my mother had to leave my family to help provide for us. At the time I didn't know what financial hardships we had, but eventually she left Florence, South Carolina, and relocated to Newark, New Jersey, where she began working as a domestic, cleaning and maintaining homes. Many black women worked as domestics during those days because their options were limited. My mama's leaving had nothing to do with her relationship with my father or with us. But with only an eighth-grade education and making little money as a cook at the Florence country club, she thought that she could do better, as many other blacks did during that time, by migrating to the North.

She told me many things that I've played back in my mind for years and years. I will always remember one of the simple things she shared with me before she left. I was with her in the kitchen as she listened to gospel music on the radio, to Mahalia Jackson, one of her favorite gospel singers. As she was cooking, I noticed she'd started to cry and I asked, "Mama, why are you crying?" She looked at me with those tears in her eyes and said, "Baby, learn how to take care of yourself." She didn't explain why she wanted me to do that, and as a five- or six-year-old kid I didn't understand why she was telling me, but over time it began to make sense. I was saddened to lose the everyday presence of my mother, and in retrospect, I realized leaving the family was probably one of the hardest things she ever had to do. Back then, where I lived, black women never left their children unless it was totally necessary.

Before she left, I remember she asked my oldest sister, Ruth, to take me to Holmes School for enrollment. I'll never forget that, as we were walking out of the house, Mama said, "Make sure you get Don Don into Mrs. Washington's class!" (Don Don was what everybody called me.) I didn't really want to go to school because I enjoyed playing by myself on those days when everybody else was either in school or working. But since I had to go to school, I wondered who this Mrs. Washington was. Apparently she was the first-grade teacher who'd taught all of my siblings. I thought if she was good enough for my brothers and sisters, then she was good enough for me. Once I was enrolled and started going to school, I realized that while she was small in stature, Mrs. Washington was a tough disciplinarian who wanted the very best not only for her students but for all of the students who attended Holmes School.

Mrs. Washington had a view of the world that at my young age I had never known. She was smart and patient with her students. She was tough, but she clearly loved all of her students as if we were her children. In those days, corporal punishment was a given. If you misbehaved, you were either going to get a whack with a strap from her or from Mr. Miller, the principal of Holmes School. At times she would leave the classroom and say, "I want everyone to stay quiet. If anyone is caught talking, then when I come back, the whole class will get a whipping." Wouldn't you know it, some smart-ass kid (sometimes me) would not keep his mouth shut, and when she returned, she would catch us making noise. So out would come the strap to dish out some Flora Washington discipline. The strap was either a skinny fan belt from a car engine or a strap like barbers used to sharpen razors. When it came to class punishment, nobody was exempt, and I mean nobody! The good kids and the bad kids, the boys and the girls, everybody shared in the misery, one lick to the hand. At that point I realized what being macho was all about! Who was going to cry and who was not? Many of the guys took the lick and put on a strong face as if to say, "I'm not going to cry." The girls . . . well, the girls were another story. Some of them started to cry before they were even struck. I was one of those guys who refused to cry. I never liked getting a whipping whether it was at school or at home. Although I might have had tears in my eyes when I got whipped at school, I would not allow those tears to fall because I refused to let others see me cry. I was never a bad kid in the classroom, but I got caught up in stuff that other kids brought to the table. Unfortunately we all were in the same boat. Whether you were a good kid or one of those badass kids, if one person screwed up, we all paid the price. I never really thought about it, but this was probably the first semblance of being a part of a team; we were all in it together.

Mrs. Washington's students were known for their excellent penmanship, and to this day, others who were in Mrs. Washington's first-grade class with me write with the same distinct style. She, along with other teachers of her generation, loved teaching. They were strict but cared about our growth and development. Those teachers were sort of an extension of the family because if they had to discipline you for a really bad reason, they would make sure they told your parents, and once that was done, you got both barrels. You got a whipping at school and then another at home by your parents. It was, in a way, similar in the neighborhood. If you got caught messing up in the street, it was not unusual to get spanked by a neighbor, who would then take you home, where you'd get another from your parents.

Mrs. Washington was not alone in her quest to get the most out of her students. All of the teachers in that system knew their responsibility was to prepare these little black kids to meet head-on what the world was going to offer or throw at us. Beyond the first grade I had other committed teachers, such as Mrs. Smalls and Mrs. Harrell, who effectively got their points across. Throughout my elementary-school years I had most of the teachers my brothers and sisters had. All of the teachers at Holmes Elementary School were cut from the same cloth: they worked hard to educate us and prepare us with a solid foundation to build on.

From the very first day I stepped foot in Mrs. Washington's classroom, it was always stressed to all of us to take pride in ourselves and where we came from. I learned to read, write, and do my math in the classrooms, but the very basic and fundamental lesson of taking pride in ourselves was also learned at Holmes School. Those words of influence were indelibly etched in my brain and on my soul so long ago. Those teachers and the staff at Holmes School knew better than us that we would in time go in many directions, but wherever we went, we would eventually come back, and when we did, they could take pride in whatever we'd accomplished. I could always sense the pride the teachers felt when their former students who were now successful adults would come back to say hello and to thank them for teaching them and influencing their lives.

As I grew older, I started spending more time being active with friends. When playing sports with other kids in my neighborhood, I was often overlooked because I was too small or because I just wasn't good enough. I remember the hurt and disappointment I felt at being left out of the games, at being only a spectator. In most cases the guys chosen were bigger and better. In those days I was not the most agile guy when it came to sports. Okay, to be completely honest, I was clumsy! When it came to God's giving out talent, I was probably at the end of that line. But as time went by and I grew bigger, I became a bit more athletic and progressed from being a player who might not have been chosen at all to one who would usually be one of the top picks among the sandlot teams.

On those days when we competed in the neighborhood, we sometimes wore T-shirts. I recall using black shoe polish to write the number of my favorite player on mine. At that time that was either #87, Willie Davis, a defensive end with the Green Bay Packers, or #86, Buck Buchanan, a defensive tackle with the Kansas City Chiefs. I focused on those guys when I watched football games on television. Like everybody else I watched the more skilled players in games, but I thought that if I was ever going to play football on some higher level, it would be as a lineman. I knew I didn't have the skills of a running back because I wasn't fast enough. I didn't have the arm to be a quarterback, nor did I have the grace, speed, or sure hands of a wide receiver. So there I was on the "make-believe" pro teams, playing the biggest games, trying to emulate my favorite players.

I developed many friendships through those days of playing sandlot football. Whether it was playing at St. Anne's Church or Levy Park, playing in pickup basketball games or spending time in the wading pool, it was always good to get together with friends to just hang out. I would watch some of the guys who were much older than me play in organized baseball games at Levy. Sitting in the stands I saw fans rooting them on and enjoying the game regardless of who won or lost. At times I would think to myself, "One day I'm gonna be out on that field and everybody will be cheering for me!" I thought it would be fun and exciting to hit a home run or strike out a batter in front of all those people at the park. It was a good feeling to be a part of that community where everybody knew one another and just had fun on a Saturday or Sunday afternoon. Some of those players who played at Levy Park, some of the other parks in Florence, or at the local black high school became role models for me. I had no clue as to what type of people they were outside of sports, but I admired their will to compete before so many people.

One thing stands out from a high school game I went to when I was in the seventh grade. At the end of the game, I remember standing next to the gate watching the players walk off the field. Some of the players were dirty, some were sweaty, some were bloodied, and some were just downright stinky. No matter how funky those players were after the games, all the pretty girls seemed to flock to them. I remember thinking, "Damn, I wanna be a part of that!"

CHAPTER 2

If at First You Don't Succeed . . .

By the time I made it to junior high, I thought I had progressed to being a decent athlete, but I was not a big badass dude on the school grounds. In one specific incident, and I don't even remember what caused it, something happened between another guy and me at school. Some misunderstanding was blown out of proportion. I clearly remember that he told me that he was going to see me at recess and "kick your ass!" This guy was a really hardened dude who you just knew could punch your lights out without much of a problem. Several of my friends and classmates wondered what I was going to do? I didn't know exactly because I had never been in a situation like that before, but I was afraid of what might happen. While I had grown to be a little bigger than most of the other male students, I was not violent and was never one to pick fights with anyone.

Usually when fights occurred around school, especially toward the end of the school year, everybody wanted to see what was going to happen. I never thought I would be called out to fight or even to have to defend myself. As lunchtime drew near, I remember the panic I felt deep in the pit of my stomach. Why me? By this time it seemed as if everybody in school knew what was going to take place. One or two of my buddies were trying to give me support, but ultimately what was going to happen was all on me. Nobody else was going to help me fight my battle.

When the bell rang for lunch, I saw a crowd had gathered in the school yard waiting for me to arrive, and the guy who wanted to fight me was already there. I had no choice; I had to show up. As I approached the group, I kept thinking, "This cannot be happening, this cannot be happening to me." I had known of fights where someone pulled a knife or razor blade and cut the other person even in a school yard. I was also aware that someone had shot a student who drove a school bus during a fight. I knew I did not want to be a casualty or a statistic. So, as this guy put his hands up assuming a fighting stance, I bolted. Yes, I ran, and as I ran, I could hear the kids laugh and call me a "punk." The guy who wanted to fight me did not run after me; I think he was relieved that I took off. After threatening me, I think he might have realized that fighting me was the wrong thing to do. After all, we would both have been suspended from school for fighting. But I wasn't really worried about him; I was only concerned about my own well-being.

My attitude was "piss on the sticks-and-stones thing, no words from anyone will ever hurt me." I realized from that one experience that I was not about violence and I was not a hardened tough guy as some people might have thought. Some people looked at me and, purely because I was this big, burly black guy, assumed that I was a tough guy. But I never portrayed myself as a hard-nosed motherfucker; I was very much a mama's boy. I wasn't looking for a fight to hurt this guy or anyone else, and I certainly didn't want to get hurt myself.

I went through a growth spurt between seventh and eighth grade and got much bigger than I was when I first arrived at junior high school. The spurt may have been a result of my spending my summers in New Jersey with my mother. Her cooking was always the best I had ever eaten. Some of my friends and I talked about trying out for the high school football team when we became eligible to do so as ninth graders. I felt I could physically hold my own on the school yard and playground so I decided to go out for the football team as a freshman with several of my buddies.

When I arrived at Wilson High School on the first day of football practice, the janitor had just used a tractor to trim the field. The scent of freshly cut grass signaled the start of football season. I walked into the equipment room and joined the other guys who were there to pick up their gear. I tried to act cool as if getting real equipment were no big deal, but it was to me! It's difficult to explain my joy and excitement at getting that helmet and those shoulder pads. For years I had seen professional and college players on television wearing their uniforms, and I wanted to be a part of that. I placed my equipment in one of the lockers, but I knew I was going to take it home and bring it back for practice the next day.

That first day was not about working on the practice field; it was about getting physicals to be certain that we were in condition to practice the next day, and about picking up the equipment to make sure it was a comfortable fit. I had never held a real football helmet in my hands before, it was so heavy! My football pants and knee and thigh pads were nowhere near as exciting as my shoulder pads and helmet. I remember walking home with the equipment and people asking me, "Are you a football player?" Just being asked gave me a reason to stick out my chest, and I proudly answered, "Yes." I went out of my way walking home so that as many people as possible could see me and my equipment and know that I was a football player. When I got home, that helmet was like a new toy; I could not put it down and I kept trying it on to see how it looked on me in the mirror. I think I would have slept in it if I could have.

The next day was the first official day on the field for practice. Normally football practices start a week or two before the beginning of school. I had my jockstrap on, and since I had never had one before, it felt a little awkward. I put my pants on with the knee and thigh pads in, then my shoulder pads with my practice jersey over it. I held my helmet under my arm, ready to practice. I went into the restroom and looked at myself in the mirror and felt good at what I saw.

Because of a little rain shower prior to the beginning of practice, we waited right inside the locker room until it was time to hit the field. As I stood inside the doorway, one thing stood out above anything else. The nervousness of doing something new was on most everyone's mind, but I was thinking of the scent that permeated the air, that smell of the grass that was cut the day before. When the rain subsided, we all started our walk toward the field, and as each man took a step, no one talked. Everything went quiet, with the exception of the sound of metal cleats hitting the pavement, click clack, click clack. Once at the field, we awaited the whistle that would signal the beginning of practice. I had never had any type of formal or organized training in any sport so I didn't know what to expect. The players were silent as if to conserve their energy and clear their heads of everything except football. Once the whistle was blown, all of the players jogged onto the field, and most of us first-timers took our lead from the veteran players, who knew the drills from the previous season.

For the first time, as I was decked out in that practice uniform, coaches were yelling and barking out commands for us to perform. They were excited just to get us on the field to see what we could do. I looked around to make sure I was keeping up with everyone and to familiarize myself with this new routine that I'd signed up for. The rain had stopped but the field was still wet as we stretched for a few minutes in the hot August humidity. After that we did push-ups and then sit-ups, and we finished by doing jumping jacks. I'd never realized that you had to do all of this preliminary stuff just to get to the part about running plays. After we loosened up, we broke into smaller groups to run at a full sprint to our position coaches. I'd chosen to be a defensive lineman after the two players I admired from the NFL, Willie Davis and Buck Buchanan.

Our first drill as linemen was the monkey roll. This drill is designed to test both a player's agility and his ability to work together in a group. It starts off with three players on their hands and knees parallel to one another. On the signal or whistle by the coach, the player in the center jumps over the man on the right as he drops and rolls under the center man, then the man on the left jumps over the center man. It continues until the whistle is blown to stop. As a new player I had to first observe from the back of the line. When it was my turn to go, my group screwed up the drill, which caused the coach to yell and scream at us. We had to keep going until we got the drill right. That was my first understanding of what "doing it right the first time" meant. We then had to do grass drills; for those who have never played the game, they are called cutaways. You run in place and move back and forth on the command of the coach. When he blows the whistle, you hit the ground, assume a prone position, and then bounce back up into a running position as fast as possible. Again, if you screwed up, you had to do the drill until you got it right.

From that drill we went on to tackling drills. Tackling is a fundamental for defensive football players. If you can't tackle, or if you are afraid to hit someone, you cannot play defense! Defensive players have to want to tackle; no, I take that back, they have to love to hit people! More precisely, they have to want to make the hits on ball carriers. At first we practiced tackling another defensive player by walking at a slow pace to learn how to make a perfect tackle. Then we increased the speed as we approached the ball carrier, placed our head across his chest, then wrapped our arms around him, driving him back to make a good tackle. As you know by now, if we did not do the drill right the first time, it had to be done over and over and over.

After those drills we went on to hitting and tackling an eight-man sled. Then I started to better understand something that I'd learned in Mr. Green's eighth-grade physical science class: the laws of physics by Sir Isaac Newton. "For every action there is an equal and opposite reaction." I hit the padding on the sled full speed and realized that it was not quite as easy as it appeared. When hitting it, you have to hit it with force and authority, otherwise it would spring back and knock you on your ass—something I discovered quite by accident. We had gone through all of the exercises and then the grass drills, and I could feel my body getting fatigued. When I hit the sled, I did not have any energy behind my blows and was rudely knocked back by the sled. The coach laughed, as did most of the other players, as they watched me pick my ass up after being blasted by a sled. I barely made it through that phase of practice and didn't know how much energy I had left.

The next drill proved to be the final nail in my coffin. I had to go one-on-one in a drill with one of the best players on the team. The coach knew I had good size, but I assume he wanted to see if I had any heart. Having heart or the will to compete and win is what all coaches want in their players. You can have all the size, speed, and quickness you want, but if you don't have heart, it doesn't matter, you're just another player. Coaches such as William Long knew how to separate the men from the boys by pressing certain buttons to see how a player would respond. With me, he pushed the toughness button. Having to compete against a player nicknamed Bubble Gum in a blocking and tackling drill pushed me to, and then beyond, my limits. Bubble Gum was an experienced guy who knew so much more than me as a player and was also much harder and tougher than I was. As he came off the ball to block me, I could do little to defend myself. My legs were like rubber from all of the other drills we'd run before that one. He must have blocked me three or four times, and with each block I felt like a rag doll being chewed up by a pit bull.

By this time I knew I was in the wrong place! I was unable to make it through the rest of practice and had to sit it out. Coach Long was pissed because I had not shown up for practice ready to compete. He made it known to everyone that in order to play you had to be physically ready and tough! While he didn't speak directly to me, I might as well have been the only person on the field.

After practice, feeling beaten, battered, embarrassed, and humiliated, I turned in my equipment. It was the first time of any importance in my life that I quit something on my own volition. I didn't think about it at the time, but afterward I realized that by giving up I would be embarrassed to go to school and hang out with some of the same guys I tried out with for the team. I had gone through this growth spurt and thought I, more than any of the other guys, should have been able to stick it out and make it. I felt like a big-time loser as soon as I decided to quit. I think being a soft mama's boy, being somewhat impulsive and a bit stubborn, all played key roles in my decision. I had just been laughed at by the coach and some of the other players. I knew I was making a mistake quitting, but I was just too embarrassed to ask for another chance with Coach Long. My inner pride did not allow me to do so. I decided to go on about my business, maintain a low profile, and wait for another opportunity, perhaps the next year.

Because I lived across town and didn't have access to a car, I had to make the long trek home from school on foot. As I began that long walk, I had the time to think about what I had gone through in practice. Making my way home, I felt a need to take a different route from the one I took the day before when I was so proud to show everybody that I was a football player. Ironically my detour took me past a field where another football team was practicing. The Florence Boys Club was having football practice for guys who wanted to play the game but, for whatever reason, not on the high school level. One of the Boys Club coaches saw me walking by and called for me to stop. He came over and asked me my name. He then said, "Man . . . you should be playing football!" I didn't have the balls to tell him that I had just tried out with the high school team but quit. He invited me to come by the club the next day at 3:00 p.m. and pick up a uniform.

When I got home, my sister Ruth asked what happened. I told her that I quit the team and she said, "After one day, you quit?" Yep! That was it. *"I quit!!"* I did not realize how that one act of giving up would affect me later. That night I went to sleep exhausted from the day's practice, and the next morning when I awoke, Ruth told me that I had been having nightmares and was doing push-ups in my sleep. I didn't believe her until my sister Rhettie confirmed Ruth's claims. I felt bad about quitting, but I felt a little better having spoken with the guy from the Boys Club.

By the next day the word had gotten out to some of my friends that I had quit the team. I did not realize that many of my friends knew that I was going out for the football team, and they kept asking, "What happened?" More important, I started to get angry with myself for giving up. Why did I do it? Many other guys just like me had stuck it out. What made me so different that I didn't have the will to compete on the field to make it through that first day with the football team? I think it came down to my not being fully prepared and not being willing to pay the price necessary to play the game!

That afternoon I walked to the Boys Club, which was in downtown Florence. More precisely, it was in "the block." Every town in America had a "block"—where the black businesses were located, where many Friday- and Saturday-night fights took place. The block was where the black barbershops and soul-food restaurants were located and the railroad tracks separated the white business areas from the black stores. The Boys Club was on the second floor over a pool hall surrounded by a dry cleaner's, several barbershops, and a couple of bars. The location was inappropriate for working with kids, but I didn't think about that at the time. To me it was better to have one there than to have none at all. I was merely looking for an opportunity, and I didn't care where it was located. Besides, the block was in the same area where my father would bring me to get my hair trimmed when I was younger.

When I walked up the dimly lit stairs to get to the club on the second floor, I didn't know what to expect. The interior of the club was dark and bare-bones but suited the young boys who just needed a place to go to have a little fun. The activities included pool and Ping-Pong but also what I wanted, football. E. J. McIver was the executive director of the club and one of the coaches for its football team. He and an assistant coach, Robert Sanders, had to put a team together to play against other clubs and smaller teams around Florence. There was little pressure at this level; it was more about fundamentals and having fun. The practice and game field was a vacant field about two blocks from the club. Every day when we got our equipment and walked from the club to the field, people on the block or in their cars smiled or blew their car horns to show their support. Once we arrived at the field and put on our equipment, we practiced against one another. There were no sleds to hit and no grass drills. This was definitely a low-budget, ragtag operation, and while it was not Wilson High School, for me it had to do for the time being. I took instruction from Coach McIver and Coach Sanders to develop my game, but also to gauge what I needed to do to make the high school team. I think those coaches knew that I was eventually moving up to the next level and that the Boys Club was just a pit stop on my journey to where I really wanted to go.

The practices and games we played were not much to talk about. A lot of instructional points were made, but most of the players were either not very athletically inclined or rejects like me from the high school programs. It was just good to be able to take the field and play organized football, especially with our coaches trying to at least guide all of the guys like me out of trouble. Ironically, the police department was a short walk from the club. McIver and Sanders probably saw more than their share of talented black boys who never realized their potential because they made bad choices along the way. They were just like my Boy Scout leader, Mr. Walton, and other black men like him who gave their valuable time to help give black boys an opportunity to do something positive instead of getting involved with things and people who would lead them to jail.

The Boys Club team only played six games. The games were fun, but it was more important for me to gain more experience on what was necessary to "stick and stay" the next time I tried to play football on the high school level. After our last football game I was ready to try high school football again. I enjoyed and appreciated my playing time at the Boys Club. It was there for me when I needed an alternative source to help me grow a little as a football player. I thought it was best to say as little as possible to my family and friends this time about going out for the varsity at Wilson for fear that I would again fail. I didn't want to feel that same disappointment if the same thing happened once more.

CHAPTER 3

Try, Try Again

With the Boys Club experience, the ninth grade, and the embarrassment of quitting behind me, it was time to commit to making another run at playing varsity ball at Wilson High. This time I think I took greater care in training my body for the tough two-a-day practices I knew would be coming. For much of the summer prior to the beginning of practice, I ran on my own. June, July, and August weather is no joke in South Carolina, so I did a lot of my running early in the morning. Several times I ran through my neighborhood in the middle of the afternoon or evening, but the bulk of my conditioning was in the early morning. I've always been an early riser so it was never a problem for me to wake up at 6:00 a.m. and get going with what I knew had to be done. I felt like that little kid who played soldier when I was younger because I was on my own mission.

As the beginning of practice approached, I got more and more anxious. I just kept wondering if I had what it took to stick it out this time, and if I didn't, what would I say to all of my friends and family? I knew I could do it, but deep down a small trace of doubt reared its head as if to say, "You're not good enough" or "Who in the fuck do you think you are to think that you could play football?" Every time that trace of doubt entered my mind, I would think about what my mom had always told me ever since I could remember: "Don, you can do anything you want if put your mind to it." I also reflected on how if my father was tough enough to beat three strokes he'd suffered and bounce back without any lingering long-term effects, I had to have the same kind of toughness within myself to stick through this challenge. This was starting to be a test of my will not just because I wanted to play football, but because I wanted to erase that bitter taste of quitting that was still bothering me deep in my gut.

On the first day of practice, as I approached the locker room, I recognized that unmistakable scent from the year before: the smell of freshly cut grass. I felt anxious. Other guys were in the locker room getting dressed, but I could hardly remember anyone being around me. I was in my own zone, basically blocking everything out of my mind. I hardly remembered putting my equipment on; my attention was so focused on the drills awaiting me. I do remember that I had to swallow a lot of pride to come back to where I was the year before. It was hard, humbling, and a little embarrassing to see the faces of some of the same guys I tried out with, who with a year of experience were now considered veteran players. We all took some of the same classes together, but in this football world I was revisiting *they* were now the veterans. Regardless of the team's record, those players had earned the respect of the older players and their coaches. I felt that I was being looked down upon by a few players because I had quit, and some probably thought that once you're a quitter, you're always a quitter. I am certain that some thought I would do the same thing again. I remembered what I heard the coaches and many of the players say the previous year, even when they were dead tired—"Winners never quit, and quitters never win"—over and over like a recorded loop.

Standing by the fence, wearing my uniform and equipment, I was ready to take the field once again. As Coach Long walked past me to the field ahead of the players, he looked at me with a smirk and said, "Hey, baby, you gonna try this shit again? Don't let me run you off again!" Some of the players heard the comment and laughed openly, while several others looked at me to see what my response would be. But what could I say? Not a damn thing! I was back, couldn't say a word, and had to let my actions do the talking this time!

Coach Long blew the whistle to begin practice, and all of the players jogged onto the field to loosen up and begin calisthenics. Stretching and jumping jacks were no big deal to me, but when we got to the push-ups, I started thinking back to the previous year. I think it helped that the temperature this August was a bit cooler than the previous year. It's amazing how stiflingly hot and humid it gets in August in South Carolina, and when you are wearing football equipment, you get even hotter and can hardly think about anything but the heat. No matter how much running you do in the mornings wearing shorts and a T-shirt, it's another thing when you are wearing all of that equipment along with a helmet and trying to keep up with everyone else. Fatigue sets in quickly. In football terms it is called having a monkey on your back.

After calisthenics and the loosening-up period, it was off to the position coaches for individual drills. This was what I was dreading, the grass drills, the monkey roll, the one-on-one tackling drills, and hitting the two-man or seven-man blocking sled. Once again I assumed a position at the rear of the line because the older, more experienced guys jumped out in front to lead the group. When it was my time to run any drill, I kept thinking three things: the previous year; the bitter taste of having to face family and friends when I quit; and what Mama said, "You can do anything you set your mind to."

I did the monkey roll with two other guys from my group and actually liked it. I did the grass drills, and while they were not enjoyable, I pushed myself and completed them. We did the tackling drills on one another, then we took on the sled. After we hit it a couple of times, the whistle blew and the period was over. The next drill was the one-on-one live blocking and tackling drill where I got my ass handed to me the previous year. This time I didn't wait for my number to be called by the coaches. I jumped to the front of the line and I wanted to go against the best. I don't remember the name of the guy I went against, but I do remember that he was a senior. As he lined up in his stance, a running back assumed a stance about five yards behind him. The lineman's job was to blow me off the ball with a block, clearing the way for the running back to run to daylight. I knew I was going to have at least two opportunities to show what I could do against this guy, and I had to make the best of those chances. My job was to destroy the lineman in front of me and destroy the play for no gain. I put myself deeply in a mental zone where I tried to block out everything that might distract me. I could hear the defense yelling for me to stuff the lineman, and I could hear the offense yelling to the lineman to blow me off the ball.

On the snap of the ball I exploded into the opposing lineman, using all of the power I had in my thighs, ass, and legs. My explosion stalemated him and then pushed him backward into the backfield, stopping the running back before he could get started. At the end of the play the only thing I heard was the whistle to stop it. From the applause and yells, I knew the coaches were pleased with the first play, but I knew I still had to go again. As I returned to my position, I could hear the cheers but I stayed in my zone trying to concentrate. On the next play I followed the head of the lineman as he tried to use a cutoff block on me to shield the back, who was trying to get to the outside. I started to come across the face of the lineman with my forearm as he tried to cut me off to my left side. In a fraction of a second I could see that the running back was about to break the run back to the inside, to my right. I spun 360 degrees off the block of the lineman to catch the back before he could break past the line of scrimmage for positive yards. I heard the thump of my helmet against his, and then I heard the cheers of the defensive players and coaches.

Coach Long looked pleased with my performance, and unlike before, I thought I held my own against the offensive lineman in the drill. After we all finished the drill, I was tired and exhausted, but I noticed when I looked around that everybody else seemed to feel the same. We all felt exhausted but couldn't stop until break time. Moving to the next drill, we could not walk; we had to at least jog. Huffing and puffing, we were all sucking for air trying to get the fatigue monkey off our backs. We made our way over to another area for the next drill, but before we got started, we had an opportunity to take our helmets off and get a swig of water from a pump canister. That water seemed like the best water I had ever tasted. I took a knee and rested my hand on my helmet. I looked down to the ground trying to catch my breath and realized, with sweat pouring from my head, that I had cleared a tremendous hurdle. It was further than I had gone the previous year. At least I could relax a little before the next drill, which turned out to be a walk-through to teach players techniques on playing within a defensive scheme. All I had to do was pay attention and learn as much as I could from watching what was taking place. I knew one thing though: I would be able to stand up to the physical demands of football just as everyone else did. If they could do it, I knew I could do it, too!

The rest of practice was tough, but the best part of being a new guy was watching the other guys do the drills until it became my turn. At the end of practice I had one last hurdle to clear: wind sprints. All players at a set of position gathered to run with one another. The quarterbacks, running backs, and linebackers ran together, the wide receivers and defensive backs ran together, and the offensive and defensive linemen ran together. This final drill was not about killing anyone because the coaches were pleased with the pace and tempo of practice, but they did want to work the players to the point where they were certain that we were getting something out of the drill. Even if players didn't know their assignments as well as they should, they must be in condition to play the game. The purpose of working us so hard at the beginning of practice was to fatigue us and then see if we could think when we were physically drained.

Walking off the field, sweaty and tired, I felt a tremendous sense of accomplishment. I remembered seeing those players after that Friday-night game that inspired me to want to play football in the first place. I realized what those players felt and the price you have to be willing to pay to earn a spot on the team and wear the uniform. One of the guys that I tried out for the team with the prior year who made it and remembered me quitting came over to me and gave me a pat on the shoulder and congratulated me on making it through the first day. Following him, Coach Long came over and congratulated me on making it through practice and told me that he hoped I could stick it out because he knew I had talent but it needed to be developed. I told him that I would give my best but it was hard. He looked at me and did a double take and said with a smile on his face, "Shit, son, if it was easy, everybody would be out there. It takes special people to play football."

It took me a few sessions to get fully acclimated to the rigors of football practice. When I say *acclimated*, I mean to the point of being used to what I was going through daily. When I got to that point, I was able to concentrate, focus, learn the game, and then have fun. As the days went by, I improved my skills. One drill I remember was a variation of the tackling drills: A running back and a defensive player would lie on their backs on the ground about five yards apart. The running back had to hold a ball in one of his hands. On the first sound of a whistle both players had to get to their feet as quickly as possible. The job of the back was to elude the defensive player, and the job of the defensive player was to tackle the back within three to five yards. This was a little different from the regular tackling drill that we did as a group of linemen: we did those drills at one-half to three-quarter speed and could not fool one another with our running since we were all a little slow compared to running backs. This drill was more realistic in that it was full speed and we had no clue as to where that back would go once he got off the ground with the ball. It was also what most people envisioned football to be: the intense hitting, but especially the sounds of the game. Pads and helmets clashing together was what everybody wanted to see and hear. In drills like this everyone gets pumped up to see how tough a player he is and what he is made of. This was a "difference-maker" drill because you can look as good as you want in a uniform, but if you can't make it through these contact drills, you will certainly be sitting your "looking good in your uniform" ass on the bench.

Taking what I had learned from my still limited amount of coaching and watching some of the other players in the tackling drills, I thought I was ready. I then heard Coach Long call my name. "Hey, Carson, get in there!" Damn, I began to get nervous because once again I was on center stage. The whole team was watching and I didn't have a clue as to where the ball carrier would be running. I didn't know if he would make a spin move to avoid a tackle or if he would try to bull-rush his way right past me. As I lay down flat on my back, all kinds of thoughts were running through my head. Then I told myself to just focus on his chest and go for the spot between his numbers. Coach Long yelled to me that the defense was counting on me to make a good stick! But I could also hear all of the other defensive players yelling and screaming words of encouragement. The offensive players were yelling the same words of encouragement to the running back.

The scene was like a gang fight with each group putting their best players in the ring to fight. The whole drill lasted only a couple of seconds, but before the whistle was blown to attack, it seemed as if time stood still. On the first sound I heard, I got up as fast as I could and saw the back right in front of me. It happened so quickly that I had no time to think, only to react. I saw the numbers and my "kill spot," where I was going to place my face to be certain of the shot. As we made contact, I wrapped my arms around the running back and then drove my legs, exploding right through the other player, throwing him backward for a loss of yards. It was a picture-perfect tackle! The only thing I heard after the whistle blew were the cheers of the defensive players. Coach Long came over, slapped me on my ass, and congratulated me for a job well done. He said, "That's the way you do it, baby. Every time you make a tackle, I want it just like that!"

Plays like that helped me go from a first-year practice player to a first-year starter on defense. It was good to finally get that "quitter" tag off my back. That play, while it may have been insignificant to most, was a defining moment for me as a football player. That play opened the eyes of the other players and earned me the right to be one of the guys. I appreciated the Boys Club taking me under its wing and nurturing me as a player, but this was where I wanted to be, at Wilson High School wearing the school colors, purple and gold, and being a Tiger like all of my brothers and sisters.

Once the school year began, I had to decide whether I was going to play football or play in the school's marching band. I took band as an elective course, but I was not good at playing the saxophone. With the knowledge that I was going to be a starter on the football team, I knew that I was not going to try out for the marching band. Instead of playing an instrument at the school's pep rally, I would be one of the players introduced in the school's assembly on Friday afternoons.

One of the great things about playing at my school was players could wear their game jerseys at school all day on Fridays. Friday-afternoon pep rallies were even more special when I was able to wear my #70 football jersey with pride around friends, who sometimes looked at me with envy and admiration. As a tenth grader, I thought I was big shit being in the same company as the juniors and seniors. Only in playing a sport such as football does everyone seem to be on the same level, when they are on the field. If you can get the job done, it matters to no one if you are a freshman or a senior. Early on, I didn't think I was one of those guys who had a lot to say as I could still remember that I'd quit. While most of the players were aware of that, the issue was never really brought up again. I figured that until I did something besides wear a jersey, it was best to let the older guys do most of the talking.

The excitement for me at Wilson was about playing football. For the first time, the game was about the students, faculty, cheerleaders, and the band. Oh, the band was something else! The bands at black schools were unlike bands I saw at schools on television. The band at Wilson played the latest sounds that we heard on the radio, not some dry standard tunes that everybody and his sister could play. The band played music that made people want to get down and dance in the stands during the game. My music teacher, Leon Harvey, was also the band director. I think Mr. Harvey was from the era of knowing that if you were at a black school, you had to bring it every time the band stepped on the field. I got inspiration from the music and the people I saw cheering for the team in the stands. I also learned that much like the band, players had to "bring it" whenever they stepped on the field.

Initially, once we opened the football season, I didn't think my play was anything special. I got used to the contact and the speed of the game. It was good to be a part of the team and able to contribute in some way. But as the season wore on, my confidence grew and I became more than just a contributor. I became a player who was able to make big plays, especially in stopping the run to my side of the ball or putting pressure on the quarterback. I was learning at lot about the position that I played, which was right defensive end. I was still the raw player that Coach Long knew I'd be, but I learned the position quickly by watching some of the other guys as well as by watching how the pros played that same position on Sunday afternoons. What I needed to do was learn as much as I could not just about my own position, but about the whole defensive scheme: better tackling, better techniques in rushing the quarterback, and recognizing screens and draw plays. I needed to be able to transfer that knowledge to my play on the field. During our practice sessions I would remember the moves I saw the pros such as Deacon Jones or Willie

Davis make on television and imitate those moves against the offensive linemen in drills.

In practice I was able to gauge the talent level of players I had to go up against, but in games I didn't have that luxury. In one game we played, the offense ran a sweep play in my direction. I saw the quarterback hand the ball to the running back, who started my way. I was so focused on the guy with the ball that I blocked everything else out of my mind; some might call that tunnel vision. When I saw the running back coming my way, I thought the tackle was mine being served on a platter. What I did not see was the pulling guard leading the way to open a hole for the back to run through. I thought I was going to shut the play down for little or no gain, but before I realized it that guard knocked the crap out of me! I was concerned about making the tackle, not about protecting myself. Just as I thought I was about to hit the ball carrier, the guard popped me on the side of my helmet. For a moment everything went black, and as I started to get my bearings again, I saw stars twinkling before my eyes. I didn't realize what had occurred because it happened so quickly, and I recovered and continued playing in the game. I remember that we won that game on the road, and when I was on the team bus coming home after it, I was pleased that I had a good game. The next morning one of my friends showed me that my name was in the paper for the first time, for making a big play to help the team win. You know I had to go out and buy at least ten copies of the *Florence Morning News*. I had to send the first copy to my mom in New Jersey to let her see that her baby boy's name was in the newspaper for doing something good.

After seeing everyone's excitement about my name being in the newspaper, my game took off to a higher level. It may have been totally in my head, but I could swear that I became a little faster, a bit quicker, and more agile, with a greater sense of confidence than I ever thought I could have. At the time I weighed about 185 pounds, but it wasn't the weight that mattered, it was what I thought about myself. It's funny how a positive moment can go a long way toward building self-esteem. From that point on, I received more and more cheers and louder applause from all of the students at pep rallies, especially from my friends who had attended Holmes School with me. While we were all in it together as a school, my friends from East Florence knew I was one of them and felt that I was representing them.

By the middle of that season the bitter taste of quitting was gone. While I didn't dwell on it, I knew I would never forget that feeling. Coach Long was pleased that I was able to stick it out, make the squad, and go on to become a key contributor on the team. I had come a long way since the sandlot teams of St. Ann's Church lot and my ninth-grade year playing at the Boys Club. Some of the same people who cheered for me while I was playing club ball were now cheering for me at Wilson. As the season wound down, I began to think about what the team could do to get better for the next season. The seniors would be leaving so it would be up to the rising juniors and sophomores to take the reins of leadership and help the team move forward.

Romance reared its head for me with someone that I had known for quite some time. I used to steal honey buns for Donna Rae Hawkins when we were a little younger. We went to Holmes School together, but she never really stood out in my mind. Then one day I looked at her, and all of a sudden, bang, I got shot by cupid's arrow and saw her in a much different light. When we were together, we looked like the old comic characters Mutt and Jeff because of the size difference. I stood six foot one inch tall and weighed about 185. She was four foot eleven inches and weighed about 88 pounds soaking wet. It didn't matter because we had a thing for one another. Her father was a fireman and her mother was a schoolteacher, far more impressive than my parents. Both Miss Janice and Mr. Lawrence Hawkins were graduates from Wilson High School, while neither of my parents graduated from high school. I think subconsciously I truly admired their family relationship. Donna Rae and her sister were expected to do well in school because her parents demanded excellence. She was always on the honor roll in school and was positioned to attend almost any college of her choice once she graduated from high school. I was basically still doing just enough to get by in my classes. Don't get me wrong, I was not a dumb kid. Let's just say I was not inspired to do my best. I intended to graduate from high school, but I did not have any goals beyond my high school years.

Donna Rae and I were complete opposites at schoolwork. When given an assignment, she wasted no time in getting the work done. I, on the other hand, always waited until the last minute to finish. We spent many hours in school and in the public library. While she worked diligently on her projects, I sometimes tagged along just to keep her company. Visiting the library, I learned that if I was not working on my own projects, it was a boring place to be. So instead of going out of my mind with boredom I started to open books and read. By reading on my own, my world started to open up. It didn't matter what I read, I began to see things that I would never have seen or known about. I did not realize Donna Rae's influence at that time and what it would mean to me later.

Wilson High was supposed to be the end of a tremendous journey for me and many of my other friends who began our education at Holmes Elementary School. At Wilson I knew I was walking the same halls where my brothers and sisters walked, and I had some of the same teachers that they had as well. It was, I thought, inevitable to do just as most other African-Americans who preceded me in Florence did: learn the school's alma mater, conduct myself with the same pride as others who'd finished their secondary education at Wilson, then go on with living my life. But that was not the way this scenario was going to end. Because segregation had been the norm for so many years in the South, federal laws were passed to help bring about desegregation of its schools. As a result, I and most of the other kids from my area of East Florence were zoned to another school closer to where I lived.

I remember the shock and then sadness most of the students felt when we were first told that we would not be returning to Wilson the next school year. Robert Durant, the principal of Wilson at that time, called me to his office and had a confidential heart-to-heart meeting with me to discuss my options. Mr. Durant told me that if I wanted to remain at Wilson, he would withhold my records to allow me to continue playing football there. I enjoyed Wilson and wanted to stay and finish my football career there, but I thought it was best for me to join my friends, who did not have the options that I had. I had many apprehensions because I had never attended a white school before. I did have several good friends who, after leaving the elementary school, opted to attend the predominately white junior high school and then the high school I was about to attend. I knew I was going to have to quiz them to get a feel for what was going to take place once the new school year started. It was sad to have to say goodbye to friends, some that I had known since junior high, and the teachers that I had gotten to know personally. I also knew that I would miss those black coaches, especially Coach Long, who, while he could brutally chastise me for my practice or game habits, ultimately wanted to see me succeed on the field and in life.

It took me a while to adjust to junior high once I left Holmes School. Then it took time for me to adjust to high school from junior high. I was comfortable where I was but I had to make another adjustment, transferring from Wilson High School to McClenaghan High School.

CHAPTER 4

Desegregation

What I was about to face as I entered my junior year was going to be foreign to me: a school that was merely four blocks away from where I lived but part of a totally different world from what I was used to.

My sister Ruth became the resident manager of an apartment complex operated by my church. One of the perks for her being the manager was that they provided housing. These apartments were built for low-income families to help them live in better conditions than those they were accustomed to. A lot of senior citizens and some single mothers with children lived there, and these two groups outnumbered the two-parents-with-children group. I don't think anyone complained because it was the first time many of these people had had a decent place to live. I know I was quite content to be living in a relatively new apartment, especially after having lived in so many homes that were not very comfortable. The apartment was our first with electric heat, so I no longer had to chop wood for the stove, haul in chunks of coal, or go to the store to get gallons of kerosene for the heater. We had a two-bedroom apartment on the second floor. Another first was that I had my own room and did not have to share it. My brother Ronnie, who was four years older than me, had already graduated from Wilson and had gone on to join the air force. Keep in mind that this was a time when the end of the Vietnam War was in sight by most Americans.

As I worked out during the summer, I did not know what to expect from a new coaching staff at the new school. I had, in a short time, gotten used to the way things were done at Wilson High. With this move I was going to have to make adjustments to the unfamiliar. I knew several people who had already been attending McClenaghan High School, and they were familiar with the athletic program as well. They convinced me that going to school would be a breeze. One of my friends thought that because I was an athlete, I would be able to meet more people and be accepted quicker than most of the other students.

When I reported to school to take my physical and pick up my equipment for football, the coaches gave me a once-over to see how muscular I looked and seemed pleased that I would be joining their program. Ladson Cubbage was the head coach; he had several assistant coaches, who also doubled as teachers in the classroom. In a meeting for the first time as a group, all of the players, including the new players from the other schools, were introduced to the coaching staff, and that staff was introduced to the players. I kept waiting to see a coach who looked like me (black) to appear, but there were none. I remember thinking to myself, "This should be interesting." Of the forty players on the varsity football team, only about eight were black. I knew each of the black players as we'd all attended Holmes School, and some of us had played sandlot ball together or were in Boys Scouts together. I thought that it was sad that there had been no effort to desegregate the football team's coaching staff as had been done to desegregate the school. I figured I could do nothing so the best thing was to focus on playing the game and making the best of the situation.

The team showed up for practice a couple of weeks prior to the beginning of school. While everyone else hung out at the beach or enjoyed their leisurely summer vacations, football players had to commit themselves to two-a-day practices sessions in sweltering heat and high humidity. I wanted to be certain that I was physically ready to play this time. During the summer I ran early in the morning or during the hottest parts of the day to make sure I was prepared. I was lucky enough to get the same jersey number, 70, that I wore at Wilson; there was a comfort in that. As I dressed for the first time in the locker room of the new school, I could tell that everyone was nervous. I could also detect a difference between the ways the white guys and the black guys interacted. Some white players tended to be quieter in the group, while several of the black guys were louder and more vocal in the locker room. I was somewhere in the middle because I was never a boastful player on the field. I was more of an observer who only spoke when I felt a need to speak.

New school, new uniforms, different players, and different coaches, but one thing remained the same: the scent of freshly cut grass signaled for me the beginning of another football season. The quietness of the field would soon be replaced with the loud grunts of players and the smashing of shoulder pads and helmets in blocking and tackling drills. The sound of the whistle and the yelling of the coaches got practice under way for us as it did for thousands of other teams at all levels around the country. The sound of that whistle symbolized the beginning of an opportunity for each player to show what he was made of. In my case, I wanted to be able to "hang" in my new surroundings. No one at McClenaghan knew that I had quit football the first time that I'd tried out for the team at Wilson. In the one year that I'd played there, I'd earned respect from many of the players, especially the older guys. I knew I could compete, but I had never participated in sports with or against white guys. From the crib I had only associated or competed with and against black guys.

The drills at the new school were the same as the ones at the old school. Once we got into the hitting phase of practice, it got a little more intense than I remembered it being at Wilson. My weight had increased from about 188 pounds when I first started at Wilson to about 210 pounds, and what I lacked in bulk I made up for in speed and quickness. As a defensive lineman I could not always run around blockers and had to take on players head-to-head who were sometimes heavier and bulkier than I was. Early on in practice during a blocking drill, I had to take on an offensive lineman named BC Correll, a white player whom I eventually became friendly with. BC was broad, a wide load; he must have outweighed me by a good fifty to sixty pounds. He wasn't fat and was certainly solid. The objective of the drill was for me to take him on head-to-head and work my way through his block. Anytime you are in a new situation on the football field and you have to go head-to-head with another player, you have some anxiety or fear that you are going to be shown up or embarrassed. I was worried as the coaches called my name for the drill.

I assumed my position along the line of scrimmage and fastened my chin strap. When I came face-to-face or helmet-to-helmet with BC, I could see in his eyes the same anxiety that I was feeling. I didn't have any knowledge of what kind of player he was, but my senses told me that I had better load up to go against him in this drill. As he assumed a three-point stance, I did as well. I knew that all eyes would be on us. Everyone was probably wondering who was going to bring the leather in this drill. We both lined up against one another with a balanced stance; my right hand was planted in the grass in front of me, and my right leg was cocked, ready to propel my body toward his body. Everything got quiet. Then the coach began to bark out signals. To a defensive player, the signal in this kind of drill means nothing! It's most important to move on the snap of the ball. When I say the snap, the snap is not when the quarterback has the ball in his hands; it's being able to focus on that blocker in front of you, yet also being able to see the slightest movement of the ball by the center.

As I readied myself, I held my helmet up with my left hand to make certain that I could see into his eyes but also be able to see the ball. "Ready, set, hut one, hut two"—on the mere flinch of his body I exploded from my stance with as much power as I had. As he came out of his stance, BC and I collided. It sounded like a massive explosion. My head hit his head and then his shoulder pads. We tussled against one another until the whistle blew. BC and I hit so hard that I saw stars twinkling before my eyes, then everything started to fade to black as I walked to the side since my turn in the drill was over. Hitting him was like hitting a solid block of ice. He was not just a big guy, he was a big guy with power! I tried not to let anyone see that I had been dinged in the drill. Physically I felt fine, but I was pumped up as the adrenaline flowed through my system. Everything was still in the right place; my legs and arms were fine, but I will always remember that shot I took and gave. Perhaps it was a defensive-pride thing, or maybe it was a black/white thing, meaning I did not want the white guys to see that I was affected by the block. I think that one block taught me to keep my head out of the action and instead use my shoulder pads to make contact with the opposing linemen or running backs. It was a good thought, but when you are practicing and playing, it's not always the easiest thing to do when the objective is to either block or tackle.

I held my own in practices and eventually earned a starting position on the team as a right defensive end. That was an ideal position for me because it gave me an opportunity to use my speed and quickness against linemen who would be larger but usually slower than me. Since my days of idolizing Buck and Willie as NFL stars, I'd also watched David "Deacon" Jones, who played with the Los Angeles Rams' Fearsome Foursome defensive line. At that time the Deacon was one of the most effective pass rushers in the NFL. He used speed and quickness to beat bigger players, but added a different element to his game that I tried to incorporate to my game as well, the head slap. To me the head slap appeared simple, straightforward, and effective. A quick or fast defensive end starts his pass rush up the field on the snap. As the offensive lineman begins his pass drop, the end just hauls off and slaps the side of the lineman's helmet with the palm of his hand. Usually when a player sees something coming toward his head or face, he closes his eyes, if only for a fraction of a second. That moment is sometimes all that is needed to give myself or any other defensive player the opportunity to get past the lineman to get to the quarterback. By watching the techniques used by players such as Deacon Jones and other professionals and incorporating those skills into my game, I elevated my play and became more effective.

I was already a pretty good run-stopper. I had this knack for putting my body against another player's body and controlling his movement to read where the ball carrier was going. Then I could quickly get rid of the block to make the tackle. At times, being able to read, react, and make tackles came easily to me. But I knew when I played at Wilson that I needed to be a more complete player by being an effective rusher against passing offenses. When I played, I found that I was stronger than I'd realized, but I didn't know why. I was never into weight lifting but I realized that I did a lot of manual labor. I grew up having to chop wood, haul coal, and carry ten-gallon cans of kerosene from the gas station to my house. So I think I got my body development and strength naturally from doing chores like that. I could attribute being physical against the run to the strength I got from my manual labor, but in becoming a better pass rusher, I found other ways to improve my play. I discovered by accident a simple way to improve my agility. As I went to and from school, I had to walk near some railroad tracks. My buddies and I would walk on the tracks, usually shooting the breeze, talking about any number of things. We started by walking on the tracks, but that progressed to running on the tracks, and then to being able to jump from rail to rail without falling off. Quite by accident I learned how to improve my agility, control my balance, and have fun at the same time. I incorporated those simple, everyday things I did naturally into what I did on the football field to make me a better player.

I was getting to be good at this game. I had come a long way from being unprepared for that first practice to becoming a player who had earned the respect of his coaches and teammates. I was not aiming to get to any specific level of play; I was just trying to survive the day-to-day rigors of football practice and have fun. At times I was unsure what I was doing on the field, but my playing at full speed all the time masked any of my confusion. At McClenaghan, I developed more confidence. I was becoming an aggressive pass rusher and a tough run defender. From the practices, I knew I was going to be doing a lot more hitting, so I decided to start wearing J-pads.

J-pads were foam-rubber arm and hand pads that protected the forearms, hands, and wrists from being battered with scars and bruises. The other purpose of the J-pads was to look cool. I saw pro players wearing them, such as Gene Upshaw, who wore a whole bunch of pads on his arms as he blocked on the Oakland Raiders' offensive line. I figured that if I was going to be smashing people around, I should protect myself. When I went without pads like some other players and hit somebody on the face mask with my forearm, that shit hurt! I learned early on as a player that to play football I had to develop a high pain threshold, but I wanted to protect myself as much as possible if it did not adversely affect my performance.

Those practices at McClenaghan were crisp and hard-hitting. As time went by, the defensive players tried to set the tempo in the drills between offensive and defensive players. While we were beginning to get to know one another and become friends off the field, we wanted to earn the respect of one another on the field. You earned respect by your toughness, aggressiveness, and showing absolutely no fear. The drills, especially the one-on-one drill, became the highlight of practice. Coaches loved to see and know who was tough and would compete. Tackling and blocking drills were the times to show what you were truly made of. I could say it separated the men from the boys; one-on-one physical confrontations have always been around to establish a hierarchy among males. In the classroom, a demonstration of knowledge evens the playing field among all, but on the athletic field men are not all created equal. I never thought that I placed myself over anyone else, but for the first time I started to feel like a gladiator.

These drills were designed to test out blocking schemes against defenses at full speed, but the drills were also run to see who had toughness. The drills might be one-on-one, two-on-two, three-on-three, and on and on, but they were the highlight of practice. I didn't mind the contact in practice. We would run several plays, then get a break, get a little water, and watch some of the other players to see what they had. Sometimes I could tell what was happening simply by closing my eyes, listening to the snap count, the crash of pads, and finally hearing the reaction of the coaches when the play was over. The excitement in the tone and volume of the coaches' voices often told the story. All coaches know that games are won and lost in the trenches. While the skilled positions get all of the attention, nothing can effectively take place on either side of the ball if you don't have strength and power in the interior of the lines. Throughout those practices, I took most of the best offensive lineman on my team. I knew what each had and what each player was capable of. After being a part of this new team for a short time, I had no fear of the players there. I respected them and knew that at any time one or two of them could knock my dick in the dirt if I was not ready, but I would not let my guard down and give them that kind of opportunity.

After being a part of the new team for a few weeks and understanding the practice routine of the coaching staff, I felt more comfortable. I focused on trying to get better at what I did. I wasn't thinking about it, but I was in another league with different kinds of competition. The previous year I was attending an all-black school playing against other all-black schools in that part of South Carolina. Now I was playing on a slightly different level against mixed and some all-white teams. In practice and games I was being noticed as a good player with the potential to become an outstanding college prospect. My teammates and coaches knew I was getting better, the fathers of those players who always showed up for practice knew, and other teams were going to get to know it.

Some of the people who followed the Wilson team began to monitor my progress as well as that of some of the other players who had played at the old school. At times I thought it was ironic that some of the businessmen in Florence who years earlier did not allow blacks to enter their restaurants or other businesses, or had separate entrances for blacks and whites, were probably now cheering for the team that I was playing for. While I had more than my share of being called "nigga" and "boy" as I was growing up, I could not dwell on that stuff. I knew racist attitudes would always exist, but as long as they were not shoved in my face, I could deal with almost anything. What I think was more important at that time was my role as a leader on the team—more specifically, my leadership role among the black players. I think this was because we had no black coaches. With no offense to the white coaches, if we had problems on or off the field, we did not always feel comfortable taking concerns to them. While they were our football coaches and we respected them as such, they did not know us and we didn't know them. They had no clue as to where we came from or what made us tick.

In the classroom, I had been taking Air Force Junior ROTC as part of my academic curriculum while I was at Wilson, and I continued taking it at McClenaghan. ROTC was influential in my development, both as a student and in my life in general. Colonel Charles Kennaw and Sergeant Ronald Moore were assigned to teach the fundamentals of military history, tradition, and knowledge to cadets at McClenaghan. From close-order drills and marching in local parades to field trips to Cape Canaveral and air force bases or learning the protocol of attending military festivities, ROTC aroused my interest and tapped into what made me tick. I'm sure part of my interest came from being part of an air force family: my two brothers, Sonny and Ronnie, had spent time in that service. But I had also developed a desire to fly and was fascinated with planes.

Because of their extensive military experience and having worked closely with blacks in the military, I felt more comfortable with Colonel Kennaw and Sergeant Moore than with the football staff. What also made the ROTC experience good for me was that many of the black football players also took ROTC. We had a kinship not just on the football field but also in wearing those dress blue uniforms in the winter or khakis during the warm-weather months. The two things that held my interest and focus both involved wearing uniforms.

As an academic student I remained average, unlike when I put on my football or ROTC uniform. I wore both uniforms well, but I also assumed a different personality when in them. I had to project confidence and dignity. Colonel Kennaw influenced me tremendously not for what he said but from the way he carried himself, standing tall, erect, with shoulders back, chest out, and gut in. I wanted to emulate his walk: smooth, with his arms down to his side. He taught us as cadets what many of our parents in the black community tried to teach us: to look people in the eye when talking to them, to use a firm handshake in greeting or saying good-bye, and overall to conduct ourselves with confidence. That ROTC course helped instill a sense of pride and discipline in me that no other class could have done. When I started as a freshmen, I was a cadet airman, which put me at the bottom of the barrel in military rank, but as time went by, I rose to sergeant, then lieutenant. I eventually assumed the highest rank a cadet could assume, flight commander with the rank of lieutenant colonel. I was the top-ranking cadet in the school, and all of the officers beneath me reported to me. It meant a lot to me to be recognized, acknowledged, and respected as a leader. Though uncertain what my future held, I knew that I might well pursue a military career or a vocation where discipline was a major factor. For me it was a good fit.

In the classroom, doing just enough to get by was not getting it done. I was dating Donna Rae, who also transferred to McClenaghan High from Wilson High School, as did many of our mutual friends. We became one of the more recognizable couples at school. It was hard to miss the two of us, considering our size difference. Donna Rae's work ethic started to rub off on me, and she quickly became a role model as to how to get things done right without procrastinating. In so many ways I wanted to be like her so I tried to do as she did in academics and extracurricular activities. While I was the jock when it came to sports, Donna Rae was far more disciplined intellectually and academically than me when it came to books. My roles as an athlete and in ROTC meant many students both black and white recognized me, so much so that I was elected senior-class president by my classmates.

As a senior, I was doing better academically, I was holding the top position in ROTC, and I was the school's first African-American senior-class president. My football career was also taking off. We played our games on Friday nights, and usually on Saturday afternoons some of my black teammates would come to my sister's two-bedroom apartment to drink sodas, watch college football games, and reflect on what had happened in our games the night before. It was always interesting to watch schools such as Oklahoma and Nebraska play and predict how many plays it would take Greg Pruitt and Jack Mildren, the Oklahoma Sooners running back and quarterback, to score. My team friends Steve Parks, who played linebacker, and Curtis Cato, a running back, and I would often visualize ourselves playing for those major football programs. We had bonded through the ROTC experience and stuck together for one another in football. We wanted the best for each other, but we knew who we were and our economic limitations.

The players on our team had very different lifestyles. Many of the white players took off for Myrtle Beach in their cars or their parents' cars the day after the games to enjoy time with their friends. Few of the black players had their own cars or access to a car, so we generally rode our bikes or walked to visit one another. We were comfortable with one another, whether it was having serious conversations about sports and world events or just bullshitting around, telling jokes, or pulling pranks on each other.

Friendship and football bound us together, but one event during my senior season changed the course of my football career. Our team played a game on the road at Hillcrest High School near Sumter, South Carolina. In a hard-fought defensive struggle, we blew an opportunity to win the game and wound up settling for a 6–6 tie. The game was not memorable, but I'll never forget what happened afterward. When we got on the bus to return to our school after the game, most of the black guys sat in the back of the bus not because we had to but because we chose to. Most of the white guys and the coaches sat in the front. As we headed home, several of the black guys started to have some fun by telling jokes. One of the white players stood up in the front and demanded, "Why don't you guys in the back shut up!" We looked at one another and wondered whom he was talking to. Words were exchanged between the back and the front passengers. I didn't have much to say because while I was disappointed that we did not win, it wasn't as if we'd lost either, so why not have some fun.

Then the coach stood up and demanded again that everyone "Shut up!" Several black players felt that the coach was taking the side of the white players. By the time the bus arrived back at our school, what happened in the game was irrelevant as several of the black players were incensed with the words and, more important, the tone, of our coach. Over the weekend, a couple of those players decided that they were going to boycott the team and practice. So, when Monday rolled around, most of the black players came to my house. We talked about the coach's attitude toward us and the evolving situation. I hadn't invited everyone to come over to my place; I think that it was just natural for the guys to show up there.

One white player's father knew something was wrong when none of the black players showed up for practice, and he found out that everyone was at my house. He came to my apartment and found all of us standing or sitting under a tree in front of my place talking about the situation. He talked with us and tried to get us to see things from another perspective. We told him that we could only see things from a black perspective. We did not appreciate what happened on that bus and the attitude of the coach toward us. We also told him that it was not our intent to stay out longer, but a one-day work stoppage was appropriate for what had happened to send a message of our displeasure. That father went back to the coach and I assume told him of our displeasure and that we intended to return the next day.

Upon our return the next day, you could sense a chill in the air in the locker room and then once we all returned to the field as a team. I could especially tell that little was being said to me and eventually felt that I was being singled out as the ringleader. I felt that I had a huge target on my back and it was just a matter of time before something happened. In practice drills I felt that I was being unnecessarily chastised for petty reasons, but I just went with the flow and kept my mouth closed, hoping that at some point things would get back to normal.

In our next game, while fighting off a block by an offensive lineman, I sprained an ankle. I hobbled off the field, and the athletic trainer taped it up tighter and got me ready to return to the game. I knew I was not able to move at full speed but I wanted to play anyway. Then, helping to make a tackle, I sprained my other ankle as I got tangled up in a pileup. I lay on the field until the doctor and the trainer came out to help me. I got my other ankle taped, but this time I would not be going back into the game. I had to have assistance getting to the locker room after the game. I felt like a cripple because all of a sudden I was in pain and could hardly walk. The next morning I remember waking up and having to go to the bathroom. As I got out of the bed and tried to stand, it became clear to me that I had not been dreaming but had actually sprained both ankles, which were slightly swollen. It was painful to try to walk to the bathroom, but I did so by holding on to the walls. I spent the weekend soaking both ankles in a bucket filled with ice water to reduce the swelling. I had been injured before, but those injuries were "nicks" that did not render me unable to walk. For the first time I was looking at the possibility of missing some playing time. I didn't like that feeling because I had worked hard to be a starter, and I didn't think anybody could play my position better that me.

Once we resumed practice, my injury forced me to miss the first and second days. I decided that I was going to try to practice on the third day in hopes of playing in the next game. It was too soon but I just wanted to get off the sideline and back into practice. I knew I was going to have a problem with pain and the inability to push off or to stop quickly. When we began to run our drills, I was slow in running from drill to drill, and I heard the coach bark out, "Hey, Carson, if you can't run any faster than that, get off the field!" With the pain and frustration I was experiencing, along with the sense of being targeted, I got off the field just as the coach demanded. As I walked off, some of my teammates thought I was joking. I heard some of them yell, "Hey, Harry, come on back!" Then it became clear to them that I wasn't joking, and I heard someone say, "Oh, shit, he's serious!"

When I make up my mind to do something, even if it's done impulsively, I go with my gut and let the chips fall where they may. I made an impulsive decision and followed the coach's orders because it seemed to be something he wanted me to do and I obliged him.

As I changed my clothes and left the locker room, I was focused. I did not allow myself to look toward the football field as I was leaving. I was lashing out, to whom I didn't know, but at that point I didn't give a shit. Little did I know where my action on that field would take me. I had been receiving college information from major universities and figured I'd be one of the captains of the McClenaghan team by the end of the year, but that would not be the case. I would probably have been selected to participate in the all-star game between the star football players in North Carolina and South Carolina, but since I wasn't representing a high school team, I knew that would now not be likely. Most important, I knew I would not be promoted to college recruiters by members of McClenaghan's coaching staff. So, I was on my own as far as looking for a college athletic scholarship. Actually, I wasn't sure if I had the grades to get into a college because I was such a goof-off in my early high school years.

When the coach yelled, "If you can't run any faster than that, get off the field," it was as if I was obeying the command of a superior just as I was taught to do as an ROTC cadet. Although, in my case, I obeyed the command with a gigantic attitude attached to it. Once I took the first step toward leaving the field, I knew I could not come back. I did not stop to think about the ramifications of taking that first step. All I knew about was that moment. I felt that I was being singled out among all of the players. No one knew the pain that I was feeling, and as far as the coaches were concerned, that I was able to get dressed and participate in practice was a clear sign that I was okay. Had I taken a couple of extra days off to allow my ankles to fully heal, even if I had to miss the next game, things would probably have been different. But I had learned playing football that you have to be tough. Not only do you have to have a certain toughness to play, but you have to learn how to play with aches and pains. With each play brings some type of contact, and when bodies collide, bad things can happen.

The next day I felt that I was in a dream as I had to attend classes with the same kids I attended classes with the day before, but now the situation was different. Many of my friends gradually found out during the day what had happened on the field and about my decision to quit. Some of my teammates continued to try to talk me into coming back, apologizing to the coach and the team for walking off the field, and reassuming my position. I found that the pride that I had to muster up to make the team at Wilson was the same pride that prohibited me from apologizing to the coach. Many lessons are learned in playing sports but especially in football. That you have to have an abundance of that "pride thing" to be the best is one lesson that is driven into you from the first day you put the helmet on. But I learned another valuable lesson those days: with or without you, the show will go on.

After school, as I was walking home, I saw some of my old teammates heading to practice. While I was not going to stick around to watch, I knew what was going to take place on the field at specific times. It was hard to go through that afternoon all alone without being a part of the team, but I'd made my bed and had to sleep in it. It was hard to stick to my principles, but I guess I can be a stubborn MF.

My high school football career for all intents and purposes was over. Only two football games were left in the season, and my best friend, Steve Parks, and BC Correll were two of the three final team captains for the year. I was happy for Steve and BC because they were good guys and deserved the honor. My college football career was also over several weeks prior to that. As was to be expected, while I received a number of courtesy form letters from various schools, no school showed any interest in me nor did I receive any firm offers of scholarships. But others refused to see my career end that way.

The assistant principal of my high school, James Madison, was an African-American and had also been a neighbor of mine as I was growing up. He took a personal interest in my post-high-school possibilities. He was the son of a barber who cut my hair in the hood. Mr. Madison caught flak from many black kids who saw him as a sellout just because he was part of the establishment in a predominantly white environment. But I always held him in high regard because I recognized that his job was a thankless one that had to be done. Mr. Madison did for me what few others offered to do. When he found out that no schools were offering me a scholarship, he packed me up in his car along with game film and took me to his alma mater, North Carolina A&T State University in Greensboro, North Carolina.

Arriving on the campus of A&T, what I remember most was seeing so many black people in one place. Because of all the beautiful black folks that I was in the midst of, I thought to myself, "This is where I need to be." I met several assistant football coaches. None stood out in my mind except for Willie Jeffries, a defensive coach I spoke with for a brief time. Without seeing film, he thought that I had the size to play ball on the college level. I appreciated his comments but he was not the man in charge. That was Hornsby Howell, the head coach at North Carolina A&T. Coach Howell was a well-respected coach in black college football. After meeting him, we spent some time watching game film. It was a little uncomfortable to sit there with college coaches and hear them critique my play. Most of the comments they made were complimentary. Afterward, Coach Howell shook my hand, told me he liked what he saw, and offered me a scholarship on the spot.

I was so excited to be wanted by someone. On my ride back to Florence I felt as if I were walking on air. I could not wait to tell my family that I was going to be heading to North Carolina A&T on a full scholarship. Most of the kids in my class who were going to college had already chosen what schools they were going to attend or whatever else their post-high-school endeavors would be. My euphoria did not last long, as several days later I received a letter from Coach Howell. I thought it was my scholarship contract to be signed, but instead the letter informed me that the school did not have the funding for a scholarship. The letter ended with regrets and best wishes on my future endeavors. I felt as if someone had hit me in the stomach with a baseball bat. I was not just disappointed; I was devastated and embarrassed. Mr. Madison was also disappointed and was at a loss for words. In a way I thought that I got what I deserved; had I not quit my high school team, my options would perhaps have been much greater. If I had just bitten my tongue, swallowed my pride, and apologized to the coach, or if I had just stayed on the field and ignored what he had said, I would have had my position back on the team.

I was senior-class president and ROTC commander, but those titles meant almost nothing to me since I was not looking at a bright future. Mr. Madison mentioned my situation to another African-American teacher, Dorothy Joe McDuffie. Ms. McDuffie was cool with the students. To me she was very much like those teachers that I had had at Holmes School. She took teaching personally and wanted students to be the best that they could be. Ms. McDuffie offered to do what Mr. Madison had tried to do. She, too, thought it would be a shame if my talent as an athlete went unnoticed. Ms. McDuffie arranged for me to visit her alma mater, South Carolina State College, in the hopes of obtaining a scholarship.

Since my mother was still a domestic worker cleaning homes in New Jersey and my father was semiretired in Florence, I knew that if I was going to attend college, it was not going to be with resources from my family. We were poor, but we managed to get by most of the time. That was the case with many of my friends as well; we didn't have the option of going to school with a college fund like some students. A football scholarship was going to be the only way for me to get there. It sure wasn't going to be my smarts. I'll never forget when Ms. McDuffie and I traveled to Orangeburg; we made small talk, but my mind was on what would happen once I met with the coaches at South Carolina State. I knew I practiced and played hard when I was on the field in high school, but I didn't know if what I did in high school was good enough to make it in college. With the exception of one game I'd attended at a small college when I was much younger, I had never even attended a college football game.

When we finally arrived on the campus of South Carolina State, Ms. McDuffie and I headed to the football office at Dukes Gymnasium in the middle of campus to meet the head coach. There we were introduced to Coach Oree Banks, the head coach of the SC State Bulldogs. Coach Banks was expecting us and invited us into his office. He then called for another coach to join us in the meeting, the defensive coordinator, James Carson. Coach Banks and Coach Carson had both been brought up to speed on my high school situation and what had occurred with North Carolina A&T. As we watched the film together, both coaches ran it back and forth to get a good picture of my speed, agility, and aggressiveness.

In some ways this was my first job interview. With the help of Ms. McDuffie, I was in search of a scholarship. They only had a couple available, and I had to sell myself to get one. After we watched the film, I could tell that the coaches felt good about what they saw, and they asked why I'd left my high school football program. I'm sure they did not want some malcontent, disruptive player in their program. I tried to be as forthright as I could to give them an understanding of my position and state of mind when I quit my team. They understood and offered me a scholarship on the spot. They also guaranteed me that I would not have the same problems I had with A&T. Coach Banks and Coach Carson also told me that if I accepted the scholarship, I would graduate! They would see to it that I graduated, not by pulling strings as might have been done at other schools, but by staying on my ass just as a parent would to help me off the field as well as on the field. For the first time in a long time, I felt that connection that I'd felt as a youngster at Holmes School and Wilson High School, that people truly cared for me as a person and not solely as a football player. Without speaking with anyone in my family, I decided to accept the scholarship and attend South Carolina State.

After my meeting with the coaches I was given a mini-tour of the campus. At Dukes Gym, I was introduced to Barney Chavous and Donnie Shell, the two primary leaders on the football team. Barney was a defensive end and Donnie a linebacker for the Bulldogs. They were working out in the basement of Dukes Gym on a Universal machine fit for a YMCA program instead of a college football program. Little did I realize that machine was the bulk of the football program's weight equipment. I remember both of them looking at me as if to say, "We've seen many players come and go, what makes you any different?" but they didn't say anything of that sort. Instead they both congratulated me and said that they hoped I could help the program.

When Ms. McDuffie and I got back into her car to head back to Florence, I felt relieved that the interview was over and it was a success. I think she felt a sense of accomplishment that she had made a difference in someone's life. Mine! I could not wait to get back and share the good news with my family and friends. I kept thinking that the situation had worked out well, especially since several of my friends, and, most important, my girlfriend, Donna Rae, were going to be attending State.

I graduated from my high school with many of my friends. In my earlier high school years, graduating was not on my radar screen. In ninth and some of tenth grade, I only did what was necessary to get by. Had I not seen the light in time, and not surrounded myself with other kids who inspired me, I would not have been graduating! As president of my senior class I was part of the graduation program and gave a speech on behalf of all of the graduating seniors. I didn't harbor any bitterness over the football situation; that was in the past. Though I'd initially felt ambivalent about the move to the new school, I eventually became popular with most of the students there. I felt honored that, having only been at that school for two years, I had earned enough respect from my peers that they'd put me in a position of power. I knew that I would never have been considered for such a position in my earlier years in school.

I felt so special when my scholarship papers arrived in the mail. I knew that once I signed those papers, it would open a new chapter in my life. I had the scholarship but I also had to be admitted to the school based on my high school transcript. I still had to hold my breath and cross my fingers because I did not have the best grades. I had to thank Donna for her influence on me because I'd been only a fair to average student. I did a lot of goofing off in school, not fully understanding that I would need the grades to get into college. Thank God for Donna Rae and her parents, who instilled in her a certain work ethic that rubbed off on me before it was too late. Before long, my application for admission was approved by state, and only the mandatory physical remained.

My family physician was Dr. Roswell Beck, who was then the only black doctor in Florence. My sister Ruth gave me the money for the physical. I was a tough football player, but I was afraid of going to doctors, even when I was ill. I equated doctors with needles and shots, and that was a huge fear. I walked into Dr. Beck's office, stated my name and why I was there to the receptionist. When Dr. Beck eventually got to me, he asked a number of questions about my own health and the health of my family members. He already knew most of my family members' health histories since he was their doctor as well. He performed the physical examination, took some blood, and pronounced me fit. I'd passed the last hurdle needed for admission to South Carolina State. As I was leaving I pulled out my money to pay Dr. Beck. He shook his head and refused the money, saying, "Boy, keep your money. The only thing I want you to do is make something of yourself." That act of kindness touched me then and has stayed with me for the rest of my life. "Make something of your life!" Dr. Beck echoed what most older black folks wanted for the younger generation. It was what my teachers wanted, it was what my ministers wanted, and it was what many adults who gave me a chance and shared their wisdom with me wanted.

I began to realize that I did not belong to just me, but also to others who had made some type of investment in my well-being and my future. One was Mrs. Rosa Key, from my church, who gave me an opportunity to earn money honestly by washing her windows after school. Another woman from my church, Mrs. Mary Walker, was like a grandmother to me. Mrs. Key and Mrs. Walker had been teachers earlier on, and they always stressed the importance of getting as much knowledge as I could to deal with life. I knew they loved me as if I were their own child. My pastor, Reverend Burgess, was another supporter. He encouraged all of the students in his congregation to strive to be great people and not embarrass their families by getting into trouble. I felt blessed that while I may have screwed up as a football player my senior year, I was getting another chance, with a scholarship to boot. When I started to think about it, I knew I was so much more than I could understand at that point. All of the senior citizens who'd really had it hard in their lives, with hardships that I couldn't even imagine, were counting on me to do something special with my life. The mantra of almost every older black person in my hood was the same as Dr. Beck's: make something good out of your life!

I also thought about all of the guys whom I'd played with and wondered, "What if they had gotten the same opportunities I have had?" Some of these guys played before me as well as during the same time I played, such as Bubble Gum, June Bug, Curtis Cato, Herbert "Lump" Nelson, Leslie Gregg, Myron

McNeil, and the Grant boys, Milton and Wesley. They were all sports legends in my town, badasses in their respective sports, but they may have made some questionable choices much as I had made. Or they just didn't catch the same break that I caught. They didn't make it to where I was going so I knew I had to represent them.

CHAPTER 5

So Hard to Be a Bulldog!

I considered myself more fortunate than many of my friends who had graduated with me. Many of them were looking for jobs while I was preparing to go to college. When I was younger, I never considered going to college. In my earlier, "limited" world, I thought going to college was something that other people did. For the longest time I thought that I would wind up in the military like my brothers. Once considered by some people as being from the other side of the tracks, I was now preparing to attend college. It was certainly going to be a different experience. Aside from my summer visits to New Jersey to see my mother, I had never spent any significant time away from home. While that was in the back of my mind, my main concern was how to physically prepare for this new chapter.

I had grown accustomed to training on my own. Who in the hell would have time or want to run with me on days of ninety-plus heat in Florence, South Carolina? My focus was on getting myself totally ready to compete once I arrived at school. My June and July days of that summer of 1972 were spent running distances and sprints, early in the morning, midafternoons, and early evenings. While others thought I was insane to run during the hottest part of the day, I knew I should not avoid the heat by running only in the mornings or late in the evenings when it cooled off. I'd underestimated the commitment it took to make the team in high school, and I never wanted to make that mistake again.

Many people in Florence quickly found out that I was going to State to play football with the Bulldogs. While I hadn't thought much about it earlier, I now realized that the State alumni base was quite strong in my town. Many people congratulated me and wished me good luck when they saw me running through town on my daily runs. Their compliments made me feel good, but also a little nervous. If I failed to make it or if I quit, I would be an embarrassment to everyone, especially myself. If that was pressure that I placed on myself, then it was good because it made me really push myself when I didn't want to work out.

My sisters gave me a ride to Orangeburg with all of the items I needed to set up my room in Bethea Hall. Arriving on the campus signaled a transition in my life. For the first time I was totally alone to make my decisions about my future. Whether those decisions were good or bad, I would not have anyone looking over my shoulder telling me what to do. This was an opportunity to show what I was made of, not just on the field, but off the field as well. That is what ROTC, Boy Scouts, Holmes School, Mount Zion Church, and my family unit were about. I felt that if I could maintain my sense of integrity, I would be okay.

Once my family helped me check into my dorm room and I was all squared away, they left. I think you feel one of two thoughts at this point. Either you jump for joy that you are finally on your own, or you feel deep sadness with bouts of homesickness. I felt a combination of both. While I felt a little homesick as soon as my family left, I knew that I was there to fulfill an obligation. With my scholarship, I knew that if I fulfilled my end of the agreement on the field and in the classroom, I would graduate. Just as other people had jobs to do in the regular world, class and football were my jobs.

My first days of practice were eye-opening. After picking up my equipment and getting a locker, I had to get used to the brand-new faces of those I would be playing with. As an incoming freshman not knowing the ropes, I found myself watching others to see how things should be done. If I had a question, I would ask, but I didn't want to appear too ignorant. As a new pup in the doghouse I tried to figure out who the big dogs were. In my mind the true big dogs were the older, more experienced, and most respected players. It didn't take me long to find out who those guys were. Barney Chavous and Donnie Shell were the two players I met when I visited State earlier. They would be the ones that I would measure my performance against in practice. They both were captains, and the encouragement they'd given me on my initial visit went a long way in earning my respect.

I knew I had to up my level of play to compete against guys not just from my town or my area of South Carolina, but from all around the country; this was not high school. These guys were from South Carolina, North Carolina, Georgia, New Jersey, New York, Florida, Alabama, Mississippi, and Virginia. And they weren't from the bottom of their high school programs; most of these guys were pretty damn good players, and many of them were tough, hard-nosed players who didn't give a shit about anything. You know, those guys that if they weren't in school, they might have been hardened soldiers who'd just fought a war somewhere. The offensive and defensive linemen that I had to practice with and against were big. Not huge, but they were agile, they could run, and they packed a pop. At the time I was about 220 pounds, but these guys were 250- to 280-pounders. To be able to hang with these guys, I would have to bring it physically on the field. I knew that I had to give my best if I was going to make this team.

Once again, it started with that very first step on the football field. That first step is symbolic of our committing to the team, the coaching staff, and ourselves. We began our practice a full week or two prior to most high schools because the college football season started earlier. But whether it was high school or college, waiting to take the football field for the first time was the same. The cast of players and coaches was different, but the one constant for me was the smell of the freshly cut grass. For me that scent meant it was time for football, and whether in the South, the North, or the Far West, it was the same for every other football player. To me it meant that it was time to go to work!

Once we began our two-a-day practice sessions, we spent a couple of days in shorts and T-shirts to get acclimated to the Orangeburg heat and humidity. Florence was only about ninety-five miles northeast of Orangeburg, but I would swear the temperatures in Orangeburg were ten to fifteen degrees hotter.

When you'd look down the street or out on the football practice field, you could see the heat rising from the surface. That alone would make some people think twice about playing, but most of my teammates were from the South and were accustomed to hot weather. Those "light" practices were good to help ease us into the full pads and helmets. Otherwise I'm sure players would have passed out due to heat exhaustion. The heat was at times unbearable, but we had no choice but to throw ourselves into it and get used to it. The coaches knew that once we began our season, our games would be played during the day in early September in the South, with no nice, pleasant seventy-degree days.

I was given #75. I wanted #70, the same number I wore in high school, but that number was already taken by Barney. The equipment manager pointed out that the last player to wear #75 was James Evans, who, while undrafted by the NFL, was a free agent in the New York Giants training camp. While I was a new puppy on the block at SC State, Evans was in the same role in New York. He had been a well-respected player the previous years at SC State, and some of the older guys made me aware that if I was going to wear that number on my jersey, I had a lot to live up to. To top that off, Coach Banks and Coach Carson, my position coach, told me individually of the respect they had for Evans, whom everyone called Mississippi. They both said that while he was an outstanding player on the field, he was a leader for the team as well. What I didn't know was that one of the other players who wore that number when he attended SC State was David "Deacon" Jones, the same Deacon Jones who played with the Los Angeles Rams and went on to become a member of the Pro Football Hall of Fame. So, while I was this lowly freshman at the bottom of the totem pole, apparently somebody thought enough of me to give me that number. Talk about pressure; not only did I have to make the team, but I also had a numerical reputation to uphold. At one point I thought, "I don't know if I want the pressure that comes with a fucking number." I had enough pressure trying to compete against the other players to earn a spot on the roster, let alone compete with myself, just to make it through each practice. Finally I thought I was either going to uphold the integrity of the number or I wasn't. And if the latter, then I probably wouldn't be at State by the end of my freshman year anyway.

Once we put the pads on and started to hit, players began to distinguish where they were going to fit on the team. Some players looked good in their uniform but you could tell that they were not big hitters, while others took great pride in looking as if they could knock the shit out of people and think nothing of it. I was sort of a cross between the two: I could hold my own in the early contact drills but I didn't seek out the contact. I wanted to scope out the environment for as long as I could before getting thrown into the mix, so I did what I thought was best for me: I hung out at the rear of the line so my name wouldn't be called. Because State's athletic program did not have a huge budget, Coach Carson doubled as both the defensive line coach and linebackers' coach. That meant that whenever the linebackers worked against the offensive linemen or running backs, as a defensive lineman I had to be a part of the drill, maybe not as a participant but as a spectator. I was able to watch what talent most of the players brought to the table. I was impressed that these guys on the defensive side of the ball were not afraid to hit.

As we went through one-on-one blocking drills, I heard my name called as the next player for the drill. My heart started to race. At last it was my time to take center stage. When placed in this kind of situation, you want to do your job to the max but you also want to look good doing it. From the beginning of my short playing career I'd learned one important thing: in football you earn respect not by talking a good game but by what you do on the field. Many players try to "wolf" or talk trash to impress others with their playing abilities. All talk goes out the window if you're not able to walk the walk.

I was called to go through a basic blocking drill where two dummy pads were placed on the ground about three to four yards apart. On the snap of the ball I was to hold my ground by defeating the blocker in front of me. In the drill the offensive lineman had the advantage of knowing the snap count and the way he was going to block me. I drew Charles Wright, an offensive guard who was good at running the power sweep, which was throwing blocks on linebackers and defensive backs to spring the tailbacks running behind him. Bottom line, this drill was about seeing who was the tougher of the two of us; it was a power-against-power drill.

As I assumed my three-point stance in the drill, my mind went back to BC Correll in high school as I anticipated what was to come. Charles got into his stance, and with our helmets tilted up, we looked at each other. I looked in his eyes, but there was so much more I had to see. Prior to the snap I had to be ready for any movement of his body, his hands, or his head. I had to see the football out of the corner of my eye to see the snap. While I used my eyes to see everything, I could hear the signals being called by the coach. I couldn't be influenced by what I heard; I had to go off at the first movement I saw.

On the snap of the ball Charles exploded off the line of scrimmage. In that fraction of a second I had to do the same—explode with as much thrust as I could muster and meet force with force. Once we made contact, I stalemated his block and used my leverage and hands to shed him. I won the match, and the defensive players cheered my victory. Charles was a leaner BC but with more pop behind his block. Coach Carson was like a proud papa sticking his chest out with pride at the work of his young defensive players. When the play was over, I headed to the back of the line to take a knee with the other defensive players. I felt good about what I had just done, but I also felt a little woozy. I saw stars twinkling before my eyes, but I had had that same feeling a couple of other times while in high school.

That block by Charles Wright basically set the bar and gave me an idea of what I was going to be facing every day in practice and probably in games as well. That Wright was a junior who started and not a freshman like me impressed many of the other younger players as well as me. That one play, in that one drill, gave me the confidence of knowing that I could hang with the big dogs. The rest of practice was a test of stamina, with lots of running from drill to drill—the tackling drill, working on the two-man and seven-man sleds, different types of agility drills, offensive and defensive drills—and to top it off, lots more running at the end of practice. I was glad I spent so much time pushing myself during the summer with my running, especially in the sun and the heat, because as each practice passed, players were dropping like flies. You can't pick and choose the weather you play football in. It is the one sport that begins in the sometimes unbearable heat and humidity of summer and ends in the cold, frigid weather of the fall or winter. You have to prepare for the uncertainty of each game's weather conditions. Right then, I could only concern myself with practice conditions. We went through our two-a-day practices for about two weeks, until all of the other students arrived and we began classes. Then we started our once-a-day practices. The intensity of those practices increased because we did not have to pace ourselves for an additional daily practice.

I learned early on the tradition the team had for the end of each practice. As a group, all of the players would clap their hands and hit their thigh pads and chant, "Bulldog!" "Tenacity!" "Bulldog!" "Tenacity!" At the beginning I didn't know what in the hell was going on or what the chant meant. Then I began to realize that bulldogs are tough and tenacious. I guess it would have been worse to have a mascot that was not so aggressive and tough, but I figured out pretty quickly that these guys that I had joined believed strongly in bulldog tenacity and having pride.

Once all of the students reported for the beginning of school, I developed the same problem as many other new college students (and not just athletes): being unable cope with the college social life. When I wasn't doing the football thing, I realized that I had entered a new world that was much different socially from where I'd come from. While quite a few students from my hometown were attending SC State, I did not realize I was going to meet so many other students from around the country. I felt like a kid in a candy store—talk about gorgeous women, oh my God! I never claimed to be the brightest crayon in the box, but I was astute enough to notice that many of the senior and other upper-class guys spent a lot of their time at the freshman female dorms. As soon as parents dropped their daughters off at those dormitories, the wolves attacked the henhouse. So, I wondered, since all of the guys were flocking to the freshmen dorms, what was going on at the senior female dorms? That's where I started to spend a lot of my free time when I was not on the practice field. I spent so much time there talking to the older, more mature ladies that I got off track and started to have problems early on with my classes. I'd been excited to attend SC State because Donna Rae would also be attending the school. But when much of my attention started going in those other directions, our relationship fizzled out rather quickly.

Going to meetings and practice seemed like a new job. I had to learn so much about the game and the defenses we were going to be playing. But going to class with all of the other students made me begin to understand the responsibility of college. I had to go to classes, get my assignments done, study for tests, and write papers. By midafternoon, I had to hurry to the locker room, change into my uniform, put whatever I had to do for class out of my mind, and focus all my attention on what I had to do on the practice field. Regardless of what had happened in class or what I had to do for the next class, I could not allow any outside thoughts to enter my head while on the field. Coaches expect to get your undivided attention during practice. I had to put the football stuff in a box when I went to class, and then in practice I had to put the classroom stuff away. My class schedule coupled with my strenuous football practices meant that I didn't always have enough time to rest.

I was doing quite well on the football field. My play was good enough to earn a starting spot as a freshman. I was happy that my work and dedication to the game were paying off. McClenaghan High School seemed so long ago, yet the taste of how I left that team stuck with me in a positive way. I was the only freshman to earn a starting spot on defense, yet this didn't make me feel much pressure. If anything, I felt honored to play along with upperclassmen such as Donnie and Barney, the two guys who, unbeknownst to them, became my role models on the field. In choosing those guys as mentors, I was not looking to be like them in performance, but I wanted to emulate their work ethic and leadership. They had a hearty sense of humor and had fun, but they were tough, and when they strapped on the pads, they were serious about their jobs. What was most important was these guys were respected by all the players as well as the coaches. I knew I needed to keep up with them in my own performance. I wanted to follow their example on and off the field to earn the same level of respect they had from players and coaches. Much like an understudy in a Broadway play, I watched my mentors push and demand the best of themselves and those players around them.

Sometimes I wondered what drove them, how did they get to where they were as successful student athletes? I assumed that they were a product of all of their past experiences. But sometimes they were more like members of my own family who talked about my ancestors; they talked about players who played before them and influenced them when they were in high school or when they were freshmen at State. They occasionally referred to players they played with before I even arrived on the scene. Whether it was the grace, the grit, the talent, or the toughness of certain players' past teams, those players must have had a profound impact on them. I began to understand that just as a legacy is passed down from generation to generation in families, legacies can be handed down from generation to generation in football. I didn't know how many generations were being played out when I watched Barney and Donnie. I'm sure they were influenced by parents and their own home life, but I could also sense in them a legacy that they were charged with handing down to many of their teammates.

Most of the players at South Carolina State had chosen to attend a historically black college. Only a few years earlier, most of the schools that you saw on television playing football on Saturday afternoon had teams with mostly white guys. Those schools, I imagined, had superior facilities for their football teams. At State we did not have the best locker room nor the weight-training equipment that most other schools had. We couldn't sit around and gripe about locker rooms or weight rooms, we just had to make do with what we had. Ironically, what little equipment we had was probably better than anything we had had in any of the high schools that we'd come from. That was probably a reason why we as a team did a lot of running. We ran forty- to sixty-yard sprints and gassers, which are sprints where you start on one side of the field, run to the other side of the field, then run back to the original starting point. Then we ran fifths, which started at one corner of the field and followed the borders of the field back to the starting point. All of these running drills were against the clock. With these running drills coaches didn't need to cut players from the team because if you couldn't keep up physically, you usually cut yourself.

You need to know several things about black college football of my era. First, players could run and were mobile. Second, every player knew the feeling of getting on the bus on Thursday night to travel to the location of Saturday's game. Traveling by jet was reserved for the major schools; black college football programs did not have the budgets to fly their players. Some schools couldn't even bring all of their players on road trips for away games. So while our team might have had eighty to ninety players dressed for a home game, an opposing team might only have forty to fifty players who'd traveled on the bus from sometimes a good distance away.

Our first season did not go well for us as a team. We won the first game we played by one point. That was it, one win my freshman year! While we had a decent defense, we did not have a good offensive team. We started the season with a senior at quarterback and finished with a freshman, my roommate, Elias O'Neal. As players from opposite sides of the ball, we got along well. At night, before going to sleep, we talked a lot, and both of us agonized over the plight of the team that season. The team had heart, but at times we just weren't good enough. I thought a couple of the older guys had some drug and alcohol issues that took away from their game. But while the team struggled, I had a respectable season and opened the eyes of some who followed the team.

At the end of the '72 season Coach Banks was fired and took an assistant coaching position at the University of South Carolina, the larger, predominantly white university in Columbia. For a while, no one knew what would happen given the change of coach. A couple of seniors who noticed I had talent and promise tried to convince me to transfer and follow Coach Banks to USC. These guys had just completed their athletic eligibility by NCAA rules and were looking at graduating and going on to graduate school or to life in the real world. I'm sure their intentions were good, and they thought that the football program was probably going to collapse. But I did not even look at the possibility of changing schools. I felt comfortable at South Carolina State. I remembered I had those coaches in high school whom either I could not relate to or they could not relate to me; why would I want to go back into a situation like that?

Also, I could not transfer because at the end of my first semester my grade point average was 1.31. A GPA of 1.30 would place you on academic probation. The transition to college, the course load, playing football, but, more important, the misplaced priorities, put me in a place where I should never have been. A 1.31 GPA was embarrassing; I even failed remedial math! I may not have been the smartest person around, but I knew I was no dummy. I came

.01 point from being placed on academic probation and possibly losing my scholarship. In my first semester I had taken great care to stay away from the alcohol and any possible drugs in the dorms. Being linked to those things would certainly have been the kiss of death to my financial aid. Nobody in my family had the means to pay for my college education, so I had to stay on the right track and maintain my scholarship. I did not share my grades with anyone, including my family, after that first semester, but I knew I had to get my ass in gear. I approached my second semester with greater determination and commitment in the classroom, and while I continued to have a social life, I began to understand that I needed to take care of my main priorities.

With the departure of Coach Banks, a search for a new head coach began. This was the first time any coach that I'd played for had gotten the ax. I wondered who would be brought in and what changes would be made in the football program. The search committee recommended that Willie Jeffries be named the next coach of the Bulldogs. Coach Jeffries and I had met less than a year before when Mr. Madison had taken me to visit North Carolina A&T State University. Coach Jeffries had been a defensive assistant under Coach Howell, then moved on to the University of Pittsburgh. He lasted only one season at Pitt before being lured to South Carolina State, his alma mater, to turn the football program around. One of the first things he did was to retain Coach Carson as the defensive coordinator. In my opinion, Coach Carson was one of the smartest and toughest coaches to play for. He demanded a lot from his players, but the most important thing he got from us was our respect.

As the team went into spring practice, we needed to improve upon many areas of our game, and every player had some type of weakness to work on. Barney was a senior with no further playing eligibility. He was scheduled to graduate but was being heavily scouted by every National Football League team. I was excited to see all of the pro scouts come to Orangeburg to run him through drills and time him in the forty-yard dash. Some of the scouts gave me and my teammates logos of their respective teams. Some of us would put those logos on cars, dorm doors, books, or whatever we could to show people that we had some link to the NFL.

One of the more memorable meetings I had with a scout was with Bobby

Beathard. Bobby was a scout or player-personnel director for the Miami Dolphins. While scouting Barney during the season and afterward, Bobby watched a lot of film on Barney. While his focus was on Barney, apparently my play caught his eye. When we eventually met on one of his visits to see Barney in Orangeburg, Bobby told me that he couldn't help but notice me on film and that I had a lot of talent and potential. He then said, "If you keep playing the way you're playing, I'll have to come back to get you." I was only a second-semester freshman, but to have a well-respected National Football League insider say that to me gave me a huge lift. While professional football was not a goal of mine at the time, it made me aware that I potentially had the talent to get to the next level. I always remembered that comment, and it made me understand that even when your team is not playing well, if you play your game to the best of your ability, you will get noticed. Even when you think no one's watching, someone is!

Toward the end of the school year all of the athletes prepared for the annual athletic awards program for all of the university's sports. Dr. Maceo Nance was South Carolina State's president and was probably the football team's biggest supporter and fan. Dr. Nance was honest in telling all of us football players that he was disappointed with the play of the team, but he promised Coach Jeffries the support of the administration.

I remember sitting with my roommate, Elias O'Neal, during the program. As various awards and honors were given out to different athletes, Elias whispered to me, "You know you're going to get the Rookie of the Year Award." I said, "Naw, I don't think so." He said, "Man, you're a shoe-in for that award." I had not thought about getting any kind of award or recognition till that point. I knew I was going to get a letter for my playing time, but I didn't think I'd get any award. Then he whispered again, "You're going to get the Rookie of the Year Award." I thought he was sharing a secret that he knew that I was unaware of, so I began to believe what he said. I began to get excited when one of the coaches presenting the awards started talking about that award. He then said, "And the Rookie of the Year Award goes to . . ." As I began to rise up out of my seat to head to the stage, the coach said, "Elias O'Neal." Already halfway out of my seat, I pretended to be making space to allow my roommate to walk past me. For the first time in a long time, I was disappointed, all because I allowed myself to believe what someone else said. I bought into it, and all of a sudden I got pissed, not at my roommate but at myself for letting my hopes get too high. Elias probably deserved the award more than me, not that I hadn't had a decent season, but I'm sure his position as quarterback allowed him to highlight his skills more than I could as a defensive end. That night as I lay in bed, I quietly made a promise to myself that a situation like that would never again happen to me. If my performance on the field was ever going to be judged again, I was going to make it difficult for anyone to pass me over for any honor.

Barney was drafted in the second round by the Denver Broncos. With his departure from the defensive line, I knew I had to step it up a notch. Donnie was a hard-nosed SOB and solid with the linebackers, but when he spoke, everyone listened. Donnie was the defensive captain and was well respected, but we guys up front needed a voice who could speak for us. I wasn't the same kind of vocal player as Barney. He was a huge guy, about six feet four inches tall and 260–270 pounds; I was about six feet two and a half and weighed about 225 pounds. Barney had the body mass and strength to go against those big linemen. Me? I was still growing, but I decided to fill in where Barney had left off. I made sure that I got myself in shape for the next training camp, as I did not know exactly what kind of camp Coach Jeffries was going to run.

At the beginning of my second season at State, I realized that things were going to be different in many ways. Retaining Coach Carson as defensive coordinator was probably one of the wisest things Coach Jeffries did in putting his staff together. I had tremendous respect for Carson; even though he was a short, squatty guy, known for his cigars and raspy voice, he was tough and wanted his players to follow his lead. The other smart move Coach Jeffries made was in hiring Samuel Goodwin as a defensive coach and, more important, putting him in charge of conditioning. While all of the coaches who were hired or retained by Coach Jeffries were good, solid coaches, Carson and Goodwin were the guys who probably set the tone for me as tough guys. Coach Carson had been a defensive lineman who probably was an overachiever when he played. He was the force who pushed us and would not allow us to drag around in drills. Coach Goodwin had been an all-star football and basketball player at

SC State back in the sixties. Just looking at him, you could tell he had well-defined muscles all over his body, including his face. There was no doubt about Coach Goodwin: you knew he probably hurt some people when he played. He was a slave driver who got the players at the end of practice and put us through our conditioning.

Coach Jeffries told the team when he first arrived that even if we didn't win a game, we were going to look good and be in condition. Goodwin's job was that of a drill sergeant putting us through the conditioning ringer. His favorite saying was "Don't cheat your body!" You could hear him yell it time after time as we ran, and ran, and ran. . . . One of the good things about a team sport is, when you have to run as we did, we all had to run. It didn't matter whether you were a big offensive lineman or the placekicker, we all had to run and make it within a particular time. The bigger people were given a longer time to finish than the smaller people, who should have been faster. We all ran with our shoulder pads on or off and had to pace ourselves to complete the drills, and when we finished, we all had the same "Thank God it's over" look in our eyes. Those who did not make their times had to do more running after practice. Those who did make it had a tremendous sense of accomplishment. It was as much a part of coming together as a team as anything else—going through like experiences. I was considered a big person because I was a defensive lineman, but realistically I was more of a medium-size guy playing a big-guy position. As time went by in our practices, I could feel myself going from dreading and struggling to make it through sprints and the runs at the end of practice, to being able to easily finish without straining at all. With Coach Goodwin's conditioning drills after practice and Coach Carson pushing us during practice, I could feel my body becoming well conditioned.

Our tempo in hitting also increased over the previous year. I realized that to make this team and raise the level of my play from my first season, I had to be a tougher player than before. I knew the coaches, as well as some of my upper-class teammates, were expecting bigger things out of me. Guys such as Donnie were going into their last year of eligibility, after which they would have to move on with their lives or attempt to play in the NFL. My approach to the game was improving as I seemed to mature more both on and off the field. Having played with Barney and still with Donnie, I had an example of what it took to hang in there and play the game the way it was supposed to be played at South Carolina State, with pride and tenacity. I went from standing in the back of the line when running various drills to assuming a place at the front, leading the way and setting an example of what the tempo should be. This was my first bout of leading by example at SC State.

One of the drills was hitting the seven-man sled. One by one we would attack the first bag on the sled, hit it with a forearm shiver, bounce back a couple of steps, avoid the second bag, attack the third bag, bounce with another drop step, then attack the fifth bag. This drill was done to simulate taking on an offensive lineman, hitting him with as much power as possible with a forearm, maintaining balance, and reacting off the block to make a tackle. (A forearm shiver is much like an uppercut in boxing, but instead of using the fist, the forearm is used.) The sled was too heavy for one person to push and move individually, so when it was hit by one person, it was like hitting a wall with springs. This sled was one of the reasons why I quit on the first day of practice back at Wilson High, but over time I had grown accustomed to hitting it. At SC State I remember hitting the sled with as much force as I could muster—the sound was a solid thud—staying under control, and bouncing back. When I completed the drill and headed to the back of the line, I started to see those stars twinkling before my eyes again. I didn't think a lot about it then; I was just happy to be able to hit the bag with power and style. I'd had similar things happen in the past; it was the feeling many people get when getting up from a chair after sitting for a while. The head starts to spin or everything fades to black. I thought I was just slightly straining myself going through the drill. Because it didn't cause me pain, was just a bit of light-headedness, I ignored it.

My experiences from high school on to my early days at SC State taught me that to truly be a player you had to shrug off injuries and play with pain. I saw that when players sustained nonserious injuries such as sprains, strains, and pulled muscles, many of the guys would joke, "You can't make the club in the tub." While the reference was never made by or to me, I heard it and knew that, although it wasn't being said maliciously or mean-spiritedly, I did not want to teased or be looked at in an unfavorable light by my teammates. Don't get me wrong, if a player sustained a serious injury such as a knee being taken out in practice or in a game or a back, neck, or a broken bone, everyone would be sympathetic. We all felt bad for those guys, but for those with nonserious injuries it was just good-natured kidding.

I came to admire and respect Coach Jeffries. You hear the expression in sports *hard but fair,* and that is the way Coach Jeff was with his team. He worked our asses off on the field. When it was time to work, we worked! But he also took an interest in us as young men, overseeing our development off the field and especially in the classroom. He constantly hammered into us that we had to take advantage of getting our education. He didn't want any of his players, whether they were starters or third-string players, to leave SC State without a degree. I saw a lot of those black teachers I had had at Holmes School in Coach Jeffries. He wanted all of his players to excel on and off the field, but he also wanted us to carry ourselves with dignity and respect and to be good people. He often stressed to us that what we did on and off the field represented not just us individually but our school and our team.

Coach and I got along well, but we did not always see things eye to eye when he first arrived. To get more practice time, he instituted 6:00 a.m. practices. For a college student, 6:00 a.m. was far too early to be thinking football along with classes all day. These early sessions were for mental preparation, as there was no hitting or even dressing in pads. We had to get up at 5:00 a.m. to be at the practice field on time. I thought the coaching staff had to be violating an NCAA rule. I was so incensed by the ungodly early practice time that I came close to writing a letter to the NCAA to report what was going on. But as with most things surrounding football, I learned to adjust and go with the flow, especially when the team started to come together and play better in practices and then in games. Had the situation not improved, I'm sure Coach and I would have clashed on the 6:00 a.m. practices. I also began to understand how important it was to mentally prepare for games. Physically, we could compete with just about anyone. We had speed and quickness at the skill positions on both sides of the football. In the trenches we had good size and strength. To mentally comprehend what we were doing and why allowed each player to get a better grasp of what other players around him were doing and to see how the small pieces of the puzzle fit together for the team.

The play of the team early that season was much better, with an improved attitude and a better commitment from most of the players. The team was starting to win, and I was having a pretty good season with my play helping the defense establish itself as a solid unit. After having been considered a "puppy" as a freshman, I think my teammates sensed that I had the potential to be a much better player now. Some of them started calling me Big Dog! To hear that in just my second year was a huge compliment. Some of the guys who were also in their second year and the incoming freshmen who were looking up to me gave me that nickname. It may not seem like much, but to be accepted and looked upon as a leader by my teammates meant the world to me. My teammates were the people I considered my family. We worked hard together, played hard together, laughed hard together, and, when needed, cried together. We ate in the same dining hall, slept in the same dorm hall, and, let's not forget, traveled on those Thursday-night bus rides to play opposing teams together. We formed our bonds as teammates going through those experiences.

Many of the nonathlete students in school pledged either a Greek fraternity or a sorority. They went through weeks of hazing and humiliating tasks to become a part of a group they could call their own. I never considered becoming part of a fraternity as I was already in one. My understanding was that in those fraternities pledges were kept up all night and beaten with paddles to prove they were worthy of belonging. If anyone is longing for acceptance in a group, try playing football. It doesn't take long for those players and coaches you practice and play with to see your strengths and weaknesses. In essence, to be able to hang you have to show what you're made of, not in private, behind closed doors, but in the open for everyone to see. Respect is not just given; it has to be earned by performing and consistently bringing your best to the table. The Big Dog title made me realize that my teammates and coaches respected my abilities.

During my second year I also settled in at State and became comfortable as a student athlete. I had a good understanding of what it took to play the game. I had good coaches and had the opportunity to play with pretty good players. Off the field, I realized that I'd dodged a big bullet by getting off track with classes. The toughest year for any college student (especially an athlete) is the first. My transition from high school to college was huge. I was not a great student in high school, and to excel and not just survive college was a challenge. No one was there to remind me to attend class, do assignments, turn in reports, study for exams, etc., and also learn my assignment as a football player. I could not continue to make those mistakes and put my eligibility in jeopardy, so I began to bear down and get more serious in the classroom.

I also wanted to be certain to stay away from drugs and alcohol. Some other athletes who came to State at the same time that I did were, in a year, no longer there because they assumed that what they did in their dorm rooms or off campus would not affect them and that no one else would find out, especially the coaches. It was amazing how those players who hid in their rooms drinking beer or wine or smoking grass eventually exposed themselves to the coaching staff and wound up losing their scholarships. The coaches found out by making surprise visits to the dormitory and smelling grass or finding seeds from marijuana plants or wine and beer bottles in players' rooms.

During football season, Coach Jeff had his own unique way of finding out what players were doing off the field. Everyone on the team took part in a twelve-minute run on the track that surrounded the football field on Sunday afternoons the day after every game. Most of the players had to make seven laps within those twelve minutes on a regular 440-yard track. To make it, you had to run your ass off. Once we finished the run, we had to walk right by Coach Jeffries, who had a sensitive nose. He could smell alcohol coming out of a player's pores if he had been drinking. Those players who felt a need to drink either lost their scholarship or were disciplined by running extra during the week, usually at five o'clock in the morning.

From the beginning, I knew my family was in no financial position to help me if I lost my scholarship, and I also felt that I was better than that. I loved where I was as an athlete! Unlike when I first went out for football in ninth grade, I had trained my body to do what I wanted it to do. But the bigger reason why I chose not to drink was that I could not intellectually understand why a person needed something to help him feel good or to help him better enjoy a party or a concert. I've always had a problem with that. I think that my pride as an athlete and my prowess on the football field would not allow me to go down that road. My fate was in my own hands, and I knew it would be crazy to go out and do something stupid such as smoke a little grass or have a few drinks. I promised myself to always be me. I also finally understood that my college football career was going to end, and what would I have when it was over if I did something stupid? While I didn't give up my social life completely, I was able to create a better balance among my athletic, academic, and social lives at State.

After my first year of adjusting to college and my second year of adjusting to another head coach, I settled down to enjoy my college experiences. Unlike many students who attended bigger universities, I got to know many of the students at State either by name or by face. Going to classes, mingling at the student center, at basketball games, campus concerts, etc., I felt very much a part of a family at State. As an athlete I was quietly establishing myself as a leader and a key player on the football team. Off the field I was gaining friends and respect largely from the notoriety of being an athlete, but also from my involvement in campus activities. I began to understand that while I was my own person, I was a representative of all of those students that I was meeting and going to class with. I represented those teachers who taught me and the coaches who coached me. Whenever the team traveled for road games, many students and alumni traveled to support us, and whether we won or lost, those people never wavered in their support. They had their opinions at times as to how things should be done, but they always supported us as a team.

My college teammates were special guys. We knew nothing about one another on the first day of practice, but by the end of each season it was as if we'd all pledged the same fraternity. One teammate in particular distinguished himself. Thomas Holliday was a rangy, on the slender side, offensive lineman who probably never played in games because of his lack of bulk. While I was only about 225 pounds, Holliday was about 210 pounds. I was able to use my speed and quickness to beat the people that I lined up against. Most of the guys who played Holliday's position were thirty to sixty pounds heavier, so he never fit into the scheme of the offensive coaches. I'm sure that Holliday knew that his chances of getting into actual games were going to be slim unless we had a sizable lead.

Holliday decided to use each practice session to play his own game. If he was going to be on the team but not get into the games, he was going to make the most of his time on the field. As a younger player looking for a challenge, Thomas Holliday decided that I was going to be his project. I remembered the first time I went one-on-one with him in practice. Coach Carson called my name to lead off the blocking drill. Before the offensive coach could call the name of a line-man to go against me, Holliday jumped to the front of the line. I was expecting to go against one of the bigger, more veteran offensive linemen, not a fresh-man. I stood in position, getting ready, and thought the offensive-line coach would pull Holliday for another lineman since it could have been a mismatch once we got into the drill. The coach said nothing and I just looked at Holliday standing in front of me. For a brief moment I thought going against him was going to be a piece of cake. Holliday looked me directly in my eyes, put his mouthpiece in, and fastened his chin strap tight. He got into his stance and dug his cleats on his right foot into the dirt to get traction. I thought because he was a bit undersized that I would be able to defeat his block easily.

On the snap of the ball, Thomas Holliday exploded out of his stance and planted his helmet right under my chin. He stunned me as he kept his feet moving and blocked me out of the box. Coach Carson looked at me and said, "Damn, Carson, maybe you need to spend more time in the weight room. That man just whipped your ass!" I immediately wanted to go again but was denied by the coach. This was a drill for the group, not just for me to soothe my rather frac-tured ego. I was a little embarrassed, but it served me right to get my ass handed to me because I took another player too lightly. I knew that I was going to have to execute every play, whether in a game or in practice, with great intensity and force. I could not take a play off or assume that an opponent was easy. Thomas Holliday taught me a valuable lesson that day, one I would always remember. From that day on, Holliday and I chose to go against each other in practice drills because we both knew that we were going to give our best stuff against each other. Ironically, Holliday's best stuff as a blocker was better than that of most of the players I played against in games. While he was not a wide load like many other players at his position, he was quick off the ball with power.

Most of the players I faced in games were bigger but slower than me. My speed, quickness, and agility, along with a quick burst of power, served me well and gave me an advantage over bigger, slower players. Thomas Holliday and I became friends while battling one another on the practice fields, and we pushed one another when times got hard, such as on those hot September Sunday-afternoon twelve-minute runs when we needed to make seven laps around the track. Usually he was my rabbit, setting the pace, and I tried to keep up with him. I could probably have done it myself, but it was good to have a supporter like Holliday to push me to be the best that I could be as an athlete and as a person.

I became a team captain during my junior season. It was a tremendous honor for me to be looked at as a leader. I had won a couple of honors such as all-conference, all-district, and all-state for my play in my second season. As a junior I was no longer in the shadows of Barney and Donnie. They were doing well on their next level. Barney was playing with the Denver Broncos, and Donnie was playing with the Pittsburgh Steelers, having made that club as a free agent. It was up to me to step up and exhibit the leadership qualities that I'd acquired from playing with those guys. I had to be an example and set the tempo in practice, not just by talking the talk but in my actions as well. While I knew that, so did the coaches. Although they never talked with me about it, I could sense that they expected me to carry myself in a certain way and take charge. The younger guys were going to be looking for guidance from me as a captain, and from some of the other older players, so we could not disappoint them.

Having gone through one season with him, I had gotten used to Coach Jeff's training and practice sessions, so I made sure I was in good shape to get through those tough hot days of practice. For the first time playing football, I was really the Man! I don't mean that in a cocky, boastful way but in a heavy-load-on-my-shoulders way. I had never been a captain before, even on the high school level, because I quit my team during my senior year. That could never happen here because of the responsibility placed on my shoulders by the coaches; I could never quit my team at State for any reason. Besides I was having too much fun on and off the field.

My college life was great! I was away from home and on my own. I was becoming a decent student and had a full social life. Many nonathlete students knew me, and my teammates respected me. It was a good place to be in my life. No major cares, just keep my nose clean and do my job. My relationship with Coach Jeffries was getting closer. The coaching staff drove us into the ground in practice sometimes, and while we did not always like it, we knew they had our best interest at heart. Whenever I attended a pep rally the night before a game, I could see the enthusiasm of all of the students in attendance. They wanted us to play well and they wanted us to win. I loved that about black college football on Saturday afternoons. Fans came to see the games and wanted a good show, but they also came to see the bands.

Our band was one of the best in the country in black college football. I never paid attention to the band when I was at my last high school, but the band at SC State always inspired me. As a captain, prior to a kickoff, I had to go to the center of the field for the coin toss by the officials. That responsibility was special to me as a leader, but once I returned to the sideline in preparation to do battle in the game, I stood at attention, closed my eyes, and listened to the Marching 101 play the national anthem. It's hard to explain, but listening to that anthem got my juices flowing much like watching a western featuring John Wayne leading a platoon of soldiers into battle as the bugler is playing "Charge!" The band took pride in their precision drills, much as we as football players took pride in our play on the field. The Marching 101 got me fired up and helped inspire me to give my all on the field, as did the students, who could really get that Bulldog spirit in supporting the team. Whether we won or lost, the students always had our back. So I knew the importance of the team giving its best effort when it was time to play. I felt that I belonged in the place where I was, with my friends, my instructors, and even Dr. Nance, SC State's president, appreciating and supporting the football program. That backing made my efforts worthwhile and more meaningful.

My junior year was one of the most exciting times of my football experience. Our team was about as good as you can get, especially on defensive. We on defense were in shape, knew our assignments, were physical, and challenged one another to get to the ball carrier first. We swarmed opposing offenses like a bunch of bees on honey. Our defense played games in which the opposing offensive ended the game with fewer yards than they came with—minus thirty, fifty, to seventy yards rushing. We set an NCAA record of giving up the fewest points in one season. It is unheard of for any team to give up a mere 29 points in a season, but we did that. I took pride in the whole team, but especially in my group of guys. Our defensive front seven worked hard in practice and then we did our thing in games. I was honored and took great pride in being the leader of that group. We weren't cocky, but we certainly were confident in our abilities. I was named Most Valuable Defensive Player in the Mid-Eastern Athletic Conference and was given all-American honors by several sources. In two years I had come a long way from being embarrassed at my school's athletic honors program as a freshman.

We had few injuries as a team that year, but I sustained one that I'll always remember. We played Alcorn State University, another historically black institution, at home. Toward the end of the first half a running play came to my side of the field. As I was fighting off a block, my hand went down to the ground. At that moment, the lead blocker went at my legs to try to cut me down to allow the ball carrier to advance. When the play was over, I looked at my hand and saw that my ring finger on my left hand was bent completely backward at the middle joint. I felt no pain, probably because I was so jacked up from playing in the game. I walked over to the sideline as the first half was ending. Our doctor thought it was best to try to put the finger back in its proper position while I was still on the field. As the rest of the team went into the locker room, the doctor thought it would be best to give me a shot of Novocain to numb the area before he put the finger back in place. Aside from snakes, I hate needles with a passion, so as I saw him pull out the needle and stick it into the small bottle of Novocain, I turned my head to look away. I never felt the needle, but I could hear the crowd in the stands, some eight thousand to ten thousand spectators, groan as they witnessed that bit of unpleasantness. After waiting a minute the doctor pulled on the finger and replaced it in its proper position.

For some reason that experience in front of all of those people made me feel a little more macho than I had ever before felt. That was one of those experiences that showed people that to play football you really have to be tough and able to play with pain. I received much sympathy from so many people, especially girls, who felt sorry for me. To this day the joint in my left-hand ring finger is still swollen and I'm unable to wear a regular-size ring.

Once junior season was over, I concentrated on my schoolwork. I decided to attend summer school as I anticipated being six credit hours shy of graduating with my class. After my final exams I went home to take some time to relax before coming back for the summer session. When I arrived at our apartment, I noticed that my father had come to stay with us. He normally stayed at his own apartment, where he lived alone, several blocks from us. When I saw him, I immediately noticed that he looked a little drawn and weak. From mid-May, I noticed that day by day he underwent subtle physical changes. It seemed that he was becoming like my grandaunt when she became ill several years earlier. He went from being able to stand to having trouble with his balance and falling. Soon he was bedridden and almost incapable of doing anything for himself. He was unable to walk or feed himself, then he started to lose his ability to speak and his right eye began to close.

I was with my father, who was there in bed but had not always been there for me. My father never came to a football practice like some of the other fathers or even to one game to watch me play. He was not an athlete, so he never talked to me about sports or anything else. But he was my father, and while he might not always have been the ideal role model, I still loved and respected him. I tried to take care of him then because I knew I was going to have to leave to return to summer school. I remember giving him a bath after he had made a mess of himself in bed because he couldn't get to the bathroom. In a weak voice my father apologized to me, his son, because I had to bathe him. I saw firsthand the embarrassment one feels when one is no longer able to care for oneself. He cried from the frustration of being unable to control his body and its functions. Some of the last things I did for him before I left for school were to cut his hair and give him a shave and a bath. He was so satisfied and happy to be clean and comfortable. I stood in the doorway of the room that was normally mine and just watched him in bed. When I had to leave for school, I told him, "Daddy, I've gotta go." He looked at me and said, "I know. Don't worry about me, I'll be all right."

One of the toughest things I've ever had to do in my life was turn and walk away knowing that I would probably never again see my father alive. I forgave him for anything he had ever done or not done for me and my family. I forgave him for all of the whippings I got as a young boy. I forgave him for every time he made my mother cry. Whatever hurt, bitterness, or pain he ever caused me, I forgave him because it just wasn't important. I preferred to think about the good times, those days when he took me fishing with him and all of those guys that he drank with. From that experience with my father I realized that every moment spent with a loved one is valuable and precious.

I drove back to Orangeburg crying and thinking about how huge that point in my life was. While I tried to be optimistic that he would eventually be okay, I knew he probably would not. I registered for summer school and found an apartment near campus to share with my roommate and teammate Neely Dunn. About a week after I returned, I was studying for class one evening when I became annoyed by the constant ringing of our phone with friends calling. I took the phone off the hook until the next morning. On my way to class the next morning, Coach Jeffries saw me from his office window and called me to his office. When I walked in, I saw he had a somber look, and he told me that my father had passed away the previous night. He said that my family had tried to reach me all evening but my line was busy. I remember feeling somewhat numb, as if I had icy cold water running through my veins. Coach was concerned about me, but I was okay. I'll never forget that I shed one tear for my dad and remembered what he had told me the last time I saw him alive: "Don't worry about me, I'll be all right." I think that I had already prepared myself for this time. It was still tough to hear what had become a reality. Coach Jeffries and I were somewhat close before, but after that I gravitated to him more as a father figure.

After my father's funeral I returned to school to finish the summer session and prepare for my final football season at State. In the hot summer sun, my teammates and I ran, lifted, and pushed one another to be in the best condition for training camp. I had been looked at by many pro football scouts by this time, and everyone knew that I would probably be a good choice for an NFL franchise. I didn't think about it a lot. I was more concerned with making sure that I did what I had to do to graduate. I'd seen a couple guys who, thinking they were going to be drafted, didn't bother to finish their degree in their senior year. Those players thought they were so good that school didn't matter; they knew they were going to go pro and make a ton of money. I also saw that when draft time rolled around, some of those players weren't selected nor did they graduate. I didn't want that for myself, but most important I didn't want to disappoint my family. While my oldest sister, Ruth, and my oldest brother went to college, neither of them graduated. I knew that my family was counting on me to get my diploma.

It was neat to have NFL teams calling to arrange a time when I could run and be tested by them. After every workout I made sure I got one of their helmet logos to put on my books or on my dorm door. I felt special even being considered for play in the National Football League. I entered my senior season making a special effort to ensure it was one that I really wanted to remember and savor. Yeah, the NFL was interested, but the NFL was not a goal for me. Don't get me wrong, if it happened, fine! But if it didn't happen, that would be okay as well. I wasn't pinning my hopes and future on playing in the NFL.

After passing my summer school classes, I knew I was on pace to graduate. That was the most important thing to me at that time. I knew that my four years of eligibility for college ball would be over after my final game of the season, and I knew I would miss it when that time came. I wanted to remember those small things such as the camaraderie of being with my teammates in practice, joking around with teammates in the locker room, and hanging out in the dorm with the guys. I wanted to remember having meals together with other players and friends in the dining hall. Those times with my teammates and close friends over the previous three years were some of the things I valued most.

When I was first offered a scholarship to attend State, the coaches told me, "You will graduate!" To accomplish that, some of the coaches acted as surrogate parents for some of us. They pushed us to excel in the classroom, knowing full well that if we did not keep our grades up, we were of no use to anyone, especially the team. It took me three years to finally get the message that not only did I have to work on the football field, I also had to apply the same energy in the classroom. It seemed as if overnight I underwent a transformation from taking shortcuts in getting my work done to giving more than required in class. I guess I wasn't as focused before as I'd thought. But by the beginning of my senior year I began to understand that within a year I was going to have to hit the road in the real world and compete against my peers who were more studious than me. My new work habits and commitment to excelling in the classroom helped me make the President's List for both semesters of my senior year. Later in the year I was honored for having the highest academic average among Black College All-Americans. Never in my life had I gotten any kind of recognition that wasn't football-related, so this was a special honor that meant more to me than any football award I had gotten. It showed me that not only was I a good football player, but I was also intellectually bright when I wanted to be.

On the field, I kicked ass! I was good at what I did as a football player, and while I did not take my playing abilities for granted, I just knew that if I avoided any major injuries, I was going to have a special year. We had good coaches who pushed us on the field when we needed to be pushed and then praised us for rising above our own expectations. I knew my assignments on the field; I was quick and agile and knew how to make my presence felt. I was elected captain for the second year so I knew that my teammates and coaches respected me as a leader.

When we began play my last season, the coaches threw a little wrench in my plans. They asked me to change positions to help the team. To fill a void at the tackle position and take advantage of the depth we had at the defensive end, I was asked to move from the outside at right defensive end to play several games at nose tackle. Initially, I didn't like the idea of change, especially as a senior. I felt uncomfortable being moved from my comfort zone. After thinking about me for a quick second, I realized that if it was to help the team be better, why not? I thought I would have problems adjusting to the change since I was so comfortable playing right end, but playing the inside position came relatively easy. Because of my quickness and the slowness of most of the centers I played against, I had a slight advantage at nose tackle most of the time. The position change altered the way that I had to play my game. On the outside as an end, I avoided a lot of contact by using my speed and quickness to get to the quarterback, usually from the blind side if he was right-handed. On the inside playing nose tackle, I was almost constantly being hit by somebody, either the center or a guard helping the center with his block. I was still an effective run stopper and pass rusher from that position.

The pro scouts were coming to see me play on weekends, and during the week they wanted to time and test me for the upcoming draft. Once the season ended, some of the scouts told me that I needed to develop more strength in my arms and shoulders. I was quick, fast, and agile, but to play on the next level I needed to work on those areas. Coach Jeffries knew some of the concerns of various scouts and went out on a limb for me by getting me access to the University of South Carolina's weight and conditioning facilities. Our conditioning facility was below average for a college football program. It was good enough for Barney Chavous and Donnie Shell, who went off to play in the pros, but I needed more equipment to increase my power, strength, and size. USC had an outstanding, state-of-the-art weight facility, in Columbia, some forty miles north of Orangeburg. It was unheard of for a player from a college such as mine to be given access to the much better equipment of USC, but Coach swung it for me. He also obtained a school vehicle to drive up several days a week for me to get my strength training.

I remember two interesting things from going to train at USC. The first was meeting and watching Steve Courson, an offensive lineman for Carolina, lifting in the weight room. Steve had to be the most muscularly developed person I had ever seen in person. I couldn't see one bit of body fat on him. I thought to myself, "Damn, if this is what players in the NFL look like, then I have a helluva long way to go!" Steve had no neck; his head looked connected to his bulging shoulders and huge biceps. He looked every bit like one of those guys from the World Wrestling Federation.

The second thing was meeting Carolina's then head football coach, Jim Carlen, in the weight room on one of my visits. In a bit of small talk about football, Coach Carlen said one thing to me that has always stayed with me: "You know, Carson, you have to be prepared mentally to play in the NFL. Playing in college is about eighty percent physical and about twenty percent mental, but when you get to the NFL level, it will be the opposite, about eighty percent mental and twenty percent physical." I didn't know if that reference was directed just at me, but I assumed that he was offering some helpful advice. I'd watched NFL games on television, and I'd seen how intensely physical those games were, so while I heard what Coach Carlen was saying, the 80 percent mental thing didn't quite register at that point.

I was a good player but I wasn't good enough to earn a spot in any of the postseason all-star games, nor was I invited to any combines to be scrutinized by the pros. Instead, all of the scouts who were interested came to visit me on campus. I visited with many scouts from many different teams as well as scouts who scouted for several teams. Most of the pro scouts projected me to play outside linebacker, not only because of my weight and size, but because my defensive end position was more like an outside linebacker's but from the three-point-down position. One scout from the Steelers projected me to be an offensive lineman. During my four years at State I never weighed more than 230 pounds. I came to State weighing about 218 and generally played at about 225–227 pounds, which was somewhat light for a defensive linemen. That was one of the reasons why Coach Jeffries wanted me to bulk up, to give myself a better chance of being selected by the pros.

Of the many pro scouts that came to Orangeburg to evaluate me, I remember two distinctly. One was Emlen Tunnell, who had been a defensive back with the New York Giants, and the other was Rosey Brown, who also played with the Giants. Both of these men spent a good bit of time scouting me. Both of them were Pro Football Hall of Fame members, so I knew they had to be good in their day and knew a lot about the game. I was impressed that the Giants would show me such attention, but I knew that when it came to the draft, anything could happen. I was told by several scouts that I could "potentially" be a second-round pick, so it didn't seem to me that I would be a player needed by the Giants.

As draft day approached, I tried to maintain my focus by continuing to attend my classes. I tried to stay as normal as I could, even though most people knew that I was a possible draft pick. Again, I knew all about those guys who prematurely saw themselves as NFL stars. Their bubble was busted when they weren't drafted at all. Unless a player went to the Canadian League or to the short-lived World Football League, the only place to play pro football was the NFL. I also could not forget that I was attending a black school in the South. The NFL chose to sign many players at black schools as free agents instead of drafting them, much as Pittsburgh did with Donnie Shell or the Giants did with James Evans before I arrived at State. While it was nice to be considered by teams to play in the NFL, I could not afford to put all of my eggs in that one basket. I could be drafted in the second round, but I might not be drafted at all. I knew that making an NFL ball club as a free agent was much tougher than it would be as a high-round pick. No thank you! If I only learned one thing at State, it would be that things are not always as sure as they seem. I made the mistake my first year of thinking an award was mine, only for it to be presented to my roommate. I learned from that experience so I promised myself not to wait for the NFL to call. I was focused on my classes and getting my degree. My family and friends had expected that of me since I'd first arrived on campus three and a half years earlier.

When I attended my last athletic awards program at SC State, because I was the team captain and an outstanding senior, I was asked by Coach Jeffries to speak to all of the athletes. It was a far cry from being a bright-eyed freshman player looking to learn the ropes. I had won fifteen different school, state, conference, and national awards and honors. What stood out in my mind was that I had just experienced the best four years of my life! That time I spent at SC State flew by! I came there as a boy but was proud that I was leaving as a man. I had gained a better understanding of leadership and had learned what a good work ethic was. I remembered after my first day hearing the players chanting at the end of practice, "Bulldog! Tenacity!" I didn't know what that meant when I first arrived, but I knew all about it as I was leaving. I grew on the football field and in the classroom as well. I learned that I had to be responsible for me. No one was going to tell me when to get up and get my ass to class! No one was going to make me study for my exams. If I didn't take care of me, nobody else was going to! I learned from my early failures such as having to repeat a remedial math course and almost being placed on academic probation at the end of my first semester.

As I spoke to the audience of other athletes, friends, and supporters of the athletic programs, I said that I wished I had another four years to go through the experiences again. The friendships and relationships were priceless. When I took the field to play football, I took great pride in playing for all of my friends, family, classmates, professors, and coaches, who truly cared for me and had my best interests at heart. Whether we won or lost, I knew that my teammates and I had the support of those people. I knew I would miss my teammates, with whom I had shared those Thursday-night bus rides to schools in Washington, Baltimore, North Carolina, Delaware, and Mississippi. Individually, we didn't have a lot of money or things, but I knew that if I needed something, somebody would share even his last can of beanie weenies with me. That kind of experience built character and integrity. My coaches were hard but fair.

I graduated from a predominantly white high school where I quit the football team over stuff that wasn't important. Unfortunately, I had made it important to me. My quitting that team left me in a difficult situation. At the end of that chapter I wanted to go to college, but I knew I would not have had a chance without a football scholarship. My attending South Carolina State was possible only because someone cared enough to help me get my foot in the door to meet the coaches. That one option, going to Orangeburg with my hat in my hand looking for an opportunity, was the best thing that could have happened for me. As a young man I had made choices that I had to live with. Over the years I would grow to see that those choices positioned me to go through what I experienced at South Carolina State, and then those experiences at State prepared me for the next phase of my life.

Two very important events ushered me into that next phase. A couple of weeks after the athletic awards program, draft day rolled around. After four seasons of my playing college football, it was time to see where I would be playing next, if at all. There would be no more forty-yard sprints and running drills by the scouts to see where I rated. On the morning of the 1976 NFL Draft, against my better judgment, I chose not to attend class but to wait for a possible call from an NFL team. I didn't have a clue as to where I might be drafted, although if I did get drafted, I wanted to go to any team in California. If I could be a pro, I thought it would be nice to practice and play in warm weather. I spent most of the morning into the afternoon listening to music. It seemed that everyone knew that the draft was imminent; guys in the dorm wanted to know, "Have you heard anything?" I began to grow tired of having to respond, "Nope, not yet." After waiting for several hours without getting any calls, I decided to spend the afternoon and evening with friends to take my attention away from the suspense of waiting.

I didn't find out that I had been drafted until I watched the 11:00 p.m. sports news. In his lead story, the sports announcer said that two players from the Palmetto State had been drafted in the first day of the NFL Draft. The first was Bennie Cunningham, a tight end whom I'd gotten to know while he played at Clemson University. Bennie was drafted by the Pittsburgh Steelers in the first round. The second player mentioned was me, selected in the fourth round by the New York Giants. New York Giants? I thought, "Wasn't that the team that showed such an interest with the scouts?" I was happy to finally be able to put the suspense over being drafted behind me, but I was a little disappointed that I wasn't taken until the fourth round. It was not a big deal, but again I had bought into believing what others had said. To my family and friends it didn't really matter; they were ecstatic that I had been drafted to play in the National Football League, and the fact that the team was the Giants was irrelevant. I took all of the stickers I had collected from scouts off my door and my books and replaced them with the NY logo of the Giants.

Two weeks later I prepared for a more important occasion, my graduation! In Holmes School, I never saw myself in college, let alone as a college graduate. Getting a college degree and achieving success was what those teachers wanted for all their students. Mrs. Washington, Mrs. Smalls, Mr. Harrell, Mr. Durant, Mr. Madison, and Ms. McDuffie wanted that for me more than anything else. I knew they wanted the best for me when I was with them, but I didn't see myself as this person who was now about to be born. Even when I first entered SC State, I knew it was going to be a long journey. I knew graduating was the goal and was possible, but I didn't always see Harry Carson the graduate! My ultimate goal in attending South Carolina State was not to go to the National Football

League, but to leave with that degree. But in the back of my mind something always said, "Something somewhere along this journey is going to fuck this up!" Not this time, I was finally here! True to Coach Banks's and Coach Carson's word that I would graduate, here I was wearing my cap and gown, walking onto a stage to receive my diploma.

My graduation day was one of the proudest days of my mother's life. She finally got to see at least one of her children graduate from college. All the prayers and all of the sacrifices she had made were worth it when she saw me in my cap and gown. For me, that degree was a powerful resource as soon as it was placed in my hands. No one could ever take it away from me. Football was not guaranteed, but the options that I had as a result of graduating were limitless. It was especially gratifying to know that I was leaving college with my class, the same individuals I arrived with four years earlier. None of the honors and awards I had gotten from football meant as much to me as my degree. I knew the stories about other schools where athletes played their hearts out only to leave with a thank-you, and sometimes not even that. I was proud that I had taken control of my destiny by achieving this goal.

I was ready to tackle this new chapter of my life. To me, pro football was like jumping on a train and not knowing the destination; I was intrigued to see just how far I could go with it.

CHAPTER 6

Welcome to the NFL!

Almost immediately after being drafted I had to travel to New York to attend a mandatory minicamp and meet with the coaches and other officials of the Giants organization. While I was excited to be a New York Giant, I was not that thrilled with playing in New York. Coming out of the South, I had heard so many negative things about New York and was a bit intimidated by the prospect of living there. The one bright spot was that I wouldn't be that far from my mother in New Jersey.

When I arrived at La Guardia Airport in New York City, I was greeted by a driver named Whitey who worked for the team. Initially I thought he was there to take several players to the facility, but I was the lone pickup. Wow! I kept my excitement under wraps, but it felt good to be treated like a VIP. I thought I was going to be taken into New York City with all of the huge buildings I saw as I was landing. Instead, I was told that I would be going to the Giants training facility at Pace University in Pleasantville, New York. Pleasantville is in Westchester County just north of New York City. I thought everything would be taking place in the city, but obviously not.

On my ride to Pace I began to realize that I had in store all types of new experiences. I didn't want to show anyone that I was so thrilled or that I was in awe of any new experience. Once I arrived, I was introduced to Ed Croke, the director of public relations, as well as several others from the Giants front office. I was then escorted to the training room, where I met several of the other players who had also been drafted by the Giants. The only two that I remembered were Troy Archer and Gordon Bell. Archer was a defensive lineman from the University of Colorado and was the Giants' top draft pick. Gordon was a running back from the University of Michigan. He was the Giants' second pick but was drafted in the fourth round. I didn't know a lot about Troy or Gordon since I didn't spend a lot of time watching their schools play. I was the Giants' third pick, but their second pick in the fourth round.

The first order of business was to get the physicals out of the way. There must have been thirty to forty players in the area dressed in shorts and T-shirts waiting to take physicals. As naïve as I could be, for a moment I thought this was the whole team, but then it dawned on me that these were only the rookies. As players came out of the examination areas, I waited for my name to be called to see the doctors. I began to introduce myself and meet other players who were also waiting. These guys were from schools all around the country. Some of them were from small schools, while others were from major universities. If I had watched football on Saturday afternoons instead of playing myself, I would probably have seen some of these guys play on ABC, but I had no clue as to who many of them were. I'm sure most of them had probably never heard of nor seen me play either.

When my name was called, I walked into a room and found two trainers, team doctor Allan Levy, and an orthopedic specialist. I had already filled out my paperwork on my family's medical history and any injuries I had sustained. The doctors did their poking and prodding to make sure everything was fine, then examined all of my joints—shoulders, elbows, knees, etc. I thought it was about as thorough an examination as you could get; at least it was for me up until that time. I'm sure the team wanted to make certain that we were healthy and 100 percent fit to play, and I passed the physical without a problem.

After our physicals, we assembled in a meeting room on the second level of the field house where the Giants' offices were located. Then our group formally met the Giants coaching staff. In 1976, Bill Arnsparger was the head coach. I didn't know a lot about him except that he was the architect of the famed Miami Dolphins No-Name Defense that helped Don Shula's team have a perfect season and win a Super Bowl. Arnsparger welcomed all of us to the NFL and to the Giants. He told us the plans and objectives for our time there. The coaches wanted to do some additional testing to see how athletic we were and how we would fit into their offensive and defensive systems. Those things included running the forty-yard dash (again), a vertical jump, and various agility drills. Sitting in that room, I didn't think about in what round I had been drafted. It didn't matter, everyone was a rookie, and we all had the same opportunity to make the team. I just wanted to show the coaches and other rookies that I was as fast and quick as anyone else in the room.

We finished the morning session of physicals and agility tests and took time for lunch. During that lunch and getting ready for the afternoon session, I thought about how, just as with every other new team I'd been a part of, players were thrown together to work. In high school I came together with guys from my neighborhood or around town. In college, it was primarily guys from the Southeast, but this was the National Football League and these guys were from all over the country. I knew these other guys around me had to be good to make it this far. From the time we'd all arrived, through the morning physicals, meeting, drills, and through lunch, we were all still getting to know who was who. I knew who Troy and Gordon were, but not some of the other guys who were either drafted or were invited to try out for the team as free agents.

When we went back into the team meeting, Bill Arnsparger again led the meeting. We then broke the meeting into two groups, offense and defense. A partition split the room right down the middle. While Bill was the head coach of the Giants, Marty Schottenheimer was the linebacker coach and defensive coordinator. He was in charge of getting the defense ready to play. I would interact with Marty more than with Arnsparger. Marty told us what we were going to do as a group once we got out onto the football field. He and the other coaches handed out our playbooks, which we would have to learn. When one was handed to me, I thought, "Holy shit!" I had never had a book so big in any of my college classes, let alone for football. Hell, I had a small three-ring binder for football while at State, and while this book had three rings, it was about three to four inches thick. When I first opened the playbook, I began to feel overwhelmed. I had never been a big book person. But if you showed me how to do something and let me go, I was good from there. That was how I functioned best. Marty eased my mind a little when he asked that we focus on a couple of basic defensive fronts that we would run during practice, along with a couple of coverages for the secondary. The purpose of this minicamp was not to try to digest everything in the playbook—that would come in training camp—but to stay as basic as possible to get a picture of how we could work together. That eased my mind for the time being.

After going through some basic defensive assignments in the classroom, the players went to the field to loosen up and run some agility drills. After those drills we broke into different groups to go with different coaches. The defensive backs went with the secondary coach, and the linemen went with the line coach. I was about to take off and go with the linemen when Marty told me to stay with his group, the linebackers. Marty said he wanted me to take drills with the linebackers to see how it felt. I obviously was in no position to say no; I had to do what I was being told to do.

When I was a senior at SC State, I played some nose tackle even though I felt most comfortable as a defensive end. I thought perhaps they might want me to play several different positions since they had assigned me the number 53 like Bob Matheson, a linebacker who'd played multiple positions in Arnsparger's defense with the Dolphins. As I went through the linebacker drills, I felt a little odd because my mind-set was to put my hands in the dirt and either rush the quarterback or stop the run. I flashed back to my days at State when I had to go through the same drills that our linebackers went through with Coach Carson. Aside from having a linebacker stance that could use some work, I thought I did pretty well in the drills.

At the conclusion of that rookie minicamp Marty pulled me aside. I thought he wanted to tell me about some things I needed to work on before coming back in July for training camp with everyone else. Instead, he told me that he wanted me to come back to Pace early and spend about a month with him before the start of training camp. He thought otherwise I would probably not be able to keep up with everything once everyone arrived. I was disappointed because I had just graduated and wanted some time to relax. Some other guys might have been gung ho and said something like "Coach, I'll do whatever I have to do to make the team," but I was not feeling that way. As much as I hated the idea of spending a month at Pace University and not with my family and my friends, I knew it was for my own benefit.

I've come to understand that during the draft, the Giants had strong discussions on whom to select. They knew they needed help on defense, and Archer was a strong pick as a defensive tackle in the first round. They had no second or third pick, but they had back-to-back picks in the fourth round. The first pick in the fourth round was going to be used on an offensive player, so the offensive coaches were going to make that choice. The second choice in the fourth round was going to be used on a defensive player. Apparently some Giants personnel wanted Carl Hairston, a defensive lineman who played at the University of Maryland Eastern Shore. That school was in the same conference that I played in, the Mid-Eastern Athletic Conference. Marty wanted a linebacker type who could rush the quarterback and stop the run, much like Matheson of the Dolphins. Apparently, some within the Giants organization were skeptical that I could play the middle linebacker position that Marty envisioned me playing. During the draft, when it was time to decide whom the defense was going to take, Arnsparger made Marty get up in the meeting to declare whom he wanted. I guess the reasoning was that if I wound up being a bust, that mark would be placed squarely on Marty's shoulders alone.

During that initial visit with the Giants I was asked to take a series of psychological tests administered by Dr. Frank Ladata. Dr. Ladata was a professor at Manhattan College who tested the mental aptitude of players for the Giants. I thought I was the main focus of Dr. Ladata's attention because he spent most of his time with me. To play in the National Football League was a huge step for any athlete, but especially for a guy who had never even seen a pro football game in person. I was going to be in a position to actually play as a linebacker, but it was up to me whether I could adjust to a new position. The Giants had drafted another player, Dan Lloyd, in the later rounds who was a pure middle linebacker in case I did not work out. While I didn't feel a lot of pressure at the time, over the years I've thought of the pressure Marty might have faced since his reputation and credibility that were on the line with me as his selection. I was comfortable playing a down lineman position in college, but I was being asked to make a change from my comfort zone and play a position that I had never before played. I think had it not been for the high test results I scored with Dr. Ladata, I would probably have been used in a much different way by the Giants.

In the mid-1970s I had few dominant black middle linebackers I could identify with. Willie Lanier was the one dominant black player who immediately came to mind as someone that I needed to model myself after. The other player was Harold McLinton, who played middle line backer for the Washington Redskins. The middle linebacker position has always been reserved for players who were smart, agile, strong, and willing to hit people. To play middle linebacker in the NFL, you had to be an impact player. The position had traditionally been reserved for white players since many people saw it as a thinking man's position. I didn't see it as that; instead I saw it as an opportunity to play and contribute to the Giants organization.

During the entire time I played at State I never weighed more than 230 pounds and never ran faster than a 4.7 in the forty-yard dash. Once I had been drafted, my weight shot up to 245 and I ran a 4.5 forty-yard dash for Marty. I didn't know if that was a result of having worked out at the University of South Carolina or having eaten well during that time, but those results pissed me off because if I had weighed 245 prior to the draft, I could probably have been drafted as a defensive lineman, a position that I continued to feel most comfortable playing. But it was too late for me; in the eyes of the coaches I was now a middle linebacker for the Giants. I didn't know a lot about the Giants personnel, but I did know that Brian Kelley was the incumbent middle linebacker. Several coaches stressed to me that the team needed help stopping the inside run. My understanding was that Brian was an intelligent player whose strong suit was playing against the pass, while being adequate against the run. But the coaches felt they needed a "stud" combination guy who could stop the inside run, rush the passer, and play relatively decent zone defense against the pass. Marty's job was to get me prepared to assume those duties as soon as possible.

The minicamp I spent with the other rookies went well. That time together gave us drafted and free-agent players an opportunity to get to know one another without the intimidation we might have felt with a bunch of seasoned veterans breathing down our necks. Our coaches emphasized what we needed to do to get into condition for training camp in July with the rest of the team and what would be expected of us them. With the emphasis on learning so much information, being physically ready to practice, play, and compete against others, it dawned on me that this was no longer just a sport, it was a business.

When I arrived back home after minicamp, I began to realize the importance of what I was about to do and how it would affect those around me. Before even making the Giants roster I could see the hope and excitement that members of my family had. To say that they were proud of me would be an understatement. What my family felt was mild compared to what my friends and other people in my hometown were experiencing. It seemed that everywhere I went I was on center stage. The parents of my friends, my old teachers, and people who had merely heard of me wished me good luck with the Giants. Their well wishes made me feel good but also a little nervous. I didn't say it aloud, but within myself I wondered, "What if I don't make it?" Sure, I had my degree and my life would go on, but a shot at playing in the NFL was what every guy wished for.

Meanwhile, I had hired an agent to represent me in my contract negotiations with the Giants. Marshall Warren was a new agent who was recommended to me by Coach Jeffries. Marshall's job was to meet with Andy Robustelli, the general manager of the Giants, to get the best possible contract for me. After several days and a number of conversations, Marshall nailed down a deal for me. All of this was so new and different for me, playing for pay. I received a $20,000 signing bonus with a first-year salary of $32,500. I was ecstatic to have the contract signed and looked forward to getting paid. I had never had a serious job that paid decent bucks. I thought the numbers in my contract could have been better, but I was told that I could realize more income in the end if I could achieve the goals in my incentive clauses. My contract would pay me $35,000 the second year and $37,500 in the third. Once I signed the deal, I could not focus on its monetary aspects. I had to first concentrate on making the club, but I knew that if I did and played, I could realistically make more. The incentives in my contract were based on a number of things, such as playing time. If I played 75 percent of the time that the defense was on the field, I could make an extra $5,000; playing 50 percent of the time the defense was on the field got me an extra $3,500; and so on. If I led the team in tackles, I could make another extra $5,000. So I could live with my contract, and with any kind of luck I could make out pretty well in the long run.

With the $20,000 signing bonus I was able to do some things that I had always wanted to do. Before buying anything for myself, I made sure to purchase two headstones. The first would be for my auntie and the second for my father. Since their burials, neither of them had had markers for their graves, and that bothered me. At the age of twenty-two and a recent college grad, I could have done a lot of things with that twenty grand ($16,000 after taxes), but a bright spot was being able to help my family. I found it amazing that by just signing my name I was probably making more than both my mother and father had made together in one year. I felt extremely blessed to be able to buy the headstones.

As I was about to return to New York from South Carolina, I picked up a car that I had purchased a few weeks earlier in Detroit where my agent was located. I got a good deal on its price by getting it directly from a dealership connected with the automaker. On my drive up Interstate 95 North, I began to think about so many things. I was, for once, all alone with hours to travel to my destination. I thought about my family and what they meant to me, about all of the sacrifices everybody had made to help me through high school and especially through college. At times in college when I did not have one nickel to spend, I would write sob letters to my sisters starting with "My dearest darling most beautiful sister in the whole world." They always seemed to know what was coming next when they got a letter from me, but they always came through with a few dollars. Even when they didn't have it, they borrowed it so that I could have something. I thought of the sacrifices my mother had made, living in New Jersey, cleaning houses so that her kids would have what they needed, even when her safety was in jeopardy. She once told us that after working one week she was robbed at gunpoint by some thug. As she got up and went to work every day in the heat and the cold, we knew that we were her priority. Her major concern was the development of my brother and me. Living in Newark, she probably saw more than she should ever have seen of young black men being murdered or killed by the police, so she wanted us to always make good choices and be good people. I wanted to be able to take care of her so that she would not have to work the way that she did. One thing that all kids, especially us blacks kids, wanted to do in going professional was to buy a home for a parent. While I didn't have the means to do so yet, I hoped to one day fulfill that wish.

On that long drive to New York I thought of my friends that I was leaving behind. I truly had to be thankful for those friends because without some of them I would probably have been a lost soul. Those friends were sincerely happy for me and the success that I had achieved. I knew that no matter what happened, those people were going to be in my corner! I also thought about all of those guys I played football with in the field near St. Ann's Church, at the Boys Club, Wilson High, McClenaghan High, and South Carolina State. I knew I had become a pretty good football player since my early years, but I also knew I was leaving behind some guys so much better than me. I never felt that I was better than anyone else, so why was I so lucky to have been drafted? Only one other player from my town had played in the NFL. Johnny Brunson had played at Benedict College and gone on to play with the Houston Oilers. Johnny played a few years before I really got into football. I'd heard that he was a good player, but he did not last long in the league.

I knew guys from where I came who should have played somewhere but didn't. Some guys at State were also good enough to have gotten a chance in the NFL, but most didn't. Donnie and Barney were the only guys who got their shot and made the most of it. I often wondered if those prayers that my mom said for me every Sunday in church were working. I knew that I tried to do what was right off the field, and I tried to be the best player that I could be on the field. I knew that I had had more than my share of opportunities to fuck up off the field. Whether it was with drugs, drinking, girls, poor grades, and on and on, I'd avoided the many pitfalls that derailed a lot of people from reaching their potential. I remembered a promise I'd made to myself when I first arrived at SC State, to be the best athlete I could be; not just a football player, but the absolute best athlete I could be. While some of the guys I played with occasionally did a little grass, wine, or beer, I stayed away from that stuff and got my rest, so in a way I felt that I made the correct choices to get to where I was.

That long drive to New York turned out to be somewhat of a transition period for me. With every mile that I drove, the reality of the life-changing event that was taking place became more evident. I had to take everything that I had acquired and place it in a memory file for those times when I knew that I would need to recall that information. I had to be ready for new experiences with new coaches, players, and people whom I would need to learn to work with.

Upon arriving at Pace, I was assigned to a room in the dormitory with many of the other regular students there for summer school. I was there for a different kind of summer school. When I finally got down to business with Marty as my instructor, I felt a little uncomfortable because I had never been in a one-on-one situation with a teacher or a coach. I hadn't even known him a month before, and all of a sudden I was attending private sessions with the guy who was responsible for drafting me. As I spent more and more time with him, I got to know him and began to understand the way he communicated. Marty and I spent loads of time studying film of the Giants defense from the previous season. After watching film in the mornings, we would go over agility and ball drills on the field. Marty saw that I needed to do a lot of work on my pass defense, especially catching the football. I had never had to catch the football in the past because I was a lineman who didn't need to have good hands except in wrapping up quarterbacks. I played a little running back in high school, but my role then was primarily as a lead blocking back in a wishbone offense. In my new role I was going to be asked not just to stop the run, which every middle linebacker has to be able to do effectively, but to defend against the pass as well.

Marty was patient and passionate as a teacher, but I could tell that he would occasionally become frustrated with my inability to do things his way. Over and over he tried to get me to do things his way, but I did them my way. I was not trying to be difficult; I wanted to do the drills in exactly the manner that he demonstrated them, but I was just unable to translate some things from what I saw in my brain into what flowed from my feet. Many things that he wanted me to do I wound up doing ass backward. Whenever he wanted me to do pass defense drills, I'd try to do it his way, but even if I didn't, I got the same or better results. He was amazed at my performance in some of the drills, even though the way I did them looked awkward. Marty eventually threw his hands up and said, "Hey, as long as you can get the job done, I'm not going to be picky about how you get to where you need to get to make the play." I was happy that Marty was willing to be flexible. What was good for him was not necessarily comfortable for me, and I had to go with what I felt comfortable doing.

In the classroom I did lots of film study. One thing I wanted to do was focus on other middle linebackers that I had some knowledge of. I requested film of linebackers Jack Reynolds, the middle linebacker of the Los Angeles Rams, Tommy Nobis of the Atlanta Falcons, and Bill Bergey. The other guys I watched were Willie Lanier and Harold McLinton, the only two black middle linebackers who were starting at that time. In watching film of those players I zeroed in on every movement they made. At that time, NFL games were filmed from the sideline angle from the press-box level or higher to get a shot of the teams going from right to left and then from left to right. Film was also shot from an elevated end-zone angle to give viewers a shot of plays coming at them and then a shot of plays going away from them to see contrasting views. I would often put myself in the position of the middle linebacker as the plays were coming at me to see what that player was seeing and determine how I would react in the same situation. Those players I studied were some of the best teachers. Just being able to put myself in their position helped me tremendously.

Those weeks I spent with Marty were priceless in getting to learn more about the middle linebacker position and defensive philosophy. When I was in college playing defensive end, I only had to know my assignments and those of the other linemen around me just in case we needed to run a "game" or a stunt to get to the quarterback on a passing play or to run a stunt with the outside linebacker on a blitz play. In playing middle linebacker in the National Football League I had to know everybody's responsibility on the defense. I had to know what the linemen in front of me had to do, I had to understand what the other linebackers' responsibilities were, and then I had to understand what the secondary had to do. The middle linebacker has an enormous responsibility. When I watched games from home, I never realized everything that went into preparing to play the game, but I was getting a glimpse from the time I was spending with Marty. I was starting to think that I had gotten in way over my head with this change in playing position. It seemed like there was so much that I had to know.

I felt overwhelmed at times, but then I remembered what USC coach Jim Carlen had told me, that playing in the NFL is more mental than physical. I had some deep inner thoughts of "You can't do this shit." But whenever I had any hint of that, I pushed myself and said to myself that if Lanier and McLinton could do it, then I could do it as well. I was drawn to the challenge of being chosen by a coach to play a position that was normally reserved for white guys on a National Football League team. I was also drawn to the challenge of being just as cerebral as others, and to not just be relied upon to be the brawn that some thought the black guys should provide.

During my weeks with Marty, we talked about a lot of things and felt comfortable sharing personal thoughts. I knew that some scouts and other "experts" thought I would be drafted in the second round, but Marty told me that I fell to the fourth round for several reasons. The first was that I was drafted out of position. Not many players are able to smoothly change positions the way I was being asked to do. Some quarterbacks, especially black QBs, had been converted to wide receivers or to the defensive secondary positions if they had the toughness to hit people as defensive players. Some players had gone from an offensive lineman to a defensive lineman or vice versa. But to go from a down defensive lineman to a stand-up middle linebacker with pass-coverage responsibilities was asking a lot.

Another reason why I was drafted in the fourth round was because I played at a smaller school. Marty said that some people thought that smaller schools did not play the same caliber of football as schools such as Notre Dame and Alabama. I understood what he was saying but I felt a little insulted by the comment. Was it that we didn't have the best coaches money could buy as did some of those major schools, or was it that "some people" didn't think much of the quality of talent at the small black schools? Talent? What about such guys as Walter Payton, Jackie Slater, and Robert Brazile of Jackson State; Ed "Too Tall" Jones from Tennessee State; or David "Deacon" Jones, Art Shell, Willie Davis, Mel Blount, Willie Lanier, and many other Hall of Fame–quality players? Even though there were talented players from black Southern universities, Marty only verbalized what many in the football establishment thought but never spoke aloud. That conversation always remained with me. I have never harbored any ill feelings with Marty about the content of our conversation. Actually I was thankful that he shared that info with me. It would serve as one of those chips on my shoulder to motivate me as I proceeded. It also served as a reality check to make me understand that some people expected me to fail. I didn't know who they were, but I could not give them that pleasure. Along with all my family and friends I had to be thankful for, I also had to be mindful that I was representing black college football, so failure to make it in the NFL was not an option.

After that month with Marty, I felt more comfortable with the position change. He tried to get me to understand that once the ball was snapped, I needed to react as a football player. He urged me not to do so much thinking that I couldn't respond. Coach Jeffries always echoed the same thing: once the ball is snapped, whether you are in a two-point or three-point stance, you have to react as a football player by reading the play and getting to the ball carrier. The time at Pace University spent learning the many defensive fronts, pass coverages, blitz packages, and adjustments gave me an edge that I might not have had if I'd learned it solely once all of the other players were in camp. I returned to Florence with copies from my playbook and spent time each day trying to stay familiar with my responsibilities.

Once I returned to New York for the beginning of the Giants training camp, I felt that I was in an altogether different world. Before then, with the exception of Giants punter Dave Jennings, I had never met any of the Giants veteran players. When I attended our first team meeting at training camp, I felt like the low guy on the totem pole. I had to start all over again as a player. In beginning each new phase, whether high school, college, or then pro, I knew what the deal was. I was somewhat familiar with some of the other rookies I'd attended minicamp with, but now I had all of these older guys to contend with. Unlike on other levels where the veteran guys were two or three years older, some of these Giants veterans were as much as fifteen years older than us rookies. I looked at them with a sense of awe since they were still able to play. I should be so lucky with my career. I remember at the age of seventeen proclaiming to my sister Ruth that anybody over thirty was old in my book.

Some of the older players were new here themselves, having played in the defunct World Football League. Running back Larry Csonka had played with the Miami Dolphins but signed with the Giants when his WFL team folded. Larry was probably the most recognizable name on the roster, but we also had two very veteran quarterbacks in Craig Morton and Norm Snead, both well into their thirties. I knew it was going to take a little time to get used to this difference as well as getting familiar with all of the other players from around the country. That first meeting with the entire Giants squad taught me something special about a team sport such as football. We had players from all walks of life. We had black and white guys of various ages from all around the country, from various economic backgrounds, various religions or no religion at all, guys from different educational levels, and on and on. Whatever differences, biases, or prejudices we had could not be brought into playing the game. We had to bring the best of ourselves to the table to compete for a position on the team and then to play together to win. I sat in that meeting feeling totally amazed with where I was.

I had not been a New York Giants fan, but I was familiar with the names and faces of many of the players I was sitting with. I don't remember a whole lot of what was said in that first meeting, except that Coach Arnsparger indicated that all positions were up for grabs. He wanted players to compete and he didn't care who started as long as they could get the job done. Arnsparger didn't really have a choice; he needed players willing to shake things up as he had experienced two prior seasons that only netted him seven wins against twenty-one losses. He knew his ass was on the hot seat and he was in jeopardy of losing his job if things didn't get better fast. I took his stance as an indication that I didn't have to make this club as a special teams player the way most rookie players made NFL clubs. I wanted to do all I could to become a starter.

After our meeting, some of the guys headed to their dorm rooms to get some rest for the next day's practice, while many of the vets took off for Foley's bar in Pleasantville to have a beer. If the Giants were in training camp, everyone knew that the best place to meet players was Foley's. Out of curiosity I went to the equipment room to check on my gear. When I walked into the locker room, I discovered that all my equipment had already been placed in a locker chosen for me. The pads were almost the same as they were in high school and college; the only difference was in the helmet. When I attended the Giants minicamp in May, my helmet had no logo on it, only a strip of tape with my name on it to identify me. Now I saw that my helmet had a GIANTS logo blazoned on both sides. It might seem like nothing, but I think it symbolized that I was finally in the NFL. I had been chosen in the draft by the Giants and I had signed a contract that obligated me to the team. This was *the* defining moment that I knew this was going to be my team. When I looked at that big blue helmet, I not only saw it as my main means of protecting myself from injuries, but it became my identity. When I stepped on the field people would not see my face, but they would see the blue Giants helmet. I was not just thinking about the fans, but that this was the team that had chosen me rather than the others that could have taken me in the draft. I wanted to be a part of this team.

The next morning after breakfast we headed to the locker room to prepare for the first of our two-a-day practices. Those first practices were to be in shorts and T-shirts, but everyone had to get his ankles taped to help prevent sprains and strains. In college we had a head trainer and an assistant trainer to do all the taping. With the Giants, we had a head trainer named John Dziegel and he had about five assistant trainers to handle the 100 to 120 players who were in camp. For some reason I gravitated to John to tape my ankles. An older gentleman, he had been with the Giants organization for a long time. While spending time alone at Pace with Marty, I got to be friendly with John, and clearly he had seen a lot in his time as a trainer with the Giants. He was somewhat of a historian since he'd taped the ankles and physically cared for many of the Giants legends who preceded me. John had been a part of the organization during some of its glory years. As he taped my ankles, John spoke in a low tone that only I could hear. He told me of the many years of "his first day of practice." He said all I had to do was give my best and I would be okay. In a whisper he told me how some of the greats of the Giants prepared for practice and played in games. Listening to John, I observed all of the other players around me getting taped and wondered what each man's fate would be in practice. As John finished my tape job he wished me good luck and stepped back away from the seat to allow me to get down and return to my locker to finish getting dressed. I appreciated John's pep talk and encouragement. Others might have looked at him as an old guy who didn't know what he was talking about, but I grew to respect the advice and wisdom of those who had been there and knew what making the most of their football experience was about. As I grabbed my helmet and made my way to the field, my focus was on the job at hand, getting through my first practice. I didn't know what to expect, but I knew that I was in good shape and was determined to stick and stay.

I felt nervous anticipation as we waited to begin practice. While most of the guys were ready to go, I noticed several of the veterans were late getting into the training room to get taped. Those guys must have had a long night at Foley's before getting in for the 11:00 p.m. curfew. I could not concern myself with those guys; I didn't know them and I was not responsible for them. They had experience and tenure in the league, so perhaps they knew some things I didn't. I took a knee with a couple of the other rookies waiting for the whistle to be blown. One of the assistant coaches gave a two-minutes-to-practice warning shout-out to make sure no one was late. Other players talked and joked, but I remained quiet and focused, looking at the field and where I was. I could see the field was newly marked off by lime, and I could smell that scent, that scent of freshly cut grass. That scent was perceptible by every football player regardless of what level he played on. From six-year-olds playing Pop Warner football to the oldest guys playing on the professional level, that scent binds all who play the game.

With the toot of the whistle, we all headed out to the practice field for warm-ups. All of the rookies had to get with the program quickly by following the veterans. Months earlier we were big shit at whatever college programs we came from, but now we were reduced to being puppies, once again following the big dogs. After our warm-ups we broke into smaller groups. I could tell almost immediately that the competition for positions was going to be more intense on this level. All of the linebackers were bigger, faster, and stronger than I had ever before been around. We all had good agility and good size, ranging from six foot one to six foot five and from about 230 to 250 pounds. These were smart, solid guys who from the beginning practiced with a sense of purpose. They performed drills crisply and with power. Even though we were in shorts and T-shirts, they all moved quicker than I had been used to. The pace of practice impressed me and showed me where I needed to go physically to compete on their level. Just as I did before, I wanted to see where I needed to set my performance gauge to fall in line as a player and get with the program.

As Marty put us through various ball and agility drills, I felt comfortable because many of the drills were the same ones I did while in college. Because of budgeting issues at my college, our linebacker coach doubled as the defensive line coach, and thus I got through our drills now without any problems. Much of the rest of the practice was spent going over offensive and defensive schemes by walking or going half-speed to prevent anyone from getting hurt. At the end of practice we broke into groups for running sprints. The sprints weren't bad because I had been running anyway, and running in shorts and shirts was a piece of cake. When we finished running, Arnsparger called everyone to the middle of the field, made a few announcements, said he was pleased with the tempo of the first practice, and then dismissed the team. I was about to leave the field when I thought to myself, "Is that all there is to this?" I knew that if I had been at State, right about that time my tongue would be dragging from exhaustion. I kept thinking, "Damn! People actually practice like that!" I told another guy how things were where I came from, and he said the coaches couldn't work you into the ground because the NFL season is so much longer than college seasons. Of the hundred or so players who were in training camp, roughly half of us would be cut by the end of camp. The remainder would have to go through a pretty long football season. We would play six exhibition games and fourteen regular-season games as opposed to just ten college football games. I began to understand that the length of the season would require us to pace ourselves. I think it was at this time that I first heard the expression "It's a marathon, not a sprint" in describing the NFL season.

After a couple of days, the team went from shorts to full pads and contact in practice. I knew that to that point I could survive in the NFL, but now I was really going to see if I could run with the big dogs. Taking part in actual hitting drills would mark whether I could hang or not. Deep inside I knew I could, but I still had that shred of doubt because of the unknown. Practices were pretty easy, as we did a lot of stretching and cardio conditioning in preparation for putting the pads on. Adding pads was like shifting gears and ratcheting up the tempo.

On the first day of practice in pads I could tell that everyone felt comfortable and was not so fearful of inadvertently hitting someone and causing an injury. I felt the same; working in shorts wasn't bad, but I knew that once I put those pads on, I would feel like a gladiator. The coaches also were licking their chops knowing the hitting was about to begin. They had a sense of what we could do if we only played two-hand touch or flag football, but they all were anxious to see what kind of physical toughness we would show in full-contact drills on the field.

Some of the other younger players and I felt we were about to play in a game, not practice. Some of us seemed a little nervous. It's one thing to run around and play football player in shorts and T-shirts; it's another thing to strap on the shoulder pads, fasten the chin strap, and go into physical combat. Not only did I have my shoulder pads broken in and ready to go, but I also had my double neck-roll collar attached to those pads just as I had in college. The other thing I knew I needed were the J-pads that I had used in college. Call me trying to be careful, but I wore every other kind of pad I could to protect myself. I didn't know what was going to take place, I just knew I didn't want to get myself dinged up or hurt.

As we took the field for that first full-contact practice, the only thing I thought about was competing with the veterans. My mind was not on the stretching or the agility drills that I used to concern myself with in my younger days as a player; now those parts of practice were merely a formality. Once we got into hitting the seven-man sled, the anticipation of contact made my heart beat faster and my adrenaline flow. Regardless of what level you play on, it's all the same: football is football with blocking, tackling, and running the ball. I felt the same feelings I felt in high school and college, butterflies in my gut. I was getting so anxious about the contact that I was beginning to feel sick. I couldn't let anyone around me know that I was nervous, so I did all I could do to hide it. I tried to calm myself by recalling that I'd been down this road before, and all I had to do was give it my best shot and let the chips fall where they might.

When we got around to the contact drills, I could sense that not only was I nervous, but that most of the other guys, both older and younger, on both offense and defense, were quiet. This was going to be everyone's chance to show the coaches what he had and would ultimately determine if he would land a spot on this team. I wasn't thinking about job security like some of the veterans because I didn't have any. Instead I was thinking about self-preservation. As a rookie I had to stand back and watch as the first groups of players were called to start the drills. An offensive guy would get up to the line, then a defensive lineman would jump in the drill to go against him. On the snap of the ball the players tore into one another until the whistle blew, then they separated and went back to their respective groups. When they hit one another, it sounded good with pads against pads, but that was all there was to it, it sounded good. After these guys went against one another, I suspected that they had prearranged what they were going to do because I saw a couple of guys smiling at one another once they took a knee to watch the others. I came to understand that looking out for one another in drills like that was called "brother-in-lawing" the play. The play looked good to the coaches, it sounded good with the pads popping, but to some with an eye for football, it might have left a lot to be desired. Regardless, those players were happy just to get it over with. Perhaps that was the way to survive for as long as some of them had, but I didn't have anybody that I knew well enough to do that with. I was a rookie, I was there to take the job of one of those vets, and I'm sure that if the coaches didn't see a better effort out of me and the other rookies, we weren't going to be there too long.

When it was my turn in the drill, I, along with two defensive tackles, had to go against a center and two offensive guards. The coach stood behind us and pointed to show the offensive linemen what type of block he wanted them to run. He wanted a drive block on one side and a fold-block technique on the other side. A fold-block technique is when an offensive lineman works with another lineman next to him to block a defensive player. In my case, I was head up on the center with a guard next to him. On the snap, the center would block down on the tackle to my right and the guard would replace the center by folding behind him. As the center cleared, the guard would block the man who had been head up on the center, namely me. When the play started to develop, I concentrated on the center, who was in front of me. When he did not come directly at me, for a fraction of a second I thought I was out of the play, but instead I saw the guard fold behind the ass of the center and come at me at full speed. The play happened so quickly that in that fraction of a second I started to relax, then I realized that I was a goner because the guard caught me unprepared to take on the block. I was standing too high and not ready to deal him a blow with my forearm to defend myself.

What impressed me the most about that play was the speed that it took to execute the block. Once we had those pads on, with the freedom to not hold back, everything seemed to move at a much greater speed than I was used to. I had to learn to respect that speed. These guys, regardless of who they were and where they came from, had talent, pretty good technique, good speed, and quickness. While I knew that play wasn't the best I had, at least that first full-speed contact knocked the butterflies away. That experience in practice was like so many I had before high school and college games. There is always that anxiety prior to a game, which disappears after that first contact, and it was no different here. From that point on I was good to go in practice. I no longer had any question of the amount of contact that would be needed to play. After the drill Marty told me that I needed to work on keeping my body low and always being ready to deliver a blow on a potential block, otherwise I was setting myself up to get hurt. He also told me to always remember that as a middle linebacker, when the center blocks back, I need to step up because that will be where the block will be coming from.

Marty was a patient coach, taking time to point out how and why I did certain things wrong and what I needed to do to correct those mistakes. He was also the first to praise me for some of the positive things I did on the field and in drills. I constantly referred back to some of the things he'd tried to get me to adjust to when we spent our time together in June after minicamp. I could clearly see now why he wanted me to come back for more individualized instruction. With all of his responsibilities as linebacker coach and defensive coordinator, he had no way now to give me the extra attention I would have needed to get a firm grip on everything. It was *my* responsibility to use every opportunity to learn everything that I could about my position and playing defense. I had a huge playbook that I had to learn in my spare hours away from practice. I spent a lot of time trying to understand the full scheme of the defense along with my responsibilities. But I also needed to learn all of those things that you don't read about in a playbook, those things that you have to learn from being on the field. I made sure that I focused my attention on the other guys who were playing the same position I was playing to pick up any little tips that might help me in my game. I watched how the starters reacted to certain blocks and passing schemes.

One of the more important things I had to learn and understand was how to read the linemen, quarterback, and backs in the backfield to fully understand where the ball was going. When the average person watches a football game from his television set, he usually sees the play from above, depending on where the television cameras are located. When you're down on the field in the midst of all the action, things happen quickly, often with backs running dive action, flow action, counter action, or delayed action. The linemen could run traps or they could block down, block back, take a pass drop, or fire out right on you. Then you have the quarterback, who could use a reverse pivot, sprint-out action, drop-back action to pass, or any number of other techniques either to hand the ball off or pass. So you had to diagnose the kind of play being run, where the play was going, know what your responsibility was, then be able to get to where you were supposed to be to make a tackle or break up the play. All of this takes place in seconds. I could clearly see that when I played as a down lineman, I had it made. I didn't have as much to think about and I didn't have to bog myself down with details. As a new middle linebacker I saw that if I took a wrong step or even hesitated, I was as good as dead in getting to the play, so I had to be sharp to be able to compete at this level.

Most of the guys I had to compete with at the middle linebacker position seemed to be lighter in weight but a little more athletic than me. That seemed logical since all of them had played linebacker on some level somewhere. They were in their natural element, but the one advantage I felt I had was, I thought, that I was a more physical player than them. Some players were more willing to run around blocks on some plays than to take on blocks aggressively as I started to do in my play.

I knew I was quick, but at times I was not as quick as I thought. Sometimes because of a blocking scheme I was unable to use that quickness to my advantage, so I was forced to attack a blocker instead of run around him. Being physical didn't bother me since I was accustomed to physical play as a former defensive lineman. I knew I needed to get more comfortable with and work on many things, but especially my pass defense, and being able to distinguish between the run and the pass so as not to be suckered into giving up big yards against play-action passes. During drills that I was not immediately involved with, I positioned myself to stand about thirty to forty yards behind the defense to watch and see exactly what the players running plays saw, and I tried to react just as those players did. The more I did that, the more I became aware of my own field presence.

As the practice days went by, I grew more comfortable and more confident in my abilities on the field. I was elevated to second team behind Brian Kelly, our starting middle linebacker. Brian was a heads-up or smart backer who was good but not quite as physical as I was. That, I think, was one of the reasons why the team drafted me. He was a good backer against the pass but not quite as strong a presence against the run. It became pretty clear to me with all of the attention I was being given that the coaches wanted me to press Brian for the starting middle linebacker job. I wasn't looking to start; I was just trying to survive.

After several weeks of camp, cuts were about to take place. This was another thing that I was not accustomed to. Where I came from, if you went out for the team and had the toughness to stick it out, you made the team! You might not have dressed for the game or played in the game, but you made the team. For the first time I was going to see what the other side of pro football was all about. I remembered thinking, "What if I get cut?" I thought I would just move on and teach. I had my BS from State and was certified by the State of South Carolina to teach. But then I thought, why would they cut me when they've spent so much time working with me? I felt that I was safe, but you never really know.

When I arrived for practice the morning of the cut, I didn't see several of the rookies I had been drafted with, nor did I see several of the players who were trying to make the club as free agents. They were already gone, back to their dormitory rooms, and were packing to go home. Their football equipment had already been collected by the equipment manager in a laundry bin with wheels, and their name written in ink on strips of tape had been removed from the top of their lockers to make it appear that no one had used the locker. I remember that two of the guys who were released were guys that I had dinner with the previous evening in the dining hall. One of them had been injured for most of training camp with a pulled hamstring muscle that he'd sustained on the first day of practice. He did not dress for another practice session. When I saw that he had been cut, a sign that hung in the training room rang true: YOU CAN'T MAKE THE CLUB IN THE TUB! Signs like that were probably in every locker room in the league, but what happened to that guy was a prime example of what that sign meant. To me, it meant that if you got hurt and couldn't play, then you could kiss your ass good-bye!

I didn't have an opportunity to tell those guys good-bye. I'd quickly met them, they were there for a few weeks, then they were gone! Once I realized who had been released, I thought about them for a couple of minutes. I wondered where they would be going from here or if they would have an opportunity to try out with another ball club. I was sad for them because I knew that they had dreams, just like millions of other boys who started playing football at age six, seven, or eight, of playing in the National Football League one day. As I sat at my locker, I could tell other guys were feeling that sense of loss for someone they might have known only for a short time or for a veteran they've known for years. After a couple of minutes I realized that I had to get taped, dressed, and on the field for practice. Whatever pity party I was having for the departed players had to come to an end; I had to move forward and get ready to take care of my own business. I could do nothing about their being released, but from that day forward, I realized that I might one day be one of those players released for a younger, more talented player.

Our first exhibition game was to be against the New England Patriots. Unfortunately, I twisted a knee in practice and couldn't play. The injury was not serious, but the trainers thought it was best for me not to even dress for the game. The team traveled to Foxboro, Massachusetts, to play the Pats. Before that game I realized that while I'd seen many professional football games on television, I had never seen a pro football game in person, so this was going to be my first ever professional football game. It was exciting to see the guys I had been practicing with play in an actual game. I thought things moved fast in the first days of practice. Seeing that game showed me just how much faster the action was going to be in a real game. When the starting players left the game and the second string came on to play, you could see a noticeable difference in the speed and tempo of the game. That injured knee was probably a blessing in disguise to allow me to see a real NFL game as it was.

The next week I got back to practice with the second team in preparation for the Giants biggest exhibition game, against the rival New York Jets. During the week I heard various veteran players telling the rookies how much we needed to beat the Jets because of the intra-city rivalry and because the game was being played in Yankee Stadium. That meant absolutely nothing to me as I was unaware of any rivalry. The only rivalry I was accustomed to was State against North Carolina A&T. I had a long way to go to catch up with this New York rivalry thing. It was big for some of the players as well as some of the Giants fans from what I read in the newspapers. Unfortunately, it meant nothing to me!

In practice we continued to prepare for the season and for the upcoming game against the Jets. I knew that I was going to have an opportunity to play in my first NFL game, even with a still-tender knee. Two things come to mind about that game. First, the game had to be postponed, from Saturday night to Monday evening, because of a rare hurricane that came through the New York area and dropped quite a bit of rain. Second, in the second quarter after the starters played a couple of series, they were taken out and the second-string defense replaced them. This was my big chance to show what I could do. Finally, I was playing in my first game. I looked over to the sideline to get the visual signal from Marty on what defense we would be playing, then I called it in our huddle. We broke our huddle, then watched the Jets offense break their huddle and head to the line of scrimmage. I looked over the offensive formation and saw the Jets quarterback, Joe Namath. For a moment I thought to myself, "Damn, that's Joe Namath!" I thought, "I wish all of my boys back at home could see me now!" Then I thought, "Damn, he really does have blue eyes!"

I was so focused on his eyes and the aura of Joe Namath I almost forgot where I was. He called signals and the ball was snapped. I stood there unable to move or focus on what I was supposed to do. I saw a running back coming right at me. Namath had called a draw play, I'm sure, to test the new players who had just been inserted into the game. Who was I kidding? He called that play because he knew I was a fresh rookie, I was the new country bumpkin who had just fallen off the truck. For a moment I turned into a spectator and took my mind off my responsibility. I could have been seriously hurt as Marty had always told me. That was the first, last, and only time that I would be in awe of anyone on the football field. I had never gotten starstruck over anyone before, so I chalked it up as a one-shot experience. The next day as the defense was watching the film of the game, Marty arrived at my first play, stopped the projector, and asked, "Harry Carson, please tell everyone here, what were you watching on this play?" I was somewhat embarrassed and said that I was thinking play-action pass and was indecisive. Marty said that if I continued to make plays like that, I would find myself back in Carolina selling insurance. The point was well taken, and I knew I had to make plays when opportunities presented themselves.

The following week we prepared to play against the Steelers in Pittsburgh in a nationally televised game on ABC. That game was also going to be a reunion as I would be seeing my old teammate Donnie Shell as well as my friend Bennie Cunningham. I knew Bennie from our college days in South Carolina. He played at Clemson University but would come down to Orangeburg to see his girlfriend after football games. She lived in the same dorm as my then girlfriend, Yvette Collins. When we arrived at our hotel in Pittsburgh, I was wandering around the hotel and ran into Howard Cosell. Cosell and the ABC broadcast crew were there to televise the game on *Monday Night Football*. When I introduced myself, he knew who I was before I could open my mouth to say anything else. He said, "Harry Carson from little South Carolina State College. Some doubt his ability to play middle linebacker, but I say he will probably become one of the best to ever play the game!" *Wow!!!!* I was impressed! That chance meeting with Cosell meant more to me than anyone else will probably know. First, as a lowly rookie, to even be recognized by someone considered a true television personality and an icon such as Howard Cosell was big stuff to me. Second, he acknowledged my school; most people thought I was from the University of South Carolina instead of South Carolina State. And last, he must have spent some time doing his homework as well as talking with club personnel to determine how good I could be.

After the game—who won is irrelevant—many of my friends and family members called and told me all of the complimentary comments Cosell made about me during the broadcast. Once again I began to understand the scope of my influence not only with my family and friends in South Carolina, but also with people in other areas of the country. It made my day to know that so many people recognized Cosell's reference to South Carolina State. To that point I hadn't realized that so many people, especially females, watched football. That one chance encounter with Cosell made me understand that people who knew me were watching and rooting for me. It also showed me that if I screwed up, those same people would know it as well.

I went through the last three exhibition games without getting hurt. More important, I survived the final cut after the last game. As a team, we then prepared for the season opener against the Washington Redskins in RFK Stadium in D.C. I was still trying to learn my position and had not done anything outstanding by that time. I was like most of the other hundred or so players who came to camp in July busting their asses to earn one of forty-seven positions on the team. I was finally able to get excited about formally making the New York Giants. Nobody came around to my locker or in a meeting and said, "Congratulations, you've made the team!" That I was one of forty-seven still with a locker was enough of an indicator that I had made it.

While it was not where I originally wanted to play, it was where I was and I had to appreciate that. I was happy to be with the Giants because my mom still lived in Newark, New Jersey. Our practice facility was in Westchester County above New York City. I found out that Newark was not too far from where we would play our games at Giants Stadium in New Jersey. I thought that I would at least be able to see my mom and taste her cooking much more than before.

With the beginning of the regular season I knew my role was going to be primarily as a special teams player, so I made sure that I knew all of my assignments. I was on the kickoff team, the second kickoff-return team, and the punt and punt-return teams. It was the norm for first-year guys such as me to earn our pay by contributing on those teams. Most veteran players tried to steer clear of playing on those teams because they can be exhausting, with a lot of full-speed running. The risk of getting hurt is also greater, especially playing on the kickoff and kickoff-return teams. The kickoff teams are usually referred to as the suicide squad because certain players were responsible for getting down the football field and busting the wedge that many of the kickoff returners run behind to find daylight to get the maximum out of the return. Because of my size and speed, that became my job, wedge buster. Coaches didn't care how you busted the wedge as long as it was destroyed and the returner got no farther than his team's 25-yard line. While I was going to be getting in on some of the action on the field, I knew that I was not going to be playing much on defense in games. My attitude was that I was going to bust my ass on those teams to do all that I could to help my team.

One incident stands out as we were about to open the season with the Washington. We were in the locker room in RFK, getting dressed to play, and I recall getting ready mentally to play in my first regular-season NFL game. Making my way out of the locker room to go to the field to warm up, I saw two veteran players about to take some pills. I initially thought they were taking salt pills since it was hot that second Sunday in September. Players commonly took salt pills prior to games to help prevent them from cramping up when playing. One of them offered me what they were taking, and I asked, "What is it?" He responded that it was speed. "Speed?" I thought to myself. "What in the hell do they need speed for?" Once it registered what it was, I politely declined their offer and went about my business. That first day of the regular season was my first exposure to drugs in the NFL. I went onto the field and stood there excited about playing. With the exception of playing football with my friends, I had never played a game on any level on Sunday afternoon. As I warmed up with the rest of the team, I could feel a knot developing in my gut with the anticipation of what we were about to do. Then I began to understand why my teammates were taking speed.

When we all returned to the locker room for our last-minute instructions, I looked around the room and could see the seriousness on every player's face. Training camp was over and so were all the exhibition games, which meant absolutely nothing; this time was what it was all about. Some veteran players had laughed and poked fun at some of the rookie players who got so nervous before playing in a preseason game that they puked. Now some of those same guys who did the laughing were themselves feeling the heat of what was about to begin.

We assembled to hear what Coach Arnsparger had to say. We could only hear the faint noise of the fans outside in the open stadium. We all took a knee, held one another's hand, repeated the Lord's Prayer, then headed out for the team introductions. As we all walked through the tunnel to the field, you could almost hear everyone's heart pumping through his pads and jersey. After the introductions and the coin toss, it was time to get it on. We won the toss and elected to receive the kickoff. I stood on the sideline because I was on the second kickoff-return team. When the Skins kicked off, I swear I had never seen players move so fast in my life. Whatever I saw before in practice or exhibition games was nothing compared to the speed the Redskins kickoff team showed getting down the field. I thought to myself, "Oh, shit!" To that point it seemed as if every football level that I had risen to had better talent and more speed than the level that I'd left, but this was off-the-charts speed. It seemed as if everyone on that kickoff team were running a four-flat 40-yard dash. I realized why there is such an emphasis on speed in football, and I really understood the guys taking speed to get an edge.

Our offense was unable to move the ball and was forced to punt to the Skins. That punt was my first play in a regular-season game. It didn't take long to see that the Skins were a bit better than we were, plus they had a tremendous home-field advantage with their fans. They were able to march the ball down the field and score against our defense. Our offense came back and eventually scored our first touchdown. It was now my turn to show what I could do on the kickoff team. My position was R-1, which is right by the kicker as he kicks the ball from the tee. My job was to get the best possible jump on the kick by watching the speed of the kicker's approach to the ball and timing my crossing of the 40-yard line, where the ball had been teed, to coincide with the kickoff. Within three or four steps I had to be running at full speed to get down the field. I saw how fast the Redskins kickoff team was on their initial kick, and we needed to do even better than them to be effective.

When our kicker, Joe Danelo, approached the ball and kicked off, I felt as if I had become a missile exploding down the field looking for my target: the ball carrier. I ran about thirty yards down the field, eluded a blocker on the way, then saw the wedge forming in front of the returner. In my mind I referred back to everything we went over in our special-team meetings about busting the wedge. Even though I knew what I was supposed to do, I was apprehensive about throwing my body around, but I had no choice as I approached the wedge of three or four players in front of the returner. I laid my body out to cut down as many of the wedge men as I could. As I felt my body make contact, I could feel what was probably a knee or thigh hit the back of my helmet. It's strange because once I threw my body, I could not hear one thing and I couldn't see anything since I had closed my eyes. When the play was over, as I began to gather myself to get up, I felt a little wobbly. My head was starting to spin and I felt as if I had been broken in half, but I was able to get myself off the field. When I got to the sideline, I shook off the effects of the hit.

The rest of the game went the way of the Redskins. We lost that game and the next three games, which were all played on the road because of the construction of our new stadium. The next game was to be our first at home after playing six exhibition and four regular-season games on the road. We were coming home to open Giants Stadium against the Dallas Cowboys.

The team had not won one game, and it was frustrating to lose week in and week out. I could sense that the coaches were under pressure to win. With the opening game at Giants Stadium coming up, something had to give. The atmosphere between the coaches and the players, as well as between the offense and the defense, was getting more hostile than earlier in the season. Losing was no fun, and winning the Cowboys game would be just the medicine that we needed for the team's attitude and the spirit in the locker room. Going into that game, I could tell that the confidence level of many of the players was low. Some had an I-hope-we-can-win attitude, but I'm sure deep down they didn't have an ounce of confidence that we could. I was still playing special teams so I felt a little helpless because there was only so much I could do personally. Besides, I was a rookie who had just fallen into this situation. Marty knew I wasn't quite ready to unseat Brian at the middle linebacker position; he had much more experience than me. I was adequate playing against the run, but I was a liability defending against the pass.

A couple of days before the game we held our first practice session at the new stadium. When the team arrived on buses, I wandered around the place totally amazed, wondering how something so huge could be my new workplace. The stadium and the artificial surface were impressive, but when I walked into the locker room, I was floored. I had never played anywhere with such a new locker room, plush with carpeting all over. I thought, "This is going to be good." What was best was discovering that the equipment manager had put my things in the first locker right by the door. At the time I didn't think about it, but at that locker by the door I would see a lot of comings and goings during my career.

What I remember the most about that first game at Giants Stadium was walking out to the field for warm-ups and seeing one of the Cowboys players standing in the tunnel before heading to the field. I saw his helmet, and just as I was in awe of Joe Namath's eyes, that blue star on the side of that silver helmet impressed me. Like many other guys growing up in South Carolina, I didn't get to see many Giants games, but I did see plenty of Cowboys games. I was about to play against the Dallas Cowboys; for a moment I wondered what my old friends back in Florence would say if they could see me getting ready to play against America's Team. I had only been starstruck a few times in my short career, but this was the icing on the cake. If there was a time that told me that I had made it to the NFL, it was knowing that I would be playing in this game against the Dallas Cowboys. I played primarily on special teams against the Cowboys, and we lost another game.

At the beginning of the next week, as we began to prepare for our next opponent, the Minnesota Vikings, Marty came over and sat down next to me at my locker. He looked in my eyes and then asked if I was ready. I looked at him and asked, "Ready for what?" He said, "Ready to start?" My heart sank. I didn't know how these things were done, but apparently this was my time. I told him that I thought I was ready, but the thought of starting caused my stomach to become tied in knots. He said that Brian would be moving from the middle linebacker position to the weak side position replacing Pat Hughes. After we talked, I couldn't believe that I was going to be a starter. Despite the happiness that I felt, I could still see the disappointment on Pat's face when I saw him. Pat had been with the Giants for over six years. He was a good player, but apparently the coaches felt that they needed to make a move to stir things up on defense. I felt bad that my starting would affect the career of another player. Pat didn't show any bitterness toward me, but he seemed to be angry that the coaches made him a scapegoat because the team was not winning. I felt bad, but that only lasted for a minute.

When we went out to practice on the field that day, the defensive coaches called for the first defense to take the field. I ran out on the field with the rest of the veterans, whom I had been watching since the beginning of training camp. As the coaches were going over the plays that we would see by the Vikings and the adjustments we would need to make, I was bursting with pride. I tried to concentrate on what was going on in the huddle, but I could not help but think about all of the people I would need to call to tell them that I was going to start. With that promotion in my playing status, my confidence took off. I didn't know if I would sink or swim with the promotion, but I did know that whatever happened would be squarely on my shoulders.

When I got home, my roommate Gordon Bell and I discussed my becoming a starter. Gordon and I were drafted together as back-to-back picks for the Giants. He was the 104th player taken in the entire draft, and I was the 105th. We had been supporters of one another and decided to live together in Ossining, New York, a sleepy little village near our training facility in Pleasantville. Gordon was happy for me and wished me luck with the move. I spent much of the evening calling my family and friends and sharing the good news with them. They were extremely excited that I had become a member of the starting defense. Some of my buddies that I called were so proud of me. They wanted me to kick ass and take names. They told me that they were never Giants fans, but they would be with me as a starter.

The morning of the game in Minnesota, I woke up looking at starting my first game in twenty-degree weather against Fran Tarkenton and Chuck Foreman, two of the best players in the National Football League. I remember looking out my hotel window and knowing that although it looked nice and sunny, I was going to freeze my ass off. I went through my pregame ritual of attending chapel service, then had my pregame meal. I was so totally focused on playing the game that I could hardly think about anything else. As we took the team bus from the hotel to the stadium, I sat alone in the back and said nothing to anyone. I kept thinking about what my responsibilities were when

I read the play action and whom I was to look up in coverage. I had to remember what the audibles were if the strength of the offense changed from the right side to the left side of the defense. I had a whole checklist of things that I had to try to remember. It was easy knowing what I had to do on the kickoff team or punt team, but now I was getting flustered with the pressure of the game coming up and not feeling completely certain of all of my defensive responsibilities. Marty noticed that my head was buried in my playbook as I sat by my locker prior to the game. When he came over, he said to me, "You know you can overanalyze what you need to do. The reality is, all you need to do is go out there and react as a football player." Then he said something that I've always remembered as clear as day: "Son, don't clutter your mind with unimportant things. If you don't know this stuff by now, you won't get it." He was right; I was driving myself crazy trying to remember all of the shit I had to remember. I decided that I was just going to go out and play football and enjoy myself.

When we went out to the field for the coin toss, I was so nervous that the below-freezing temperature didn't bother me one bit. Once the game got started, our offense received the ball and had a three-and-out series. After the punt I jogged onto the field with the rest of the defensive unit. I wished that the game had been a nationally televised game so that all of my family and friends could see me on the field with the Giants defense. I'm probably wrong, but I think every play that the Vikings ran was either a delayed draw, an inside running play, or a play-action pass. I should have known that being the new guy, I was going to be exploited. Nobody prepared me for the heavy dose of running plays and play-action passes that would come my way that day. I saw purple helmets with wings coming at me all day. Not only that, but the Viking center, Mick Tingelhoff, was doing a good job of holding me on almost every play. When I came off the field and complained in frustration to some of my teammates, my tackle John Mendenhall told me that the best way to keep a guy from holding me was to hit the motherfucker in the mouth! I was waiting for the play to come to me, giving the offense the edge, instead of attacking the play when I saw it developing. On the following series of plays I did what John told me to do, attack and deliver a blow, shed the block, and make the tackle. The game was an educational for me, the first of many. Once the game was over, I felt a tremendous sense of accomplishment for getting my first game as a starter under my belt. After the game Marty came over to me. He told me I had some things that I needed to work on, but he was pleased with what he saw of my play. We lost the game, but I was already thinking about the next game.

One of the mistakes I made against the Vikings was waiting to make plays. During the week, as we prepared for our next opponent, the Pittsburgh Steelers, Marty kept emphasizing that I needed to be quicker diagnosing the play and getting to the point of attack. Marty told me that the Steelers would be running a heavy dose of trap plays with Franco Harris as the feature runner. Marty told me that as a middle linebacker I had to be able to read the direction of the center's block much quicker than I did in the Vikings game. He told me that when I saw the center block back away from the flow of the play, I needed to step up and brace for impact because that was where the play would be coming. All week I kept saying to myself, "When the center blocks back, step up. When the center blocks back, step up."

This week I knew the battle was going to be tough, or even tougher than the previous week, because the Steelers had had an opportunity to see me play against the Vikings on film. I was still the new kid on the block on defense, and until I could prove that I could hold my own and stop plays in my area, I was going to continue to be exploited by opposing offenses. That is what the National Football League is about. No, that is what football is about: finding a weakness in some aspect of the game and taking advantage of it. A team running plays and throwing passes at me could not be taken personally by me. It was simply the way it was. Until I started making plays, I was going to see it week in and week out. Marty knew it, my teammates knew it, and I knew it.

As we prepared for the Steelers game, I could sense a tenseness among the coaching staff. Stories in the newspapers were calling for the head of Bill Arnsparger. I had come from an area where we had one or maybe two newspaper reporters around during the week, but in the New York area, it seemed as if twenty to thirty members of the media were around every day, and these guys were like sharks that could smell blood in the water. They knew that

Arnsparger was about to take a long walk on a short pier. To them it was just a matter of when, not if, he was going to be canned. When I saw Bill outside of our meetings, he looked as if he had aged in only the few short months I was with the Giants. I felt bad for him because he seemed to have the weight of the world on his back, and all he needed was to get one win to stop the bleeding.

We played the Steelers in our second home game at Giants Stadium. This was my second time playing against the Steelers, as we had played against them in the preseason. In that game I played against the other rookies and reserves toward the later part of the game. This was my first chance to play against the regular starters such as Terry Bradshaw, Franco Harris, and the strong Pittsburgh offensive line for the entire game. I knew things were going to be a little different when I watched the players as they came onto the field to run their first series of plays. Before the game I made a serious mistake in thinking that because we almost beat these guys in the exhibition season, we could beat them during the regular season. Teams had a different mind-set in the regular season from the exhibition season. The Steelers had gotten off to a good start that season, and it was up to us to slow them down. When the Pittsburgh offense broke the huddle, their linemen didn't walk to the line of scrimmage as on a lot of teams, they sprinted. The five linemen all wore skintight jerseys to keep defensive players from being able to grab them on a pass rush. These offensive guys also looked as if they had been lifting weights while they were in the locker room before coming out to play. These Steelers were pumped up! I could see that they were in attack mode, and they were going to come after us.

When Bradshaw called the signals and said "Set," they all snapped into their stance and put their fingers on the ground in unison as if they were soldiers taking part in close-order drills. They were crisp, alert, and on a mission. On the snap, they exploded low off the ball with force and power. When the play was over, they went back to the huddle and repeated the routine. As they were driving down the field, they lined up near midfield in a split-back formation and on the snap of the ball the center blocked back on my defensive tackle John Mendenhall. I thought of the rule Marty had tried to drill into my head: "When the center blocks back, you step up." In that fraction of a second after seeing the center block back, I stepped up, and when I did, I felt the block of their offensive lineman on my right side trap me. When Sam Davis hit me on the side of my face, it felt as if I were hit by a sledgehammer. I had never been hit so hard in my life! That hit turned my helmet around on my head and had me seeing stars and feeling woozy. He didn't just hit me; he never stopped blocking me until I was on the ground, and even then I'm sure he kept digging his feet until he heard the whistle blow.

When the play was over, I had to feel my face to see if all of it was still there. I never liked going to the dentist, but that shot I took from Davis was like getting a massive shot of Novocain without having to wait for the effects to take place. When the center blocks back, step up! Like hell, I stepped up and got the shit knocked out of me. I felt good that it didn't take long for me to recognize the play, but I also felt as if I had just had a train going at full speed run over me. That was truly my "Welcome to the NFL!" shot. Almost every player who plays in the NFL will at some point get a hit that is so devastating that everybody sees it and goes, "Oh, shit, that has to hurt!" I had been through all of training camp and the other games, but not until that game did I get what I thought was the measuring stick of playing in the NFL.

We lost another game, and this time heads rolled. Bill Arnsparger was fired, and John McVay was named head coach. McVay had been a head coach the year before in the then recently defunct World Football League. Of all of our coaches, John apparently was the only one who had head-coaching experience. He did his best to make us players feel that we weren't that far from winning a game. I didn't think we were a bad team, but I felt that we had players who had developed a loser's mentality. I was new to the team, but I could see that some of the players desperately wanted to win by laying their guts on the line. But I could also see that others had the heart but didn't have the talent. While Arnsparger got the ax for the team's failure to win, we as players had to be held responsible for the outcome of many of those games with our sometimes lack of effort and nonbelief in one another and the team.

In the next week's game against the Philadelphia Eagles we lost 10–0 in John McVay's debut as head coach. We played so poorly that as we were leaving the field, the Giants fans began throwing eggs, apple, oranges, and toilet tissue at us to show their displeasure. That didn't surprise me since I could tell how the fans felt from remarks I heard from the stands. I noticed a huge difference in the tempo of that game from the tempo of the Steelers game the week before. Don't get me wrong, it was a physical game, but nowhere near the intensity of playing against the Steelers' offensive line. The Eagle linemen were pretty good veteran players, but they played more of a finesse game. The difference was like night and day. After playing against the Eagles, I felt fine, almost good enough to go out to dinner and socialize with my teammates. But after playing against the Steelers, the only thing I wanted to do was go home, lie down, and watch *60 Minutes* on CBS. The Steelers just beat you up physically. Whether a team is physical or finesse, you have to be able to compete against them and we were not.

In those two games, I focused on the guys who played my position. Jack Lambert of the Steelers was indeed the best middle linebacker playing at that time. He played behind a superior defensive line with great players such as "Mean" Joe Green, Ernie Holmes, Dwight White, and L. C. Greenwood, as well as two of the best outside linebackers in the game, Andy Russell and Jack Ham. Their defense was super all the way around. Lambert was great, but so was the rest of his group. I didn't get a whole lot from watching Lambert except to see the greatness of a defense working together and playing on the same page.

I think I gained more from watching Bill Bergey, the middle linebacker of the Eagles. Bergey was more like me in stature, speed, and power. He had a good defensive line just as I did, but he had to do much of his work on his own. Bill was one of the linebackers I watched during those early one-on-one sessions with Marty. He was not about finesse. He was a straight-ahead, smash-mouth, power-versus-power player, as I was. When our defense came off the field and the Eagles defense took the field, I made sure that after I sat with my coaches and went over the adjustments we needed to make as a defense, I positioned myself as close to the field as possible. I wanted to get a clear view of what Bergey was doing so that I could emulate him. I found a spot on the sideline where I placed my helmet and took a seat on it and watched. I didn't watch the offense or the defense, I zeroed in on Bill Bergey. I watched his every move as he called the defensive signals, broke the huddle, then made the adjustments according to the offensive formation. When the ball was snapped, I watched his reaction to the play and his effort to get to the ball carrier.

On one play, the ball came toward the Giants sideline and most of our players there scattered to avoid being accidentally hit. I was so unaware of my surroundings that I hardly moved because of my focus on Bergey. When he reached the sideline, I could see that he had a huge wad of chewing tobacco in his mouth, causing his bearded cheek to protrude. I was so impressed with his aggressive play that I wanted to copycat him. When I went into the locker room at halftime, I went to the equipment manager to get some chewing gum. I must have taken about ten sticks of gum, put them in my mouth, chewed them until they got soft, then held the gum in my mouth just as Bergey did with the chewing tobacco. I felt like a kid again imitating my favorite players. But here I really was, playing in the National Football League, playing not against the Philadelphia Eagles but against Bill Bergey, one of the best pure middle linebackers in the league. From that point on I knew Bergey was going to be my benchmark as to how I played my game. Whatever he did, I was going to try to do a little better.

We finished the year by winning three of our last five games. It felt good to get a dose of winning as a professional. With that first victory, you could feel the weight being lifted off our backs and especially off the shoulders of the coaches. With a win, people start to smile and feel better about themselves. We would not go winless for the season, which would have been embarrassing as well as an insult to us as players and the fans. I played well enough to earn some recognition. Not only had I become a starter at middle linebacker, I played well enough to be named to the NFL's All-Rookie Team. It was nice to be recognized, but the best part of being All-Rookie was that an incentive clause in my contract thus paid me an extra $5,000. A playing-time incentive clause in my contract also earned me some extra dollars. At that time the $32,500 salary was good, but I didn't realize the amount of money that would be taken out for federal and state income taxes as well as for my agent's fee.

Just after the last game of the season Giants general manager Andy Robustelli called me into his office and told me how pleased the organization was with my play. Before joining the organization as an executive, Andy was a Hall of Fame defensive end, and he knew good talent when he saw it. The team was pleased I was able to make the transition to linebacker and to hold my own as a starter. He saw my play as one of the few bright spots for the team that season. He told me that he wanted me to be happy with my "contract situation," so within two weeks he was going to contact my agent to strike a new deal for me. Leaving that meeting, I was thrilled that the team took the initiative to reassure me regarding my value to the team. Ironically, I'd joked with my teammate George Martin a couple of months earlier that I was having so much fun playing football that I would play for nothing. I remember George looking at me as if I had gone nuts and saying, "Tell me you feel the same way in a couple of years." The two weeks went by without a call. I never pressed the issue and just thought the team had a change of heart. But I've always felt that if you say you're going to do something, you have to do it! Don't lead me on or tease me. I'm glad that I didn't totally buy into my contract's being restructured, and the extra $8,000 to $9,000 in incentives that I made helped sustain me during the off-season.

I enjoyed my first year as a professional football player with the Giants. I was challenged as I had never been challenged before. To learn the new position of middle linebacker at the professional level was a lot to take on, but I did it and excelled at it. I learned a lot that year about playing the game on and off the field. I knew that while it was fun to play the game, it was very much about business. In training camp I saw how businesslike it was. Many players who thought they had a good chance of making the team and playing were either cut or traded to other teams. Those decisions regarding their careers were not theirs to make because they were the "property" of the Giants.

Whatever the team wanted to do, the players had to abide by the decisions. I knew that while it was a beginning for me, it was an ending for others, such as some of the veteran players who no longer fit into the plans of the team or could not physically compete because of an injury. I used the experiences from my play on the football field to help me not repeat mistakes. I tried to do the same off the field, through my own experiences as well as from the experiences of others. I knew that at some point my turn to be shown the door would come. Until that time, I was going to try to make the most of every opportunity.

I went back to Orangeburg during my off-season and attended graduate school to begin work on a master's degree. I realized that while it was nice playing professional football, whenever my career ended, I needed to have a plan and not be dependent on football. I knew that most people and even I to some extent believed the mistaken myth about professional sports and athletes that when a career was over, the athlete would be rich and would never need to work again. My limited time playing had taught me that football was merely a temporary job, just like the substitute teaching I did at one of my old schools in Florence on my college breaks. I had to be able to do something else, so while I had my certification to teach, I knew it would help to gain more knowledge as well as to get back on campus and in touch with some of the people I left there. While in school I spent some time with the football team trying to give them some insight on the ways the pros ran their drills and practice. That time on campus also gave me a chance to work out with some other former Bulldog players who were also playing pro ball, such as Donnie and Barney.

When I returned to the Giants the next year, I was in great shape and was ready to pick up where I'd left off the previous year. With a season under my belt I felt much more confident in my role as the middle linebacker for the team. I gained more and more confidence every day with every play on the field. Teams stopped trying to exploit me with the run because I was a young, inexperienced player. I was no longer a rookie and I had to stop making rookie-type mistakes. I had to take my game to the next level. I had gone through the disappointment of my team's failing to win all but three games my first year. While I wouldn't be the one to run the ball or protect the quarterback, I had my own responsibilities within the defensive system so I decided to make my own game within the game. I came from a winning tradition at SC State, and the other players that I had played with while there felt the same way I did, that instead of worrying about the outcome of games, I should just do everything I could to help my team win. One of the things that got me through my practices with the Giants was to constantly refer to my roots at SC State. They had instilled such a sense of "Bulldog pride" in me that it would have been crazy not to reflect on it and use it to help me. I was more assertive in practice since I knew my assignments; I didn't second-guess myself the way I did in my first year. My second season was uneventful except that I grew from my play. I played in all fourteen games and we went 5-9 under John McVay.

As I entered my third season, I got better and better as a player. With a year and a half of experience under my belt, I knew how to play middle linebacker and was confident in my ability. I felt comfortable on the field and didn't feel as if I needed to think so much. With my film and classroom preparation I had a good feel for what teams would try to do during games. I relied on my physical play as well as working with my outside linebackers, Brian Kelly and Brad Van Pelt, to make plays on defense. We started the season with optimism, but as the season progressed, we realized we would probably be home for Christmas. We struggled, winning six games in an expanded sixteen-game season. I played in all sixteen games, and I began to get tired of the same old shit happening year after year with the team. This year, the team would reach one of its lowest points in franchise history.

In a hard-fought home game against the Eagles, we were leading 17–12 with less than two minutes left in the game and we had the ball. All we had to do was just take a knee and run out the clock for a sweet victory over one of our division rivals. Running a simple play to end the game like that was much too simple for us. No, we had to run the damn ball. But a botched hand-off to Larry Csonka from Joe Pisarcik resulted in a fumble. The Eagles' Herman Edwards scooped up the ball and returned it for a touchdown, giving them a hard-to-believe 19–17 victory in the New Jersey Meadowlands. I was stunned, just like everyone else in the stadium. At the conclusion of the game I could not move. I sat on the bench for another fifteen minutes staring at the ground thinking, "How in the fuck did I get myself into this situation with this team?" We were awful and a poor excuse for a professional football team! I came from a winning tradition, and while my goal was to do my job, I started to get tired of some of the other guys on the team not doing what they needed to do both on and off the field to help the team win. It also pissed me off that some guys on the team took losing in stride. At times, I wondered just where their fucking pride was! All my life I had been taught to have a sense of pride in what I did. Not all, but some of these guys liked wearing a football uniform and driving a nice car but didn't know what playing with heart and passion was about.

With that fumble, everyone knew major changes were coming, starting with our offensive coordinator, Bob Gibson, who called the hand-off play. The very next day he was gone! At the end of that season, all of the other coaching staff members got the boot as well. John McVay, whom I had grown to like, was fired as head coach, and my mentor Marty Schottenheimer was not invited back.

That was a difficult season. I was beginning to think that the Giants had pissed off the football gods. We could not get a break and became one of those teams that everyone wanted to play against to get a win. We became everyone's Homecoming Game opponent. We were so bad that year that I heard that many of the fans protested the team by burning their season tickets in the parking lot. While I didn't personally see tickets being burned, I did see the planes flying overhead during games with banners streaming behind them complaining about the many years of lousy football by the Giants organization.

With the season behind us, I had one bit of good news: I was elected to play in the NFC-AFC Pro Bowl. It was a tremendous honor to have been recognized by my peers. I thought (on a small level) that I should have been selected to play in the Pro Bowl the previous year, but I wasn't. I didn't feel slighted in any way and it really didn't bother me, but I knew that if I kept playing my game and stayed healthy, I would eventually make it. The significance of being selected for the Pro Bowl was that the people I played against were the only ones who could select me, not my teammates. That honor told me that I was doing the right thing in my play. Even though the team as a whole was not doing well, the players and coaches I played against had to know that I was a bright spot for my team and I kicked ass!

Other middle linebackers that I respected played well during that season, but I was certainly not going to downplay my play. That year I was also honored by the National Football League Players Association as the NFC Linebacker of the Year. To be recognized and honored in those ways made me feel a tremendous sense of accomplishment. To hear my teammates offer words of congratulations made me feel terrific deep inside, but I knew I could not allow the recognitions to go to my head. Football had taught me many lessons; the biggest was to always be humble. I had come a long way in what seemed like a short three years. I went from being a fourth-round pick out of a little, predominately black school in South Carolina where "we didn't play the same caliber of football as they did at the big schools" to being acknowledged as one of the best linebackers in football.

My family and friends kept up with my progress, as well as my old coaches at State. Coach Jeffries and Coach Goodwin pointed out the progress and character traits of Donnie, Barney, and me to players at SC State in hopes that they would strive to carry our legacy both on and off the field.

To get to the Pro Bowl that year, in spite of what the team did, I had to work my ass off to open the eyes of players around the league. When I got to Los Angeles, where the Pro Bowl was being played, I tried to savor every minute being around the other All-Star players that I was chosen to play with and against. I felt especially fortunate to have been chosen to play with Bill Bergey, one of the players I had grown to idolize and respect. In Bill's presence, I was like a sponge trying to soak up everything I could to help me improve my game. I was just a player trying to find my way in the game, but here were players who were really good and confident in what they did on the football field. I had to learn to be just as good and confident as they were to remain on the All-Pro level.

During those few months after the Pro Bowl, several game-changing events happened for me. It was a blessing to have been named to the Pro Bowl when I was because it gave my mother an opportunity to see me play on that level. My mother had sacrificed so much for not only me but for all of her family to have a decent life. We eventually convinced her to come back to South Carolina after spending many years working as a domestic in New Jersey. When I was selected to the Pro Bowl, I was extremely happy that she and my sisters could make the trip to Los Angeles for the game. My mother enjoyed the trip and I could sense how proud she was of me. Little did we know that would be her last trip and her last time seeing me play football. Tomorrow is not promised to anyone, and she went to bed one night in May of 1979 and did not wake up the next morning. She lapsed into a coma and was hospitalized for several weeks. It was tough to see my mother in the condition she was in, not knowing if she would recover. What was even tougher was my having kept a secret. Being the procrastinator I could be, I'd kept from her the news that I was going to be a father. When I first joined the Giants and began living in Ossining, I began dating Ann Cherry. After we dated for a while, she realized she was expecting. I didn't tell my mom for fear that she would be disappointed in me. I was her baby! I was the one that she constantly prayed for. I hoped that she would recover and I could tell her she was going to be a grandmother again. She already had four grandsons from my sisters Loretta and Louise, but no grandchildren from her sons. None of her sons was married, and during those times (the late seventies) other people had children out of wedlock, but certainly not her baby son.

The hospital in my hometown did all it could to help her. They thought she might benefit from more specialized care at Duke University Medical Center in Durham, North Carolina. After discussions with the medical staff in Florence, I chartered a small plane with medical personnel to take her to Duke, hoping that my mother would wake up at some point. For several weeks I traveled between Duke and New York, where my daughter was about to be born. On Saturday afternoon, June 2, at 4:59 while I was at Duke with my unconscious mother in intensive care, my daughter, Aja, was born in Tarrytown, New York.

I didn't know how much of a blessing Aja's birth would be until my mama passed away exactly two weeks later. My mother's passing was tough for me. While she had the minor ailments of a woman in her sixties, she appeared to have been in good health. I was always her baby boy, even to the end as I, all six feet three inches of me, would sit on her lap only weeks before she was stricken. In not telling my mother about Aja, I was probably being a selfish ass because I had always known that my mother loved me despite my actions, and totally unconditionally. Not telling her that she was going to be a grandmother was one of the biggest mistakes of my life.

I thought I was a better person than that and my mother deserved better from me. I am very much my mother's son. From my earliest memory she taught me right from wrong and was proud to know that I had learned to take care of myself just as she wanted me to do when she left the family. She taught me to be a gentle and caring person. And she taught me that no matter how badly someone treats me, I can kill a person with kindness. One of the best things she taught me is that no matter what heights I reach, I should always be nice to people.

My mama's death was tough enough to deal with as, just like that, she was gone! As I was grieving and trying to get past that loss, just one week later I had another hurdle to contend with: my teammate and on-the-road roommate, Troy Archer, whom I was drafted with in 1976, was killed in a horrible automobile crash in New Jersey. Troy had so much talent and was taken much too soon. So much was happening in my life that I didn't know what day it was from day to day.

I still had to find a way to focus on what I had to do as a football player to get ready for the upcoming season. I didn't have time to grieve for my mother or my teammate. Aja was here, but she came two to three months premature. Even though she weighed only three pounds and fourteen ounces when she was born, she was physically strong. Aja spent several days in an incubator in the intensive care unit of the hospital until she was released to go home. Before long, all the love I'd had for my mom was redirected to my daughter.

While dealing with these adjustments in my personal life, I had to be certain to be mentally prepared as I approached training camp. I had to know my stuff and not take steps backward in my learning. It was a given that I could physically compete on the professional level. But I understood that the fastest way to leave the Giants and the NFL was to make mental errors by not knowing my assignments and responsibilities. I had seen guys come into the league with so much promise and ability. I mean guys who had the ideal size that coaches love, with great speed and agility, and who went to those big-name schools. I saw many of those same guys fail to make it because of mental errors. When coaches get fired, it's not necessarily because of the lack of physical effort of players on the field; it's usually because of mental mistakes players make. The speed of play in the NFL is significantly faster than in the football I had played on other levels, and when mistakes were made, they usually happened in a fraction of a second. That is all it takes to blow a play and lose a game. Indecisiveness or uncertainty during a play that causes a player to take a false step or hesitate can be the difference between winning and losing a game. I was proud of my accomplishments to that point, but I was even prouder of being able to learn and master the systems and defenses that I was asked to play. Having the opportunity to work with such players as Brad Van Pelt and Brian Kelly for an extended period gave me the confidence to do my job effectively. Even when we blew assignments, we were smart enough to understand one another's style of play and work off each other.

I had more than my share of down moments during that off-season, but at the beginning of the 1979 season my football career was beginning to shift gears in performance and responsibility. George Young was the new general manager of the team. George brought in a new head coach, Ray Perkins, to re-instill discipline in the organization. Perkins proved to be a tough, no-nonsense, strict disciplinarian right off the bat with his training camp. The hot, humid days at Pace University were physical and tough to adjust to even for seasoned veterans; things such as not being able to take off your helmet during practices, even on the sidelines, became issues, especially for players on the NFL level. I had gone through easier practices in my earlier years, but under Perkins it was almost as tough as being back at State. I took the training in stride because I knew we needed that change in direction as a team.

I was elected defensive-team captain by my teammates. Only in my fourth year on the team, far from being a senior member of the squad, I was flattered and humbled to have been accorded that title and honor. But I also knew the responsibility that came with it. I had been captain for two of my years while at State, but this was the National Football League. Not only was it the NFL, but it was the Giants, a team with a tremendous history and legacy.

I accepted the challenge and made myself understand that I was probably the first black team captain in the history of the organization. I could have been wrong about that; after all, strong leaders of African-American descent played in the fifties and sixties, such as Emlen Tunnell, Roosevelt Grier, and Rosey Brown, and then Spider Lockhart in the seventies, but I didn't inquire if there had been a black captain in the past. Even if I was wrong, I wanted to believe that I was the first so that I did not ever take the position lightly. It had never been pointed out to me by anyone that I was playing a "thinking man's position," or the quarterback of the defense; and then I was charged with the responsibility of leading the defense as captain of that unit. While I never talked about it, I knew deep down where I was in both cases. I knew I had to conduct myself in such a way as to bring honor and pride to those players and coaches I'd played with on all levels of the game. All those folks I'd left in South Carolina and those Giants fans who were watching from Newark to Harlem and around the country were watching my actions both on and off the field.

The Giants' 1979 season was nothing to write home about, but I had a decent year and earned a spot in another Pro Bowl and was again awarded NFC Linebacker of the Year honors. Two things stand out in my mind about that season. The first was scoring the winning touchdown on a fumble recovery and return against the Kansas City Chiefs. The second was playing against one of the greatest runners of all time, O. J. Simpson. It wasn't so much what happened during the game as what happened after. After the gun sounded ending the game, I started to walk off the field, having been a part of a 32–16 victory. Simpson came up behind me and tugged at my jersey and said, "Hey, bro!" I turned and said, "Hey, Juice, what's up?" I was surprised that he would seek me out after the game, but he said, "Man . . . I've been hit by some of the best, but I've never been hit as hard as you hit me today!" I said, "Thanks, Juice, I appreciate that!" It didn't really matter what happened in the game; to have O. J. Simpson say that made my year. That statement has always stayed with me because of whom it came from. I had watched Simpson play at the University of Southern California, win the Heisman Trophy, then have a great career with the Buffalo Bills, even breaking the all-time NFL single-season rushing record during those days with the Bills. I knew that he had faced all kinds of talented defensive players, and that if in his eyes I was the hardest hitter, you'd better believe that was big shit for me and probably meant more because it was an unsolicited compliment!

CHAPTER 7

Injured Reserve

The beginning of the 1980 season set the tone for what would be a frustrating season for me. I'd finished the '79 season as a Pro Bowler for the second time, but right off the bat in training camp in '80, while taking part in a live scrimmage, I saw how the season was going to go for me. Our head coach, Ray Perkins, was hard-core and no-nonsense and demanded high performance from both the offense and the defense. The best way for him to get a feel for the ability of his team was to put them through live-contact drills almost every day in training camp. If you shied away from a lot of contact, our training camp was not the place to be.

Before we were to play our first exhibition game, against the Chicago Bears, we went through a live-contact and tackling scrimmage at Pace University. During the scrimmage the offense ran a wham play from an I formation with Leon Perry as the lead blocker for the halfback. The play was designed to come right up the middle of the offensive formation with the fullback acting as the escort leading the running back through the hole. On the snap, as I saw the play develop, the center blocked to the back side. When I saw the center's blocking action, I automatically reverted back to what Marty had drilled me to do. Center blocks back, step up into the hole. When I stepped up, I looked for the guard to try to block me, but there was no guard. Instead I saw Leon coming right at me with a full head of steam. I only had a fraction of a second to react—with the blocking of the center to the back side and the guard on the front side, the hole really opened up. I had to throw my body into the hole and destroy the lead blocker to shrink the space the running back could run through. As I attacked the hole, Leon and I collided at the line of scrimmage. I collapsed the hole and stood my ground by throwing my body across the block of Leon. When we hit, I immediately felt a burning sensation in my right shoulder. With that hit, I knew something was wrong and that I was hurt. I realized for the first time I had something serious to contend with because I could no longer continue with practice. I was concerned about the injury and immediately thought that I might not be able to play in the exhibition game against the Bears and see my old friend Walter Payton. I also thought that if I couldn't practice, it would give someone else an opportunity to play my position. That was a no-no in the NFL!

In the world of pro football or any other competitive sport, giving someone else an opportunity to play your position with the starters gives coaches, general managers, and even owners the chance to see how the team can save on the payroll with a less expensive body playing the position, especially if that person is even half-decent. From the moment I started against the Vikings in 1976, I considered the middle linebacker position to be mine, and I certainly didn't want to lose it because of an injury. I could do nothing except give way to my backup until I knew exactly what was going on with me physically.

The pain in my shoulder was intense but bearable, but I still needed a diagnosis of the injury. It took a couple of days for me to find out that I had severed the nerve leading to the posterior deltoid muscle. As the days went by, I could sense a decrease in the sensitivity of my shoulder, along with my ability to use my right arm as I had once been able to do. Because I am right-handed, I could definitely tell a difference in my strength when I did normal things. Not being able to play as effectively because of the shoulder injury was going to be a serious problem. When sitting in the driver's seat of my car, if I tried to retrieve something from the backseat by reaching back for it, I was unable to do so. I experienced difficulty doing other minor things like that. I also saw my deltoid muscle atrophy over a short time. Eventually the pain in the right shoulder eased, but the doctors couldn't assure me that the nerve would ever regenerate and my shoulder would get back to normal. After a few weeks I realized that I might have to live with this for the rest of my life.

When I'd sat with my teammates in the locker room, in the dining hall, or on the bus or plane when we traveled, we occasionally talked about the length of pro football careers. During my first season I heard veteran players talk about a 3.8-year span as the average career. I didn't think a lot about that at that time. Why should I? I was a "young guy" then and time meant nothing to me. But here I was at the point where 3.8 years began to resonate with me. I was no longer a kid; I had surpassed the 3.8 years that most players talked about, and I was actually going into my fifth season. While I had had more than my share of bumps, bruises, sprains, and strains during my career, I had not sustained any really serious injuries before.

The shoulder would be somewhat of a medal or a souvenir that I would show people to prove that I'd played in the NFL. The only regret I had was that the injury was sustained in practice and not in a big game. Even with it, I was eventually able to continue my play in practice and games. I lost a good deal of strength and power in the right shoulder and found myself favoring my left shoulder to avoid contact on the right one. It was clear in practice and in watching film that I had developed bad habits because of the shoulder. For several weeks I had to do quite a bit of rehabilitation work to keep the strength I had. With so much therapy focused on that shoulder, I began to gain more strength in the muscles around that area. Unless the nerve healed itself, that posterior deltoid was gone forever, but the muscle around it compensated for the loss. I began to wear an extra protective cover over the area because even though I wore shoulder pads, I was getting hits on it, the bony area at the point of the shoulder.

When I got to the point where I stopped thinking about the shoulder, I was able to play on the field pretty effectively. I don't think I realized it at the time, but that shoulder injury was a lesson learned. Not that I didn't know before, but I gained more knowledge of adversity and working my way through a difficult situation. It was much about learning what it takes to play the game, especially at that high level. That injury was a symbol of adapting to situations and conditions. Things won't always be perfect so you have to make adjustments to get what you want. While I couldn't help but think of the 3.8-year longevity of players, I was determined to play until I was ready to stop playing, and I wasn't there yet.

With the success I had had the previous years I thought I would be able to continue that trend. I didn't think I was being overconfident; I just wanted to continue to get better at what I did. The teams that I played on were awful teams. When I arrived in 1976, we went 3-11; in 1977, 5-9; in 1978 and 1979, it was no better, even though the NFL went to a sixteen-game schedule: we finished 6-10 in those years. Three of those four seasons the Giants finished dead last in the NFC East Division. It was not what I was used to, having played at South Carolina State where one year our defense set a record by giving up only 29 points the entire season. The Giants were one of the laughingstock teams in the NFL. And I was one of the players on that laughingstock team. I tried to make the best of the situation. Many days I felt so frustrated that I wanted to quit the team. I remember calling Coach Jeffries to talk about the situation. He told me to do the best that I could do to help the team win. That was probably the best advice he had ever given me. I went into practice with the attitude that regardless of what might be going on around me, I was going to do my best to help put my team in a position to win. I couldn't concern myself with anyone else; I had to take care of my own backyard before looking at anyone else's.

I made the adjustment with the deflated shoulder, and the team started the regular season on a positive note, defeating the St. Louis Cardinals on the road. After that win both the team and I went into a downward spiral. We lost the next three games, giving up almost 28 points per game on defense. We were awful as a team then, but my adversity was just getting started. We had to travel to Dallas in the beginning of October to play the Cowboys. When we left New Jersey, the temperature was sixty-eight degrees. When we arrived in Dallas, the temperature was one hundred. The next day as we left the hotel to go to Texas Stadium, we were told that the temperature was close to one hundred. We arrived at the stadium and got dressed. When we went to the field to loosen up, a thermometer on the sideline said the temperature on the artificial surface of Texas Stadium was 130 degrees. It was so hot it seemed unreal. I had played in all kinds of weather, but I had never played in weather that hot.

Once the game began, everyone was affected: Cowboy players, Giants players, the officials. As I was making a tackle on Cowboys running back Tony Dorsett, I collided with my linebacker mate Brad Van Pelt. While we made the tackle, it seemed that I absorbed most of the blow. This was one of the few times that I could understand what running backs felt like when we tried to knock the shit out of them. When I went down on the hot turf, it felt as if I had the wind knocked out of me. When I got over the shock of getting nailed by my own guy, I realized that something was wrong: I could not move! I didn't know why but I could not move my arms, legs, or any other part of my body.

Once the trainers and doctors realized that I could not move, they took extraspecial care in attempting to move me for fear that I might have injured my spinal cord. I had been down on the turf for several minutes, and while I could not move, I could feel the intense heat over my back and legs. My body was finally placed on a backboard and secured, then I was placed on a stretcher and wheeled off the field to a waiting ambulance. I was still wearing my helmet and shoulder pads since I was being directly transported to a hospital from the field. On that drive to the hospital my mind raced as I could only look forward with my helmet strapped down to the board. I looked at the ceiling of the ambulance and thought of so many different things in my past, but I also flashed forward to what might be my future. I saw myself in a wheelchair being pushed around, not being able to move independently. I had never before shed a tear as a result of pain that I'd sustained playing football. I was a big boy and big boys never cry. When I was left alone by the paramedic, I could feel a tear round out of my right eye and down the side of my face.

By the time I finally arrived at the hospital, I was beginning to regain the use of my limbs. I was able to walk from the ambulance into the emergency room to undergo a brief examination. The doctors wanted me to stay and undergo further examinations, but I felt well enough to leave and return to Texas Stadium to be with my teammates. When I arrived, I took a shower and changed back into my regular clothes. Then I went out to the field to cheer on my team, but we had to swallow another loss.

When the team boarded our charter flight to return to New Jersey, I wished that I could have finished the game with them. It was not a normal flight because many of the players had lost so much fluid that they needed IV solutions to reduce their cramps. The interior of the plane looked like a MASH unit, with wounded players all over the place. Our trainers were extremely busy the entire trip back. I was feeling guilty over not finishing the game with my teammates. What I should have been more concerned about was the bullet I'd barely dodged. I was temporarily paralyzed, and when I could not move in that ambulance, I had serious reservations and regrets about playing football. For a time I lost the ability to be the "me" that I was. Getting movement of my limbs back was a blessing that I would never again take for granted.

It was ironic that I was injured by my own teammate in Dallas. I was able to come back for a good week of practice and prepare to play against the Philadelphia Eagles at home. But when we played the Eagles, it seemed that the worst people for me to play with were my own teammates. Again, I was making a tackle with my outside linebacker Brad Van Pelt when I injured my right knee. In the mass of confusion on the football field, we were gang-tackling an Eagles runner when someone hit my knee with his helmet. When the pile of players unraveled, I could hardly stand up. When it became apparent that I could not get off the field under my own power, a time-out was called by the officials on the field, and the team trainers came out to help me off. From the pain I felt in my knee, I knew that my day was over. We were playing the game at home, so when I came to the sideline, I was immediately taken to our locker room to be examined. As I was walking to the locker room, the fans in the stands gave me a loud ovation. I could hear some fans yelling, "Hurry back, Harry!"

When I entered the locker room and took my pads off, I threw my helmet out of frustration. No one was there to hear or see it except the trainer John Dziegel. John could see my frustration and tried to settle me down. Our team orthopedic specialist, Dr. Kim Sloan, accompanied me into the training room to examine my knee. He tested its flexibility and stability and determined that I had torn cartilage that had to be removed surgically. When he told me that, my heart sank into my stomach. I had never had any kind of surgery. I had seen other players with zippers on their knees where doctors had repaired ligaments and removed cartilage. I was not amused at the prospect of having surgery and was slightly afraid.

When the team came in at halftime, many of the guys came into the training room to see how I was doing. One of my linebacker mates, Dan Lloyd, came into the training room and said, "Hang in there, buddy. I'll hold it down until you come back!" Dan and I were drafted in 1976 together. He was a true middle linebacker in college (meaning that was his natural position). I beat Dan out as the starter having never really played the position. Over the years we played together, I always thought Dan was a strange bird, but we were able to work together as teammates in spite of my being a starter over him. In our training camps he would tell me that he had a voodoo doll back in his room that had my name all over it. Dan was a serious guy, but I always took that as a joke and never believed him.

We lost the game to the Eagles 31–16, but my mind was not on the Eagles loss or the rest of the season; it was on getting cut for the first time. Coach Perkins came into the training room after finishing his press conference with the media and asked how I was doing. I told him, "I've had better days." He asked Dr. Sloan, "How is this guy going to be?" Dr. Sloan, the trainers, and Perkins stood over me and discussed the knee as I lay on the table. Dr. Sloan indicated that I would be fine with a new type of surgical procedure to minimize cutting the knee, and with rehabilitation I could be back on the field in four weeks. Perkins looked at me again and asked if I could do it. I said I didn't think I had a choice, and he said, "Okay, let's get it done!"

Perkins told me that I was going to be placed on the injured reserve list. Being placed on that list meant that I would have to sit out a minimum of four games, and it would give the team an opportunity to sign another player to that roster spot. I told Perkins I understood and was ready for the surgery. He looked me in the eyes and said, "Hey, if you want or need anything, let me know." The only thing I needed was to place a call to my family in South Carolina and let them know that I had been injured and would require surgery. With my mother having passed, my sister Ruth saw it as her responsibility to make sure everything was okay with me. She was concerned and wanted to come to New York to be with me through the surgery. I knew the procedure was going to take place the next day and persuaded her not to come. I assured her that I would be all right! Ann, my daughter's mother, and I, were living together, so I told Ruth that Ann would be there for me if I needed anything.

I went home that evening feeling depressed. I had been given all of the information needed to check into the hospital the next day for the surgery. I was given Tylenol with codeine to handle the pain if it became a problem. I had to take my time getting into my house and I sat myself on my bed to watch television. Even though the television was on, my mind was on the surgery. I was a player and a person who always wanted to be in control of my own self. To let go and allow myself to be subjected to the unknown was tough. I had this fear of being sedated for surgery. I knew that just because you're put under by your doctor, it doesn't necessarily mean you're going to come back from being under. What if something happened and I died?

I had a restless night thinking of all that could happen. When I arrived at the hospital, I answered a thousand questions about my health and my family's health history, gave blood to be tested, and was then given a private room that I would be in after my surgery. One of the nurses asked me to remove my clothes and put on a gown. I then waited for an orderly to take me to pre-op. As I lay on the table before going into the operating room, I experienced the aloneness of facing surgery. I thought, here I was all alone, lying on a cold table, waiting to be cut, to get better just to get back on the field. This was not what I'd been thinking when I first put on the football pads and a helmet. No one ever told me about this part of the game. I'm not afraid to admit that even though I was a grown-ass macho man, for a moment I reverted to my childhood, wanting my mother or someone close to me to be there to hold my hand, comfort me, and assure me that everything was going to be all right. When I wore that Giants uniform, I had to maintain a macho attitude, especially around my teammates and in front of fans, but the reality now was I was scared to death. Maybe it was because I played a team sport and it helped to go through like experiences with the guys I practiced and played with, but now I had to go through this all by myself.

I was wheeled into the operating room, where I saw Dr. Sloan ready for surgery, his mask covering his face. He was joined by several others to assist him. Sloan told me that the procedure should run smoothly and I wouldn't feel a thing. I took him at his word and settled back. I watched as I was administered a solution through an IV and was asked to count backwards from one hundred. The last thing I remember was ninety-six. The next thing I knew, I was back in my hospital room. When I woke up, it seemed that I had merely blinked and it was all over. I didn't even dream as I would probably do if I had taken a short nap. I woke up but I couldn't stay awake. I had anesthesia in my system and it kept making me drowsy. I sat up in the bed and tried to read the newspaper, but every time I turned a page, I'd bow out for a couple of minutes, wake up, turn the page, then fall asleep again. Only a couple of hours later could I stay awake for longer periods. I was concerned about my knee and what had been done with it.

When Dr. Sloan came by to see me as he was making his rounds, he took the postsurgery wrapping from around my leg and showed me the three or four incisions he'd made. Each incision was approximately one-half inch in length. He told me that he'd inserted a camera through one of the incisions to get a good look at the damaged cartilage, removed it, then filed down the remaining cartilage to smooth it. I was amazed at the wonders of then-modern technology. I was also lucky because in the past, a procedure of this kind was normally done by opening the knee to make the repairs needed, putting a player out of action for a much longer time. I learned that the arthroscopic surgery performed on me by Dr. Sloan was his first use of the procedure on any Giants player. I didn't think about that as being a big thing; I only thought that I wanted to get back to practice and play.

I returned to the stadium the next day for treatment and rehabilitation. The trainers made sure I got plenty of ice treatments to reduce any possibility of swelling to my knee. They also put me through a variety of flexibility drills to see if I could bend my knee. I tried to do everything they asked with the hopes of getting back on the field soon. The next day I arrived at the stadium early, got my treatment, and proceeded to my meetings. I wanted to get filled in on our next opponent, the San Diego Chargers. As I was sitting in the meeting, the trainer came to the door and asked for me. I went with him as he told me that the coach didn't want me in the meetings that week because I was not going to be traveling with the team. Instead, I needed to get more treatment. At the time, I didn't agree with what was going on. I thought even if I wasn't playing, I needed to stay up to speed with what was going on with the defense. I missed games against the Chargers (which the Giants lost 44–7), the Broncos, the Buccaneers, and then the Cowboys.

After several weeks of rehabilitation and waiting, I was able to come back to play against the Green Bay Packers at home. My knee felt fine and was strong, but I felt anxious because I didn't know how it was going to hold up under serious contact in a game. Practice was practice and under control, but you don't know what can happen in a game. It helped my psyche that the game was at home on a surface that I was familiar with. Before the game, all I could think about was getting hit on my surgically repaired knee. After the kickoff, once the defense went on the field, I knew that was going to be my moment of truth. My heart raced during the kickoff, and now it was beating so fast that I could hardly breathe. After I called the defense and saw the Packer offense break their huddle, I knew it was "on." On the snap of the ball the Packers tried to run a sweep to the outside with the running back. I read my keys, determined where the ball was going, and worked my way to the point of attack. One of the Packers linemen took a shot at me, throwing a block near my left thigh. I was able to protect my leg and maintain my balance. While I didn't make the tackle, at least I got that first hit out of the way, which was so important to get myself back into the flow of playing. We won the game, our third win of the season, having already lost eight. We had five games left to play, and I thought we could easily finish the season 8-8, giving us a .500 record.

The next game up was a long road trip to Candlestick Park to play against the San Francisco 49ers. I had played a decent game against the Packers, and now with the Niners on deck I needed to turn up the intensity level of my game and contribute more. Bill Walsh was the head coach of the 49ers and had installed a pretty good West Coast offense that kept many defenses off-balance with lots of passing to backs out of the backfield. Walsh also did a good job of scripting the first fifteen or twenty plays, which made opposing defenses nuts because they had absolutely no clue what was going to be run from play to play until those scripted plays were exhausted. We got through the first half of that game and kept the offense out of the end zone, but we did give up a couple of field goals. In the second half we gave up a fourth field goal to trail the 49ers 12–0. I was so pissed off about giving up 12 points and being about to lose the game.

On the next play, in an effort to run out the clock, the ball was handed to running back Earle Cooper. Cooper ran the ball a couple of yards before being tripped and falling to the ground. I should have run over and touched his backside to make sure the officials knew he was down by contact. Instead I ran over and lay out in a prone position and landed on his body. My upper body landed on his body and my lower body made contact with the ground. Just as that happened, I felt a burning sensation in my lower back. I turned over on my back and could not get up off the ground. Within a few seconds the trainer raced out to the field to see what was going on with my back. The trainer would not allow me to move since I was complaining of my back's burning sensation. The medical staff was especially cautious in treating me since they did not know the extent of the injury. The only thing I could think of was the stupidity of what I had done. I should have played smart, but instead I reacted angrily to losing the game. I was eventually moved and placed on a stretcher to be transported from the field. As I was being wheeled off, I could hear a few of the 49ers fans cheering for me. That showed class and also made me feel a little better. Once off the field, I was taken to the X-ray facility right there at the stadium.

After twenty to thirty minutes of X-rays, it was determined that I had cracked vertebrae in my lower back. No one had to tell me that my season was over! I was told that it would take several months for the bone to heal, and with four games left in the season, once again I knew I was going to spend more time on the injured reserve list. The doctors wanted to leave me in San Francisco overnight for observation, but no way was I going to do that. I came with my team and I was going to go home with my team. I was fitted with a brace to keep my back stable. I knew that if I had to stay like this for several months, I was going to be a problem child, but I also knew that I was to blame for what had happened.

The team won only one of the last four games on the schedule. We finished the season 4-12. It certainly wasn't a season that I wanted to remember: a posterior deltoid muscle that had been injured and began to atrophy, temporary paralysis, a knee operation with several weeks of rehabilitation on IR, and finally a busted back and once again a trip to the IR. Those early years with the team when I played well and felt strong stopping running backs cold in their tracks seemed like so long ago. I realized that I had been humbled several times in a short time. I didn't know if it was God's way of telling me, "You're not the badass you think you are," or if it was my own stupidity in the way that I chose to play at times.

Even with the bad luck I had that season, I think I learned a lot, not only about myself, but also about the game. I had never really had to worry about serious injuries before; those were things that happened to other guys. Not only did I come to know that injuries could happen to me, but I grew to understand clearly that the next play in a game or even in practice could be my last. I knew that before, but I really knew it now. Injured reserve taught me that the game could be taken away from me at any time. I finally knew what so many other players knew: I was merely a cog in the machine, and if I didn't function properly, the Giants only had to go out and find another cog to replace me. The 1980 season showed me that when I was injured, the team could win without me and it could lose with me. That young athlete who thought he was tough realized that he was vulnerable at all times. Nineteen eighty was also the year that I lost a sense of what "normal" felt like. Because of my shoulder, I knew my body would never be as it was before.

CHAPTER 8

"The Crunch Bunch"

The 1981 season marked a change in the philosophy of the Giants defense. I'd had my share of personal success and personal adversity. I'd gone through several years where I had been extremely frustrated with the play of the team. There was the infamous fumble named by some the Miracle of the Meadowlands. That miracle was for the Philadelphia Eagles, not for the Giants. I'd been to a couple of Pro Bowls, had been named NFC Linebacker of the Year twice, and was elected defensive captain by my team. But I had also gone through a tough 1980 season with several injuries that I had to come back from. I had developed a good relationship on the field with my linebacker mates Brad Van Pelt and Brian Kelley. Brad had tremendous athletic ability. He stood six feet five inches with a wide wingspan, but also had good speed and covering ability. Before being a top pick of the Giants, he was an all-everything in high school, where he played football, basketball, and baseball. He went on to play and excel in football at Michigan State University. Brian, while not quite as tall as Brad, was a heads-up player who had a great feel for zone-coverage defenses and was tough stopping the run. Brian was a hard-nosed player who did not shy away from contact. He played rugby in college and during his off-seasons and had to be tough to play that sport. As a group we were good! No, let me restate that: we were a damn good trio of linebackers.

There had been talk during the off-season that the team was going to use the second pick in the draft to pick some guy from the University of North Carolina, Lawrence Taylor. Lawrence Taylor? Who in the hell was this guy and why would George Young and the Giants feel a need to use the second pick in the whole draft to bring in a guy to play in a group that was already pretty solid? We wanted the team to win, and as a group of linebackers we grumbled among ourselves. When we were asked by the New York media whom we thought the team should take in the draft, we told them, "No, we don't need another linebacker!" That pick would be better used on a running back or some other offensive player who could immediately make an impact on the team. Apparently the word got back to this Taylor guy in North Carolina that we didn't want him to come to New York. Before we knew it, an article appeared in the paper saying that Taylor didn't want to upset our boat in any way and asking the Giants not to draft him if there was going to be a problem with the players, especially the linebackers. I realized that I was guilty of prejudging a player before he ever stepped on the field. I put myself in his place and could fully understand how he felt. We meant no offense to him personally; instead, we were looking at what we thought was best for the team. The Giants did draft Lawrence Taylor with that second pick.

When we arrived at training camp, it didn't take us long to see what the guys in scouting and personnel already knew. If you saw a number of players drafted that year in the locker room without clothes, you'd know that they were well built. Taylor was one of those guys. While many players whom I had played with in earlier years were in good shape, a definite difference in the body structure and development of players occurred during that time. Players had had different mind-sets regarding physical training and preparation for training camps. Some hated lifting and running on their own and were not disciplined about being in shape; others relied on the experience of years of playing to get by. A shift was going on, separating the players who came to camp to get in shape for the season from those players already in shape, ready to compete. When you looked at Lawrence Taylor in his T-shirt and shorts, you could tell that he was in phenomenal shape.

Once we took the field, you couldn't help but watch him as he went through drills. He made some agility drills look so easy. As we settled down to do a one-on-one drill against the offense team, Lawrence got everyone's attention. As I can recall, Lawrence started the first day of practice on the third-team defense. That is where all new players have to go when they first arrive at training camp, so that was no surprise. In that morning session when he went up against players on offense in drills, he was almost immediately elevated to the second team. When we watched him, his body structure, his speed, and his power, he was clearly a man! It's one of those things that guys don't talk about out loud unless they're in a male prison, but I think we all were thinking, "Damn! That motherfucker is built like a fucking brick house!" We, as veterans, marveled at his huge shoulders, long arms, narrow waist with a six-pack, and long legs. What was more impressive was to take a knee on the sideline while the second team was running drills and watch him in action as he went against players on the offensive team. I was accustomed to seeing little scatback runners such as St. Louis Cardinals back Terry Metcalf make sudden moves on linebackers, including myself, on the field and losing us in the dust, but I had never ever seen a player so big, so fast, and so strong move the way Lawrence moved on the football field. I saw him make a mistake and miss a tackle, but he was so quick that he recovered and still made a great play, giving up few yards. He would make plays that would make players turn to one another and ask, "Man, did you see that shit?" Lawrence Taylor was something special.

There was no question as to where he was going to play, as our coaching staff had decided we would play a 3-4 defensive scheme. In that scheme we would play two defensive ends and a nose tackle on the defensive line, with four linebackers beside and behind the lineman. In the scheme, Brad and Lawrence played the outside linebackers, and Brian and I played the inside linebackers. Brian's position was designated the Sam or strong inside backer, with pass responsibilities toward the tight-end side. My position was designated the Will or weak inside backer, with most responsibilities away from the tight-end side. Brad normally lined up on the tight end, and Lawrence's normal responsibilities were to line up away from the tight end. I had grown accustomed to being the only man on the inside, having played the Mike or middle linebacker in the 4-3 scheme but this was a little different. I had different reads that I had to make to determine what I was going to do and what would be my responsibilities. I also had to work primarily with the other inside backer and the nose tackle. The main goal was still to stop opposing offensive teams, but it was going to be done in a slightly different manner.

In training camp I made the adjustments needed to feel comfortable and confident in the new scheme. I had to discard much of what I had learned in the 4-3 in order to play the new scheme, but repetitions in practice and focusing hard on the new responsibilities helped tremendously. It also helped to be working with the guys that I worked with on the field because we could talk about our responsibilities aloud to be completely certain. I would tell Brian to press the front side if the play came his way to force the ball carrier to come my way, or Brian would do the same to me, forcing the running play to bend back to his side, and I would attack my gap, eliminating any hole on my side to run through.

Once we started playing regular-season games, I could see that as a linebacker unit we were good before, but with Lawrence Taylor joining us, we were really fucking good! We were big, with Brad, Lawrence, and me in the 250-pound range and Brian not too far behind at about 235, and we were all six feet three or better, which made our linebacker unit one of the biggest in the NFL. Ray Perkins was our head coach, and Bill Parcells was our linebacker coach and defensive coordinator. I don't know who should get the credit, but we used Lawrence at many times, especially in passing situations as a rush backer, putting him in position to get to the opposing quarterback. We knew what he was capable of from what we saw in practice, but we didn't know if the same could be said once he started to face stiffer competition in games. With each game we played that 1981 season, we all could see that Lawrence was the real deal. We saw week in and week out an athlete with superb mental and physical abilities will himself, like an artist, to be better than most other players on the same field. We often watched film on Monday after Sunday's game and thought that it was unfair for some of the players who had to contend with the ability of Lawrence. I remembered thinking, "Damn, I'm glad he's on my side!" By the middle of the season, teams opposing us were very much aware of the play of Lawrence Taylor, and they had to go to their own drawing boards to figure out ways to defend against him. With the attention of others being focused on Lawrence, it made Brad's, Brian's, and my job a bit easier. We had an impact player who could wreak havoc on opposing offenses, and we could elevate our game and apply pressure from areas that were less defended. Those runs that might have gotten outside before were being turned back to the inside by Lawrence for Brian and me to blow up for no gain. Those quarterbacks that had time to get the pass away because of the lack of pressure by the defensive lineman were getting little time to get the pass away because they could feel Lawrence breathing down their necks. Because he usually lined up on the offense's left side and most quarterbacks were right-handed, it meant that oftentimes Lawrence was coming at them from their blind side.

One of my favorite early memories of playing with Lawrence was standing on the field after breaking the defensive huddle, ready to play. As the opposing team's offense broke their huddle, we watched the quarterback scan the field to find out where Taylor was lined up. Nobody did that any better than Philadelphia Eagles QB Ron Jaworski. I could see the fear in his eyes. When I saw that fear, I knew we had the game; no question about it, the game was ours unless our offense did something stupid to screw things up. That was not that unusual during those days because while as a defensive unit we grew better and better as we played, sometimes the offense did things that pissed us off, making critical errors at the most inappropriate times, turning the ball over and just overall fucking up!

Over time our group gained the reputation of being the best linebacker unit in the NFL. We all took great pride in that. I was especially proud because of the road I had to navigate to be where I was. To be considered part of the best linebacker unit in the league, being able to adjust from 4-3 to a 3-4 scheme and not skip a beat in results, and to help the team make it to the playoffs that season was special. I had come a long way from where I had been the previous year, plagued with injuries. I was a leader and the captain of this group! I did not take that responsibility lightly. I recognized myself as a black man who without any fanfare had risen through my play on the field to earn the respect of my teammates and opponents alike. For me, life was pretty good! I was into my second contract and earning pretty good money doing something that I really liked. I liked the guys I played with and just wanted to do my part to help my team win. On the field I was doing my thing. I wasn't as flashy as Lawrence when he got sacks and tackles behind the line of scrimmage. I looked at myself more as a hard-hat worker who was not going to be spectacular but solid in what I did. I had been a lineman in college, and most of the time I played like a lineman in that I had few interceptions even when the ball was thrown at me. Some of my teammates told me that I caught a football as if I were trying to beat it up. No, I wasn't known for getting my hands on the ball, but I was known for knocking a player's dick in the dirt if he came my way and I got a good shot on him.

Lawrence and Brad, by some sense, knew where the pressure was going to come from when the ball snapped, but Brian and I were not always aware of where we were going to get hit from along the interior of the line. While we saw where the play was initially going, once we began our pursuit of the ball carrier, we had to be ready to hit or be hit by offensive lineman or get cut by lead running backs or tight ends, then to make it to the runner for the tackle. While we were hailed by many for our exploits, unless you played the positions and were disciplined enough to do the things we had to do, it's hard to explain what playing inside linebacker on the NFL level is about. Every week you're going against badass linemen whose job is to knock your ass out of the way to allow their runners to advance. Our jobs were to stop the offense using any legal means possible.

I always remember those first days of practice in high school and college when the coaches would go over the proper techniques to make tackles. We would walk through the tackling forms, watching the runner's number, sliding our heads across the chest as we made contact, then wrapping our arms around the runner, driving him back for little gain. I understood the techniques of tackling at that time, and if I was coaching my own kid's defense, I would probably give him the same instructions. But I lived in the real football world at the NFL level, and with the fast pace of the game, you are lucky to make one of those picture-perfect form tackles that coaches like to see. Sometimes the only way to get a man down is to grab a shoestring to trip him. I always remember what Marty said my first year: "Do whatever you have to do to get the job done." I had excellent balance, agility, and coordination, but more important, the toughness to mix it up with those big, strong guys on the inside. Somebody has to stop the inside run and plug up the hole. Lawrence was great at sacking the quarterback, but my specialty was plugging those holes that power running backs tried to explode through.

Often in plugging those holes, I would find myself being blocked from two or three different directions. If on a short-yardage play the offense lined up in an I formation, I knew that the play might be a toss to the tailback to get outside or a wham play right up the middle. Wherever the offense thought they could attack and gain yards was where the ball was going to go. On wham plays, I could not sit back and allow the play to develop. I had to attack in the center of the line and shut the play down in the backfield if possible. In my attack, I usually delivered a forearm blow to the offensive lineman to my right, then took on the lineman on my left. With both arms occupied and holding my ground, if the ball carrier or lead back got in my face, I might have to use the upper part of my body or even my head to make the play. With bodies being tangled up and with force against force, you have to do whatever it takes to shut the offense down.

I used to hear football players say, "You have to be a little crazy to play the game." That is one of the most accurate statements I ever heard; you do have to be slightly off-balance to play football. Hell, I knew that, especially when we had to practice in heavy equipment in the brutal heat and humidity of July and August. Mixing it up in body-to-body combat with torsos colliding at full speed takes a toll on a person. Even in close quarters the contact gets intense. Seldom did I get to make spectacular plays like the ones Lawrence made in sacking quarterbacks. Brian and I were the hard-hat guys who did all that we could to stop the inside running game.

While I usually had solid games with my linebacker mates, I remember one game as my absolute worst. We were playing against the Eagles in Philadelphia on *Monday Night Football*. I never cared for Monday-night games because I was a creature of habit and I was accustomed to playing games on Sunday afternoons. Monday-night games always threw me off. First you had extra practices, then you had to watch everybody else play on Sunday afternoon, then you sat around all day Monday with next to nothing to do except attend team meetings, then finally you played that evening. As we geared up to play the game, I knew in my head what to do since Parcells did a pretty good job during the week of drilling the defense on the habits of the Eagles offensive attack. Once we started to play the game, I could sense that I was not quite in sync with what I was supposed to be doing, destroying the running game. At several crucial times I missed tackles that I would normally have made. I was playing on *Monday Night Football*, the only game on, being shown across the country, with everyone watching. I missed about five tackles that were obvious to even the average viewer. I thought to myself, "What is everyone saying about my play?" I knew I embarrassed myself and my team, especially the defense. We lost that game, largely on what I thought was an unexplainable failure on my part.

In the locker room afterward to take my shower, I didn't want to be around anyone because of my poor play. I kept thinking to myself, "How embarrassing!" I didn't know what in the hell was going on with me. I had not made tackles that were normally easy for me. The locker room was quiet with guys getting dressed and packing up their equipment to be shipped back to Giants Stadium. After showering, I could see the team's secretary, Vinnie Swerc, circulating around the locker room handing out game checks to players. He eventually made his way to me and said under his breath, "That's all right, Harry. We'll get 'em next week." I could hardly look Vinnie in the eyes when he said that. He then handed me my check, and impulsively I said, "I can't take it!" Vinnie looked at me over his glasses in amazement and said, "You have to take it!" Just like that I was back in high school remembering our honor code from ROTC: "We will not lie, cheat, or steal, nor tolerate anyone among us who does!" Years later, the lessons I learned in that one course stayed with me! I told Vinnie, "I did nothing to earn the check." I felt that if I had accepted the check, it would have been like stealing. A few players I played with in earlier years would have thought nothing about taking a check after having such a horrendous game. Vinnie told me that I could donate the check to charity, but I had to take it. I did, then split it among several charities.

I then went to Ray Perkins, our head coach, and told him that since my play was not helping the team, I felt it was best for me to retire. Perk, who had just finished his press conference with the media, looked at me with a straight face and said, "Don't do anything before talking with me tomorrow." I agreed to meet with him, but I had already decided that it was time for me to quit the team.

On our bus ride back to the Meadowlands, I replayed the game in my head to try to understand what had happened and what I could have done differently. I wondered how my skills could have eroded so quickly. But one thing was certain: I was more embarrassed than I had ever been as a football player. It weighed on me from the end of that game until I met with Perkins the next day. I went in to meet with him on my off day, and I took my daughter, Aja, with me for support. Aja was only about two and a half, but she was one of the things that kept me rational at that time. During our conversation Perkins convinced me that I could still help the team in spite of my poor performance. He'd watched the film that morning and also couldn't understand why my play had taken a tremendous drop since I had been playing well.

The next day in our defensive meeting, some of my teammates who'd found out that I turned down the game check came to me and said, "Man, you must be crazy for giving up that check!" I told them that if I had taken the check, I would have felt tremendous guilt. I know most players wouldn't think twice about taking the check, but my basic foundation would not allow me to do so.

That day I continued to struggle to understand why my play had taken a nosedive. I remembered Dr. Frank Ladata, the team psychologist who'd given me my battery of psychological tests when I first arrived to play with the Giants. Dr. Ladata was on the faculty of Manhattan College, and over time in speaking with him I'd grown to respect him and I thought he respected me as well. I contacted him and told him that I had a problem that needed his attention. Dr. Ladata told me to come over to his office at the school. When I arrived and sat down with him, I told him about my play in the Monday-night game.

He told me that he'd seen the game and wondered what I was thinking during it. I told him that I didn't know what was going on. He asked me about my practice habits. I told him that I wasn't having any problems in practices; I thought my practices were going well. It was the game that caused me so much concern.

Ladata then told me about task analysis, basically playing the game in my mind but taking it one or two steps further than in practice. I had gotten into the habit of getting my reads down in practice and in games, pursuing the ball carrier in practice and in games, but in practice we weren't allowed to hit or tackle the ball carrier. I'd always heard the expression "You play the way you practice!" That was ever so true in this case because I did everything I was supposed to do in practice as in the game except contacting the runner and wrapping him up. Dr. Ladata told me that I had to visualize tackling the ball carrier in my mind, which I was not doing. The mental aspect of the game went back to what Coach Carlen of the University of South Carolina had told me when I was about to be drafted. He said football on the pro level was about 80 percent mental and 20 percent physical. What he'd told me certainly rang true in this case. I relied too much on the physicality of the game; I needed to try to play a more cerebral game to continue playing in the NFL.

I prepared that week to improve my play and reestablish myself with my coaches and teammates, but the person I most had to impress was me. Dr. Ladata had given me the information I needed, and I had to prepare myself and use the information to my advantage. During the week of practice, as a play developed, I made my reads and pursued to where I was supposed to be, then took the play two or three steps further in my mind, wrapping up the runner and stopping him for little or no gain. As we approached the next game, I had the same anxious feelings I had when I was coming back from an injury. I was uncertain how my new techniques would work in an actual game. Once the game began, time after time when the ball carrier came my way, I played my responsibility, and if I had the chance to jack him up, I did. Tackle after tackle I was getting back into the flow of what I did best: play strong against the running game. I ended the game with what seemed like a dozen solo tackles.

I had to be effective in that aspect of my game because part of my contract was structured around tackles. If I led the team in tackles, I could earn an extra $15,000; second place would net me an extra $10,000; and third place, an extra $5,000. As a linebacker in a position to lead the team in tackles, that money was there for the taking. With what I was making at that time, an extra $15,000 at the end of the year would help tremendously. The time with the doctor was wisely spent. It was good to understand that my problem was mental and that I had the sense to get some assistance with it.

I was extremely happy with the task analysis results in my play on the field. I told a couple of my teammates that I'd sought help from Dr. Ladata. From their reaction, you would think they thought I was crazy; merely saying that I went to see a psychologist became a joke to them. I guess for football players or athletes in general, a group that is so in tune with working with their bodies, to hear that a player had to use a shrink puts some kind of stigma on that player. I saw absolutely nothing wrong with it, but apparently others saw it as a sign of weakness or of my being a little off-balance mentally. I didn't appreciate a bit of the joking because of those innuendos, especially when it came from some of the white guys. I got the impression that they thought it was beneath me to be into that kind of stuff. Or maybe I felt supersensitive about it. Perhaps they caught me on the wrong day for joking around. But I couldn't allow it to fuck with me because, as Marty told me early in my career, "Do whatever you have to do to get ready to play the game." I could easily have been sitting at home by this time if I had followed my impulses, but I sought alternative means of dealing with what I knew was my own problem.

I had temporarily gotten off track with my horrible game in Philadelphia, but I eventually felt even more confident playing the game. I'd played the game mentally many times before, all players did that, seeing themselves making the big catch or scoring the winning touchdown, but for some reason I didn't take it that seriously. After all the years I'd played, I finally began to understand how truly mental the game was, and how much my thoughts controlled my performance in practice and in games. Playing better was important to me personally, but I also needed to get back to being part of the best group of linebackers in the league. I couldn't stick out like a sore thumb as I had before; I had to represent well when I stepped on the field. Brad, Brian,

Lawrence, and I had become, through our play, one of the more dominating groups of backers in the league. We had learned how to play off one another well, and I knew that we were only going to get better if we all brought our A game every week. I knew that while I might not always be happy (because of contract issues) playing with the Giants, these were guys that I wanted to go to battle with on the football field.

We earned a spot in the play-offs as a wild-card team, beating the Cowboys in overtime 13–10 in our last home game. It had taken me six years from the time I entered the league to reach the play-offs with the Giants. Perkins drove us like dogs at times to get the best out of us. The team had always been a stepping-stone for all of the other teams to get to the play-offs. No, wait, *stepping-stone* is a bit too nice of a term to use. We were more like the whipping boy that teams thought they could beat up on to get to the next level. We finally put together a decent offensive along with a pretty good defense to earn that spot. We finished the season third in the NFC, beating the Eagles in the first round but falling to the San Francisco 49ers in San Francisco 38–24 in the next game. I was lucky to have been chosen for another trip to the Pro Bowl in Hawaii for my play that season. I had my ups and downs, but overall I thought I had a good year. I was doing pretty well financially, having achieved many of the incentives in my contract. I made All-NFC, second team All-NFL, Pro Bowl, and led the team in tackles. That money, along with the extra bucks I made from playing in two play-off games, helped me tremendously during the off-season.

Off the field, I started to realistically look at where my career was going. I knew I needed to start making plans for my life after football. Seeing the turnover in personnel every year, I was aware of how temporary my career was. I had played six seasons and the NFL's average career was a tad below four years, so I knew I was playing on borrowed time. It was the nature of the game: players came into the league, played, and because of an injury or diminished skills were shown the door. That door was right next to my locker so I literally saw a lot of players come and go! I knew that in time I would have to say good-bye and leave the stadium for the last time as an active player. As much as I enjoyed what I did with my guys, I knew that they were also playing on borrowed time. We had come so far as a team, and making the play-offs had become a reality for the Giants organization. Change is a part of the game that I had to respect, and while some players might have lasted one or two seasons and others fourteen or fifteen, the end comes for everyone; no one is exempt. I wanted to be certain to prepare for the inevitable.

After I returned from playing in the Pro Bowl in Hawaii, I secured a job at Grumman Aerospace working in the personnel department's college-recruitment division. I understood how important it was to have contingency plans during a game and to be able to make adjustments for unforeseen circumstances. Off the field, that is what Grumman was about for me. I secured a gig at a company that made jet planes. That in itself was extremely pleasing to me, but I was also able to work in a position that was more or less seasonal, recruiting college graduates with technical expertise to work at a great company. The only downside was that I lived in Westchester County, New York, and Grumman was located in Nassau County, New York. My commute by car was roughly fifty miles each way. After my day at work I commuted to Giants Stadium to work out for football, then headed back home to Westchester. I was driving about 120 miles each day in New York/New Jersey traffic. Many people who knew of the situation wondered why I did it, but it was that important to me to prepare for life after the game. I knew that making two hundred tackles a year and being an all-star player for the Giants was not going to cut it in the real-world job market. Who was going to give a shit about that stuff? I was happy and fortunate that I had earned my degree, but what if my game went downhill as it did against the Philadelphia Eagles? What if I had torn up my knee and couldn't come back from that injury? What if I had sustained a career-ending injury the way I thought I had when I hurt my back in San Francisco? What would be my options? I needed that work experience on my résumé to add more power to sell myself.

I grew to enjoy my time at Grumman Aerospace. It was good going to work wearing a different kind of uniform: a suit and tie. I felt very much like the executive, having two secretaries and my own office. The most interesting thing about my work experience was my first paycheck. Employees were paid every other week so I had to work two weeks before getting a check. When I was handed my check, I opened the envelope and saw my pay was about $310. I thought to myself, "What the hell?" At that moment I realized that I was living in a fantasy world playing in the NFL, and I began to understand what people in the "real world" made. What I made in that first check at Grumman I would consider walking-around money in the NFL. In the NFL, whenever a player took a big hit on the field, we would yell, "Welcome to the NFL!" When I saw that check, I quietly thought to myself, "Welcome to the real world!" That one experience brought me back to earth. In the NFL I was making so much more ($250,000) than what the average person in the United States was making. I know I was making more in a year than what my mother and father probably ever made in their lives. It took stepping out of my box as a professional athlete and venturing into the real world to learn what I needed to do to prepare for life, period!

CHAPTER 9

Change, Change, Change . . .

Over the next two years many changes took place within the Giants organization and the National Football League itself. Most noticeably the players' union initiated a strike against the league that would start after the second game of the 1982 season. The Giants were scheduled to play the Green Bay Packers in a *Monday Night Football* game. This was to be the last game before everyone took their belongings and stepped out on the picket lines against the league. Before that game, I knew it might possibly be the last one of the season. I didn't know a lot about the collective bargaining agreements between the league and the Players Association, and I didn't concern myself with the major issues of the impending strike; I left that up to our union player representative. With so much uncertainty riding on the impending strike, I decided to have fun and just let it all hang out! If this was going to be my last game of the season, it was going to be one that I wanted to remember always. The previous year I stunk up the place on *Monday Night Football* against the Eagles. I was so bad I was tempted to retire. I swore to myself that I would never let something like that happen to me again. This time I made sure that if I got anywhere near anyone with the ball, I was going to hit, drive through, and bring that ball carrier down.

I kept my promise to myself because I came out of that game with twenty-five tackles. I was all over the field plugging holes in the interior of the line and at the corners. I was making tackles down the field on tight ends and wide receivers. During the game I knew I was active, but I didn't know I was that active! Twenty solo tackles and five assists—what a way to redeem myself on *Monday Night Football*! Unfortunately, because of the strike, hardly anyone noticed the game I played, but I remembered. At least I knew that if the season was indeed over, I had an outstanding two-game season.

After eight canceled games due to the strike, the players returned to finish out the season. When we did, another change was in store for us: Ray Perkins, who had been pursued as a candidate, accepted the head coaching position at his alma mater, the University of Alabama. Back in the day, Ray played for the legendary coach Paul "Bear" Bryant. When he met with the team, he told us that he'd agonized over the situation but the Alabama job was the only job that he would even consider taking over the Giants job. Ray had earned the reputation, even before coming to the Giants, of being a strict disciplinarian. He made quite a few changes to turn the Giants program around and become more respected in the NFL. Ray did what we all felt he had to do: he took advantage of an opportunity that came his way. We all respected Ray's decision, knowing that if we were in the same situation, we would have done the same thing.

I think our general manager, George Young, was thrown for a loop with this matter that affected the team at such a high level. With Ray's decision for himself, George had to make an important decision for the franchise. George decided to promote my linebacker coach, Bill Parcells, to head coach of the Giants. I was happy for Ray and Bill, but I was a little concerned about who would become the new linebacker coach. Bill Belichick had been the secondary coach for a couple of years, and he was promoted to linebacker coach and eventually defensive coordinator. The other linebackers and I were considered "cagey" old vets. We had developed a good relationship with Parcells and felt comfortable agreeing or disagreeing about on-the-field matters. It was one thing to be a linebacker coach, but another to be the head guy. We all liked Parcells, and most of us had hated Perkins at one time or another. Ray was not a bad guy, but he did treat everybody, players and assistant coaches alike, like dogs, so in Parcells we got a guy who was one of us, but now he was going to become one of them.

I was happy to get back to playing on the field. No football in September, October, and early November felt strange, but once we returned, I tried to make the most of the abbreviated season. We played seven games to finish the season, winning four and losing three. I played well enough to earn another trip to the Pro Bowl, then I went back to Grumman Aerospace for another off-season of work. It was important to get as much work experience as I could. I learned from the players' strike that, aside from injuries, any career could be over at any time for any number of reasons. Those eight games we missed during the season hit everyone hard, especially financially. Those eight game checks would not be made up. Ouch! Our wallets were a little slimmer during the off-season than in other years. Most of us had to put ourselves on strict budgets to get from one season to the next. It helped that I made certain incentives built into my contract. Making the Pro Bowl and leading the team in tackles earned me at least an additional $25,000 to $35,000 for the off-season.

When the '83 season rolled around, the new sheriff was in charge. It was Bill Parcells's first head-coaching job in the NFL, and he tried to impose his brand on the team. As a group of veteran linebackers, we knew that we had to make adjustments in our approach to Bill for his sake. When he was with us as a group, we could talk shit to him just as we could with one another. In his new role as head coach, we all knew that we had to show respect for Bill, because if we didn't, the younger players would have taken a cue from us to treat him the same way. As much as some of us hated Ray Perkins, he had done a good job of reestablishing discipline with the team. Bill Parcells's job was to carry forward what had been established, and I looked forward to playing for Bill.

The Parcells training camp was tough, but not quite as tough as the previous ones. I welcomed the bit more humane treatment we got from Bill as opposed to Ray. I was once again elected defensive captain, and I wanted Parcells to be successful since I thought we had a pretty stable core group making up what I thought was a pretty good team.

The third game of the season was to be an omen of my own season. We were in Dallas playing the Cowboys. A simple screen pass to Tony Dorsett with two of his offensive lineman out in front of him was not a good scene for me to see. I dropped to my zone of coverage, reacting to the slow screen, and two offensive linemen threw their bodies on me at the same time, hyperextending my left knee. When I went down, I knew immediately that something was wrong. I could feel a shooting pain in my knee going down my leg. I lay on the ground as the trainers and doctors came out to attend to me. They asked what the problem was, and I told them that I had a pain in my left knee. Dr. Warren, the Giants' orthopedic surgeon, quickly examined my knee on the field, then two of my teammates helped me to the sideline, where I sat on a bench. I could tell my knee wasn't just sprained or twisted; I felt that this was going to be one of those "big ones." To me, those big ones were like those big NASCAR wrecks on a super-speedway. I knew it was going to be a major event with some serious ramifications. I might possibly need major surgery, with a doctor cutting the knee open to repair it.

As I was being examined by Dr. Warren, I kept one eye on the field and saw Brad Van Pelt go down with an injury. We seemed to be in the middle of a war taking heavy fire. When I saw Brad I thought to myself, "I have to get back into the game." I told Dr. Warren to let me see if I could stand. He asked if I was sure, and I told him yes. I took my shoe off because I needed to pull a rubber sleeve over the knee to keep it warm and give it a bit more support. After putting the sleeve on, getting my game stocking back up, and shoe on, I tested the stability of the knee and decided to go back into the game. I think because I was in Texas I had for a moment developed the John Wayne mentality I used to see in westerns. You know, one of those scenes where the hero gets shot but doesn't give up and keeps going after the bad guys until he gets them. It sounds dopey, but the sight of Brad going down made me feel like Robert Duvall in *Apocalypse Now*; I felt invincible even in the face of tremendous danger around me.

Amazingly, when the ball was snapped, I was able to move around and get to the ball carrier and even make a tackle, but when the official blew the whistle signaling the play was over, I could hardly walk. I dragged my bad leg and wounded body back to the huddle, called the defense, and got ready for the next play to develop, all the while feeling the pain in my leg. While I was on that field, I was in my domain, where I was supposed to be. When I came off the field, I walked over to Dr. Warren and asked, "So, Doc, what are you doing Tuesday morning?" He asked, "Why?" I said, "I think we have a date in the OR." I was realistic enough to know that I was going to be back on the injured reserve list. It was just a matter of how severe the injury was and how long I would be out of the lineup. I played the rest of the game with that bad leg.

It's amazing how much you can learn from situations like this. For me, pain was a state of mind. Everyone who plays football knows from day one that in the NFL you have to be able to play when you are hurt. No one expects players to play with broken legs or arms, but with injuries that were not considered "major," such as sprains, strains, and contusions, players were expected to play. That expectation was not necessarily officially expressed by the trainers or coaches, but it was felt by the players. We all knew from the beginning that you had to be tough to play this game. At times I had my best games when I was hurt, so this was nothing new for me. I seemed to be able to focus more intensely on playing when I also had to focus on some kind of pain.

After the game, and after further examination in the locker room by Dr. Warren, I was told what I already knew, that I would need a surgical procedure the following Tuesday morning. He knew that I had damaged cartilage, but he didn't know what damage I had done to the ligaments. When I returned to Giants Stadium after our flight back from Dallas, my knee really started to ache. I didn't have the game to focus on anymore; I only had the knee, which demanded my attention with its intense pain. I was given Tylenol with codeine by our trainer Ronnie Barnes. The next day I sat through our team meeting and watched several times the play that I was injured on; it wasn't a pretty sight to see, especially when the linemen hit my knee and it bent in the wrong direction. Some of my teammates squirmed when they saw the hit and couldn't understand how I could go back into the game. After the film session the team went out to the practice field to run and loosen up as we normally did after a game. Not me; I headed off to the Hospital for Special Surgery in New York City. I needed to get my blood work done and prepare for the procedure the next morning. I hated hospitals! Even when my parents were hospitalized I hated hospitals, and here I was again in a place that seemed so cold and impersonal, getting ready for another operation.

The next morning I awoke before sunrise to head off to the operating room. Dr. Warren explained what was going to take place. He could not guarantee me that the entirety of the work could be done through the arthroscope. I knew that if the work could be done through the scope, I could possibly be back on the field in a couple of weeks; if not, my season was over. I could only trust that Dr. Warren would do his best. As I was about to be put under by the anesthesiologist, my mind was not on the operation, but on how I could have played the screen differently so I would not now be undergoing another surgery. Perhaps I should have done what I did on the kickoff team as a younger player—throw my body to cut down the blocking to give someone else a chance to tackle Dorsett. I could always second-guess how I could have done something differently when I had time as now lying on that cold gurney. Unfortunately, when I was on the field, I often had to decide in a second or less what play would help my team win or contribute to a loss. It is the same with injuries. If you take one course of action, you'll break a leg; if you take another, you might survive to play another play.

As with my first surgery three years earlier, it seemed as if I merely blinked, then it was over and I was back in my room recuperating. This time when I reached down and felt my leg, I knew it was not like before. What I felt was hard; it didn't feel like an Ace bandage like the first time. This time I had a full leg cast from the top of my thigh to my toes. I didn't feel a great deal of pain, but I knew that the cast would restrict my mobility and I needed to talk with the doctor to get my questions answered. When he arrived, he told me that he had to remove damaged cartilage and repair a partially torn ligament, but he did all of the work through the scope. He didn't have to cut my knee open as I first thought he might have done. The cast was to limit my ability to bend the knee to give the ligament an opportunity to heal properly. Dr. Warren told me that I should be able to get back on the field within six weeks, but I would probably only have to keep the cast on for about two to three weeks. That sounded like an awfully long time, but it was shorter than I initially thought it would be. I didn't have a choice, it was what it was.

After this second knee surgery, I did a bit of soul-searching during my weeks on the injured reserve list. If you cannot play or contribute, you have a deep feeling of inadequacy. Being on the injured reserve list was tough. For me, to only be able to stand on the sidelines and be a spectator was especially hard. It was tough to see someone else playing *my* position, but I was a little better with it this time than during my first stint on IR. I promised myself then that I would always respect and go out of my way to make my teammates feel worthy while they are on injured reserve. It's not a pleasant position to be in when you're also dealing with the pain of the healing and rehabilitation.

After about two weeks my cast was removed, and I could see that I had suffered a little atrophy of the muscles in my leg from inactivity. It was such a relief to have the cast taken off and to finally be able to do something as simple as scratch an itch on my leg without using a wire hanger to get down into the cast. I got through rehab and set the next Dallas game as my target to return to the field. During the five weeks I was out, the team won only one game, then had one of the ugliest ties in the history of the organization on *Monday Night Football*. With hard work during rehabilitation, I got back just in time for the Dallas game at Giants Stadium. The knee held up quite well in spite of my being anxious about getting that first contact in game conditions. It felt good to be back on the field even though the team was not playing well. We had played nine games and had only won two and tied another. I guess I could have taken more time to recuperate, but I wanted to play, regardless of the way the season was turning out. We certainly weren't going to the play-offs, but for me it was not about going to the play-offs or even about winning. I wanted to get back on the field to play and be with my guys.

The 1983 football season was not a good year for the team as a whole, which suffered an unusually high number of injuries. We had a number of guys who basically had to come in off the street to fill positions of players who suffered season-ending injuries. I can remember seeing guys across the locker room and wondering who they were. I had gone through a full training camp and I was game-ready (injury aside), but these guys were just being thrown in as starters to get the job done. They were more a makeshift measure to slow other teams down rather than to stop anyone. I felt bad for Parcells because he was getting all of the bad luck any coach could get in his first year; nothing went well for him on the field.

Off the field, we all had adversities to deal with. Most of the players had to come to grips with what one of our old teammates, Doug Kotar, was going through. Doug had retired two years before after playing running back with the Giants for eight seasons. Doug was one of the more respected players on the team, having made the team as a free agent during the 1974 strike season. He was small in stature but was one tough son of a bitch when he stepped on the field. Doug retired after the 1981 season and went back home to spend time with his family in Canonsburg, Pennsylvania, just outside Pittsburgh. Apparently Doug had been playing in his pool with his kids when he was accidentally kicked in the head and began to experience severe headaches. The headaches became so severe that he was brought back to New Jersey, where he was examined by the Giants' doctors. To see what was going on, doctors opened Doug's skull and determined that he had brain cancer. They did what they could for him and closed him up, giving him six months to two years to live. When I found out that Doug was hospitalized, I, along with George Martin and my roommate on the road, Frank Marion, made sure that we visited Doug often to see if we could do anything for him. After practice we would drive to University Hospital in Newark, only several blocks from where my mother had lived in the sixties and seventies. I was more familiar with the area than George and Frank, but we were all on the same page: we had to be available to support Doug!

The first time we arrived at the hospital and walked into his room, we didn't know what to expect. We were all big, strong professional football players and could take almost anything. I, more than Frank or George, had grown accustomed to visiting teammates or family members in hospitals and was used to tubes and needles. When we entered the room, we saw a man who was once the gutsiest and toughest guy lying in the bed with an almost clean-shaven head with a zipper going from one side to the other. I could see how the doctors took Doug's head apart to explore his cancerous brain. Doug was weak yet excited to see us whenever we came to see him. He had some paralysis, which was to be expected since his doctors had cut through parts of the brain to get to the cancerous area. We knew that we had to keep our spirits up to keep his spirits up. That first day was one of the hardest I have ever had to go through as a man, but it was tough for all of us.

When we went back to the locker room, we gave the guys an update on Doug's condition and encouraged other players to go see him. I was disappointed that several players who were his good buddies while he was on the team did not make the time to see Doug while he was in the hospital. I began to understand that we were all built differently emotionally. Some guys could deal with a teammate in that condition, while others could not, but, shit, c'mon, when it's your teammate, you fucking bite the bullet and go. Deep down inside I lost a bit of respect for some of my teammates and coaches who had time for other bullshit stuff but not to see their fallen teammate.

Eventually Doug was transferred back to the Pittsburgh area, where I continued to travel to see him. I never considered it a hardship to jump on a plane and travel to lift the spirit of a teammate. Whether it was visiting a teammate who had to undergo surgery due to an injury and had no family members in the New York area, or a teammate such as Doug who needed the support of friends, I thought it was important to let them know that somebody cared! I cared! During my visits with Doug we would talk about all kinds of stuff that we never talked about while we were players with the Giants. Even though Doug was aware of his situation, he still had a good sense of humor. I thought I was looking out for my teammate, but in so many ways he was looking out for me.

My life was enriched by visiting Doug and helping to keep him in the loop with what was going on with the team and all the players. For a time Doug became one of my best and trusted friends. And as a friend I had to care about what was happening to him. I couldn't stand back and be passive as some others were; I had to be involved. Doug was one of "my guys." As I mentioned earlier, I took inspiration from the character Lieutenant Colonel Bill Kilgore from the movie *Apocalypse Now*. I loved my guys; they were the reason why I loved to go to battle on the football field. Whenever something happened to one of them, I took it personally and tried to find ways to take care of him.

We had an exhibition game in Pittsburgh, and once we arrived in town, I organized a busload of players to travel to Doug's home in Canonsburg to see him. Again, certain players as well as coaches should have made the time to at least say hello to Doug but didn't. Doug and his wife, Donna, were thrilled to see all the guys who did make the trip. Perhaps I was missing something or maybe I was too much of a softie, but I feel that you have to genuinely care about those around you to achieve true success. It was hard for me to understand that some of those same guys who drank beer with Doug at Foley's bar in Pleasantville didn't have the fucking balls to see him when he needed their support the most.

My time with Doug taught me that if I had a zipper in my head and needed the support of my teammates or friends, a few true friends would rise to the occasion while others probably wouldn't give a fuck. I don't think I've ever questioned my commitment to my teammates, but Doug's situation caused me to question others and their commitment. From football, I learned through the mistakes and experiences of others. I was able to put myself in scenarios that I hoped would allow me to manage my expectations of others.

Mercifully, the season was coming to an end when Doug Kotar passed away. We were about to play our last game, against the Washington Redskins on the road. I played with a heavy heart, and we dedicated the game to Doug's memory. Some of us didn't care whether we won or lost. The game became irrelevant because of Doug's passing, and others were already on vacation. I knew giving our best effort would have mattered to Doug had he been on the football field that day, so I tried to play my best even though it was a "shit game" and meant nothing to us. The Redskins eventually won and were on their way to the play-offs and eventually to the Super Bowl.

One thing that stood out in my mind about that game was the running game of the Redskins. They had one of the best running backs in the game, John Riggins. He played behind an offensive line that was composed of five offensive tackles: Russ Grimm, Joe Jacoby, Mark May, and Jeff Bostic. What made them so tough was their size, their explosion off the snap, and the push they were able to get on defensive players. With the push of the linemen, the back would get three or four yards down the field even if we were able to make the tackle. Riggins was a north/south power rusher. Unlike so many other running backs,

John didn't try to run around you, he tried to run over you! He was the kind of running back that I enjoyed playing against. His running style simplified my game because it played to what I thought was my strength: his power game versus my power game. That day the Skins got a lead on us, and once they did, they went to the rushing attack to consume time on the clock. Once the running attack kicked into full gear, I knew that we were going to see a lot of the "Hogs" blocking for Riggins.

One play from that game stands out in my mind. The ball was snapped and handed off to Riggins. I came off a block and attacked Riggins, who was running full speed with the ball. When we hit, it sounded like a huge explosion of two diesel locomotives colliding at full speed head-on. Everyone in the stadium could hear that helmet-to-helmet shot, and we went down on the grass turf. While I was gathering myself on the ground, taking inventory of my senses, and making sure I was okay, I could see stars flashing before my eyes even with my eyes closed. As I got up and walked back to the huddle, I could feel my legs getting wobbly. I didn't want anyone to notice that I had been stunned by the tackle on Riggins since I was known for dishing out the hits. When I returned to the huddle, I joined hands with my teammates. We shared that type of unity on defensive at that time. I looked to the sideline to get the defensive signals from our defensive coordinator, Bill Belichick. When I was able to focus and determine where he was on the sideline, I could feel my vision start to fade to black for a moment. I squeezed the hands of the guys beside me to balance myself and keep from keeling over in the huddle. Squeezing their hands helped me snap back to full consciousness because I was nearly out on my feet.

I looked to Belichick again to get the signal but could not understand what defense he was calling. We had an understanding that if we did not get the original signal, the linebacker, safety, or any other person responsible for making the defensive call was to tap the top of his helmet to have it flashed again. I tapped my helmet to get Bill to flash the signal again, and again I didn't understand it. The Redskins were breaking their huddle, and their quarterback, Joe Theismann, led them to the line of scrimmage. At the last moment my linebacker mate Brian Kelley made the defensive call to the defensive unit. None of my teammates knew that I was almost out on my feet! The football field, especially someplace like RFK Stadium, is not a safe place to be when you don't have full command of all your mental facilities. I was amazed that for a moment I didn't understand the basic calls that we had gone over thousands of times in practice and in games. On the next play I had my wits more about me and was able to shake off the effects of what had happened. I didn't think about it any further at the time and continued to play and finished the game.

When the game ended, I think we all gave a huge sigh of relief that the season was finally over, but we still had to deal with Doug's passing and his funeral. The next day I traveled to Pittsburgh for Doug's funeral, which was to take place the following day. That Tuesday I was joined by several other teammates, along with officials from the Giants front office, for the service. The previous game and loss seemed as if it took place weeks earlier. The focus was on our friend and helping his family through a difficult period. At the funeral I could feel the deep grief felt by all of his friends and relatives. I wished I could put my arms around the whole Kotar family and take away the pain they were feeling. But I was also able to see the strength and courage they displayed during that time of adversity. It was much of what I admired in Doug himself. He was a young man with much to live for: his wife, Donna, his kids, and all of his relatives and friends.

I grieved in my heart for Doug, but I did the macho thing and tried to keep my emotions in check. Football players are trained to be tough guys, and we had been conditioned to deal with pain and loss. But I kept thinking, "How could something like this happen to Doug Kotar?" As a player you learn a lot from watching others' experiences. We spend much time watching film of one team playing against another to see what one did to win or to see the strengths and weaknesses of an upcoming opponent. We were forced to learn quickly about others' situations. With Doug's illness and eventual passing I learned a valuable lesson: if he could develop cancer seemingly out of nowhere and eventually succumb to it, the same or even worse could happen to any of us at any time.

After the services for Doug we were forced to move forward. During that off-season many more changes would take place within the Giants organization. Parcells went 3-12-1 in his first season and almost lost his job. But he also had to deal with some personal loss himself as both his father and his mother passed away within six months. I'm sure it was tough for Bill. Getting back to football, he knew that he had to make personnel changes if the team was going to get better. He dodged a huge bullet because George Young was ready to pull the trigger and let him go, but didn't. Bill was going to make certain that he was going to control his destiny by doing things his way the next season. Sweeping position personnel changes took place throughout the team, including on the offensive line and among the linebackers. Gone were Brian Kelley and Brad Van Pelt from the defensive unit. While they were still both good players, apparently they were not the players Parcells felt he needed to get to the next level. I'm sure the decision to let them go was especially difficult because Bill had been our position coach before he became the head coach. He was one of "us," and on a certain level we were all friends. But as you might hear in a gangster movie, this was not about friendship: "It wasn't personal. It was business."

Parcells wanted guys with more speed, agility, and toughness at the point of attack. The Giants used their first pick in the next draft on Carl Banks, an outside linebacker who had a great career playing at Michigan State. They also went with Gary Reasons, a linebacker from NW Louisiana State University. Parcells felt Carl and Gary could be an upgrade in the inside linebacker and outside linebacker positions. I was saddened when I learned that Brad and Brian would no longer be my teammates. We had gone through so much together on and off the field, I knew their thought processes and their movements on the field, and they knew those things about me as well. After playing for so long together, we felt that we were in sync. If one guy screwed up, often the others would be able to cover for him. With the personnel changes, I had to familiarize myself with the new guys on the block. In my professional career, making adjustments and changes were a given. If you were so rigid that you could not adapt to change, your ass would unfortunately be left at the station.

CHAPTER 10

The Dawn of a New Day

I learned many lessons on the fly as an athlete. For every beginning there is an end. The end of every season marks the end of careers in the National Football League. Every draft is the beginning of promising careers for a few players, and I knew well enough that, as in life, we all will have our day in the sun, and then it will pass. While I never said anything aloud, I knew that I had just become the senior member or elder statesman of the linebacker unit. I also knew my clock was ticking and I would eventually be shown the door as a younger player took my place. It was the natural order of things, which I accepted. I had already had two knee surgeries and was starting to feel myself slow down a bit. The direction of the team was changing, the league was changing, and I knew to stay competitive, I had to change. As the "new" old guy, I knew that on a performance level I could still hang with anyone on the football field, but I had to be able to stay healthy during the season. I didn't have a choice but to work my ass off during the off-season to stay competitive.

After several off-seasons working at Grumman, I decided to step back and focus most of my attention on my "day job." Grumman was a great experience, but with all of the changes pending I had to become more committed to the game. I was still a tough ass, but I was very aware that I wasn't as young as I used to be. The younger guys would remind me by saying things like "Wow, Mr. Carson, it's an honor meeting you. I remember watching you play when I was in tenth grade!" I appreciated being respected and being held in high regard by the younger guys, but hearing shit like that started to make me feel ancient.

The team held its own conditioning program at Giants Stadium, but I preferred to train on my own at my gym. With Doug's cancer diagnosis and other similar situations around Giants Stadium, I became uncomfortable spending so much time in that area. The stadium had been built on a dump in the Meadowlands. I knew that chemical plants in the area might have discarded their waste into the ecosystem, so I thought it was best for me to do my own thing rather than spend so much time there during the off-season. I didn't know for certain that anything was wrong with the area, and perhaps I might have been paranoid because we had another player, John Tuggle, who developed a strain of cancer. Working on my own forced me to be more self-focused and self-disciplined to push myself even when I didn't feel like working out. I had no coaches to prod me along, yet I knew that if I wasn't in shape when training camp rolled around, Parcells was going to have my ass on a platter.

When training camp began, we all had to participate in a fitness test on the first day of practice. We had to run a certain distance, like a quarter of a mile, within forty-five to fifty seconds. Mind you, it wasn't just one lap, we had to make five laps within that time frame. The first lap was pretty easy and the second wasn't so bad, but once you got to the third, that was when the monkey jumped on your back and you had to fight the fatigue setting in. With fitness tests like that, it was easy for the coaches to see who had been working out during the off-season and who hadn't. It was a bitch to do, but I made it through the test without major problems.

Then I began to think about the rigors of training camp. I could definitely sense a change in the attitude of the coaching staff, but I also saw a shift in the players' personalities. In the past when players got a little free time after practice, many of them would head to Foley's bar in Pleasantville to have a cold beer. These younger players were more inclined to head to McDonald's or Pizza Hut when they got some free time than to drink alcohol. There was definitely a shift as well in their attitudes regarding conditioning. The dollars that were being paid to players were greater now, and it made sense for us to devote more of our attention to being more physically fit in training camp and for games.

The competition for jobs had gotten more intense with younger players vying for a spot on the roster. It was just what the coaching staff wanted: guys competing, busting their ass, and doing whatever they had to do to make the club. Bill wanted players to be hungry every time they stepped on the field. He told the team that every position was up for grabs, so whether you were an incumbent veteran or a new rookie, an All-Pro player or a free agent, if you were willing to bust your ass you could make the club. Parcells saw all the injuries the team sustained in 1983 and made moves to decrease that number through better conditioning. If players didn't "bring it," even when nothing was at stake in games, Parcells was going to get rid of those guys. He'd tried to be Mr. Nice Guy his first season as a head coach, but that was history; this team was going to have his mark all over it.

I had one of my better training camps for a number of reasons. The first was because I was in great shape. I worked hard during those months leading up to camp because I knew Bill well enough to know that he was going to shock people, and I didn't want to be caught up in that. I was the captain and I had to set an example for everyone else. I didn't need to give Bill any reason to consider taking that title from me. My camp also was good because I had shed a deep-seated anger against the organization and especially George Young. I'd felt that I wasn't being paid what I should have been paid. I saw what other players playing my position were making, and I saw that Lawrence's salary leapfrogged mine tremendously. During the past couple of years I felt that I had established myself and made myself a valuable asset for the team, but yet I always had to fight to get what I felt I deserved. At some point Lawrence had signed a futures contract with Donald Trump and the new USFL. I think that move was an embarrassment to the Giants organization so they reworked Lawrence's contract and he got a shitload of money out of the deal. He never played for the USFL and finished his career with the Giants. Lawrence had leverage when he was drafted as the second player chosen in 1981, and then when he was signed by Trump, he had additional leverage to force the Giants to buy back his contract. I had never had that kind of leverage; instead I was just happy to have an opportunity to play. Had I been available when the USFL came along, who knows, I might have been in the same bargaining position Lawrence was.

It was hard to admit, but I felt a tiny amount of jealousy toward Lawrence. I was there before him, and while I was a fourth-round draft pick in 1976, I thought I had proved to the organization that I was an asset. When he was drafted, it was clear to everyone that his talent was off the charts in comparison to everyone else. I fell into the jealousy trap when he came on board and shot past everyone with his play on the field, but more so with his contract off the field. I took great pains to submerse myself in books and music to motivate myself to stay focused and give my all. I wasn't envious of Lawrence for long. I kept the poem "Desiderata" by Max Ehrmann on my wall and referred to it periodically. I would sit in my office, and as I read it, two lines of the poem jumped out at me. *If you compare yourself with others, you may become vain and bitter; for always there will be greater and lesser persons than yourself.* No one knew it, but I was becoming vain and bitter. All I needed was to read that to shake me back to reality.

One day early in training camp, I arrived on the practice field and found a spot away from the fans and my teammates where I could lie on the grass, close my eyes, relax, and clear my mind as I prepared for the day's practice sessions. As I tuned everything out, I looked up at the sky and the clouds and thought to myself that I was pretty damn lucky to be where I was. So many people could only wish to be where I was, as an athlete and as a person. I was healthy, I was good at what I did, I was well respected, lucky, and blessed. How could I be pissed about anything? I promised myself not to sweat or get bent out of shape over things that didn't really matter, not to compare myself again to anyone else, and to just enjoy the ride because it would come to an end. Okay, while I felt that I deserved to be paid more, I was under contract and I had to abide by that contract. Nobody put a gun to my head and made me sign it, and when I originally signed it, it was a damn good contract. But every day things change. What looks good today might not be so attractive tomorrow. Besides, what I was doing was bullshit compared to what others did. How could I bitch and complain about doing something that in the overall scheme of things wasn't that important? I thought about teachers, who had more of an impact on other lives and were being paid but a fraction of what I was making, and I only worked half of the year. My anger over my contract had caused me to walk out of training camp days earlier and was so festering in my soul that it was ruining my attitude. Now, within few minutes, I could feel my ego and attitude begin to reshape themselves. By the time the whistle blew to begin practice, I felt much better. I felt lighter with a smile on my face.

We started the season playing against three of our division opponents. Bill wanted to win every game at home, but especially the ones against teams within our division. The first two weeks of the season we did that, squeezing out a 1-point win against the Eagles and then beating the Cowboys. The following week we were going up against the Redskins in RFK, and they were the defending Super Bowl champions. They had beaten us the last five times that we played, and they felt that they had our number. We had confidence having beaten the Eagles and the Cowboys, but playing them in their house wasn't going to be easy or pretty. They were running on all cylinders: special teams, defense, and offense. Their running game was once again their strong suit; when they were ahead in a game and had the ball as the clock ticked down, it was a bitch to stop them.

One play the Skins ran with perfection was the countertrey special, where the running back faked in one direction and ran back the opposite way. That fake was all it took to allow the linemen to get out in front of the runner. Defensively, we generally knew where the ball was going to go, but we still had to stop it. On this particular play, the back was running the ball, and Russ Grimm, the guard who had been head up on me, tried to cut me off from making the tackle. I could feel pressure from Grimm as I was trying to get away from him, moving to my left. Before I could clearly get away from him, he threw his body on the back of my right leg and tripped me from behind. Going down, I could feel a pop around my ankle. I immediately thought, "Oh, shit! Not another injury."

I could only imagine what this was going to be about. Getting off the ground, I had a little trouble putting pressure on my right ankle, and then when I fully stood up, it was hard to walk. For a moment I started to go ballistic on Grimm because I thought that he had intentionally tried to hurt me. Then I caught myself because I knew if I did, I'd get a penalty and perhaps get thrown out of the game. I was frustrated, but I had to weigh whether it was worth it. The price was too high to pay, so I made sure that whenever I got a chance to fuck him up with a strong forearm to the head or a fist in the gut legally during a play, I was going to go for it.

I continued to play the series of downs until the Skins scored another touchdown, then headed to the sideline to see Dr. Warren. After examining the injured ankle he told me that it appeared to be a high ankle sprain. It was slightly above the ankle, not immediately around its main part. He told me that those injuries usually took an extended time to heal. I got another tape job from the trainer to help with my mobility and to protect the area. He told me that I probably wouldn't hurt it any more than it already was, but the question was how much pain I could take. I had thirteen games remaining in the season and was not about to sit down, especially with Bill being in the mode that he was in. All injured players were going to be left for dead on the side like road-kill. I had been on the injured list every day. I had to get as much treatment as I could to help speed the healing. I should have taken myself out of the lineup for a couple of weeks, but I was stubborn. I was also tough, so no matter what, I was going to play.

From what he saw in practice, Bill knew that I was not 100 percent. My teammates also knew I was not at full speed, but many of the fans didn't know or didn't care. After a game on the road, I overheard a fan say to another after I had just given him an autograph, "Carson *was* a great player, but he's over-the-hill." And no matter who you are, when you hear someone say something like that about you, it cuts deep and bruises the ego. Few people outside of the team knew that I was playing hurt, and I never wanted to use that injury as an excuse for the quality of my play. I played because I thought playing at 80 percent was better than me not being on the field at all. I played because I thought I was putting the team and my teammates first, that was what I was about. After a couple of games with that bummed ankle I got used to the pain, and then I started to thrive on it. I used it to motivate me. I already felt like a gladiator at times being able to play with pain, so I used it to push myself and my teammates. If I could run sprints in practice and lead the group, then everybody else could do the same. If I could bust my ass and play with an injury in a game, then everyone else could bust his ass the same as I did.

This team was different; it was a younger, tougher group of guys who were learning to play together and with more confidence as the season went on. The next time we played against the Skins it was at our place and we had something to prove. I personally had something to prove to Grimm, who probably knew that he had given me a cheap shot in the D.C. game. I was not going to ease up on any play until well after the whistle blew. Some guys go a bit overboard, trying to show position coaches their aggressiveness in games when they watched the game film on Mondays. Most coaches applaud that kind of aggressiveness in games even if that effort has nothing to do with the outcome of the play. I saw a few guys get hurt easing up at the end of a play because they saw the ball carrier down on the ground. Grimm's shot on me was not after a whistle or when I was easing up; it was within the rules; but I thought it was unnecessary. I'd had many opportunities to take guys out legally and illegally if I wanted to. While I always tried to play an aggressive attacking game, my mind-set was that I wasn't going to go out to intentionally hurt another player. If I saw a player going down and if he wasn't a threat to make a first down, I normally held back from giving him a full-fledged hard-nosed tackle. It may sound strange coming from a middle linebacker, but I never wanted to hurt anyone on the football field. I wanted everyone to finish the game the way he started it, in the vertical position and in one piece.

I recall a game we had against the Seattle Seahawks in Seattle. On a run by the fullback I got a great hit on him and then pulled him back to keep him from getting a first down. One of my teammates had him around the legs, and when I twisted him making the tackle, I could hear him scream aloud in pain. When the play was over, I knew from the sound of that scream that he was not going to be getting up. He stayed down holding his knee as we waited for the medical staff to get out to the field to tend to him. I felt shitty because I knew my action caused him some serious pain. When they helped him off the field,

I gave him a pat on the rear end and told him, "Hang in there." He said, "Thanks," and made his way off the field with the assistance of two of his teammates. I continued to play but my thoughts remained on the injured player. We lost the game, and after I got dressed, I went to the Seahawks locker room to see how the injured player was doing. I was told that he had already been taken to the hospital. The point is, while I played hard, I always tried to play fair, and with the exception of one or two players who didn't think twice about trying to hurt other players on the field, the vast majority of the guys I played against played fair. Oh, I was ready for Grimm when we played the Redskins several weeks later. We kicked their ass, 37–13. And the ankle? Well, it never felt better than after that win!

We made the play-offs with a 9–7 record, winning six games at home. We had come a long way from the previous season when we won just three games. Parcells had done it his way, and the new personnel had fit in nicely with some of the older veterans such as me and George Martin and now Lawrence Taylor. I didn't know how far we could go in the play-offs, but I felt that we had a strong nucleus of players and a solid coaching staff that demanded a lot out of our team. I think the happiest man on the team was Parcells; he had to feel vindicated going from one end of the spectrum to the other.

In the first round of the play-offs we played the Los Angeles Rams on the road. What stands out in my mind about the game isn't a play or a player, but the head coach of the Rams, John Robinson. A Rams player was injured on the field during the game. Usually the team trainer and the team doctor would go out on the field to tend to the injured player. I noticed that Robinson went out on the field during the injury time-out to see how the player was doing. To others it was probably no big deal, but to me something like that was huge. I had never seen a coach on the NFL level care enough about any of his players to stop what he was doing on the sidelines and attend to an injured player on the field. I know that's what the trainers and doctors are there for, but seeing a coach concerned enough to remove his headphones and walk out on the field to check on his player showed me a tremendous amount of class.

I had been playing in the NFL long enough to know that most coaches don't give a shit about players unless they are stars. We are pieces of the machine to make it run. When one part becomes defective or damaged, it is replaced with another, newer part, but the machine must keep running. I knew from my own experiences that getting hurt was a lonely thing, and while injuries are a part of the game, it was good to see Robinson show his humanity, compassion, and care for his guys. Even if he was faking it, I still appreciated the fake; no other coach ever bothered to even go that far. We won the game against the Rams, but John Robinson earned my respect. Several years later I saw him at a restaurant in Hawaii during the Pro Bowl. I was finally able to tell him how much I appreciated his concern for his guys.

We didn't have a lot of time to celebrate after winning our play-off game, but we didn't have to travel too far. The next game was up the coast of California against the San Francisco 49ers at Candlestick Park. We knew that if we won the game against the Rams, we would have to remain in California to play against the 49ers, so we packed enough for two weeks when we left the New Jersey area for the first game. This was the second time I had been in the play-offs, and the second time that we had advanced to the second round. Ironically, it was going to be against the same team we played against several years earlier. I learned from the first time that the play-offs are played at a much higher tempo and intensity than a regular-season game, and it helps tremendously to play in front of your fans at home. If not, you'd better buckle up, because it will certainly be a bumpy ride going into another team's stadium and trying to beat them with their fans behind them and against you.

The Niners had beaten us in 1981 and again during the regular season on *Monday Night Football* at Giants Stadium. We knew they had a good defense, and their offense was also one of the best when they were clicking. Their quarterback, Joe Montana, was one of the smoothest players I had ever played against. They had a solid running game and a lethal passing attack. But you always had to be alert for their quick-strike capabilities early in the game. Bill Walsh, the 49ers head coach, ran the first twenty or so plays off a script. When the 49ers offense started a game, they never gave a clue where the ball was going. It didn't matter what the down or distance was or where they were on the field, they were going to run all of those plays on the script. Once they finished the script, their offense usually settled down and became a bit more traditional and predictable. You just had to hope that you weren't down by three touch-downs by that time.

Two plays that season I really remember; one served as a lowlight for my season and the other was a highlight, and both plays happened against the 49ers. During the season, in the game that the Niners beat us on *Monday Night Football,* I was assigned to cover running back Roger Craig on a blitz play if he came out of the backfield for a pass. When the play developed, Craig knew it was a blitz and hid in the backfield momentarily and I lost sight of him. He then released on a flare pattern and Montana hit him right in stride toward the sideline. I ran as fast as I could to cover Craig and make the tackle. Craig saw me coming like a bat out of hell and gave me an outside fake and came back to the inside. I should have slowed down and used the sideline to force him out of bounds, but instead I missed the tackle (damn, I sucked playing on Monday nights), largely because of the high ankle sprain that I had sustained three games earlier. After missing the tackle, I turned to see Roger Craig high-step the ball into the end zone for a touchdown. I was embarrassed, especially since this was on *Monday Night Football* and the entire country was watching. I was embarrassed again when we as a defense had to sit down after the game and watch the film. It was pretty bad watching me get taken to school by Craig. The only thing I could do was learn from the mistake and not let it happen again.

Now fast-forward to the play-offs in San Francisco. One of the highlights of my career was having the Niners offense backed up near their own end zone. We were playing a 3-4 defense with two-deep zone coverage in the sec-ondary. As the ball was snapped, I read the back flaring out again toward the sideline. This time there was no blitz so the outside linebacker was responsible for coverage. My responsibility was to read the patterns of the wide receivers and help if one came inside across the field. Montana either didn't see me going to the curl area near the numbers that line the field or he tried to force the ball to the wide out. I was in perfect position to make a leaping catch with outstretched hands and come down with the ball at about the 15-yard line. When I secured the ball, whom did I see in front of me? Roger Craig! My mind immediately went back to the game earlier in the season. My mind said to my legs, "Make an outside fake," Craig went for the fake, then I cut back to the inside where I used my blazing speed to beat the offensive lineman, taking the ball into the end zone for the Giants' only touchdown in that play-off game. It took a long time to get to that point, but I felt a bit of redemption scoring that touchdown for my team. We didn't do anything offensively and lost the game 21–10, but I felt great being able to contribute, even in a losing cause. More important, even with my injuries I was able to play in and complete all sixteen games that season.

CHAPTER 11

Harry . . . We Have a Problem!

I could see that the team had made tremendous strides from one year to the next. We didn't have the same number of serious injuries we had during the 3-12-1 season. Because of our strength and conditioning coach, Johnny Parker, the team was in much better physical condition, but the most important difference in the 1984 team was the change in our attitude. We had so many players who were like strangers in our locker room in 1983. In '84 we had a lot more stability and continuity in the program. We went from being a team that at times lacked confidence early in the season to one that learned how to win even in adverse situations. We were beginning to believe in ourselves and one another. Parcells had clearly begun molding the team in his image. That team would be tough, hard-nosed, big, smart, and disciplined. Bill knew what he wanted and he knew how he wanted to get it done. The team knew that more changes were going to take place during the off-season. Some of us would be back the next season and some of us would be gone, either to other teams or away from football for good. Nobody's job was going to be safe, that was a given. He was going to work our asses off until we got to the top.

During my off-season I started to notice subtle changes in my own life. While I enjoyed another trip to Hawaii and the Pro Bowl, I then focused on getting ready for another season. I started to take a critical look at my health. I could feel the physical wear and tear on my body having played nine seasons. My knees and ankles were starting to ache more not only from playing on hideous artificial turf such as at Veterans Stadium in Philadelphia or the Superdome in New Orleans, but from having to practice on it in my own stadium. I could feel that I had lost a bit of speed as a result of wear and tear. When I first came into the league I enjoyed playing on artificial turf, but by this time I hated it. With the exception of one postseason bowl game we played while I was in college, I had never played on artificial turf in high school or college. I was accustomed to playing on grass fields or even those combination baseball/football surfaces such as in Atlanta. Playing on artificial turf initially let me use my speed to roam from sideline to sideline, tracking down running backs. But with so much stress and strain, starting and stopping, on the lower body, the effects had to go somewhere, so it ended up in my knees, ankles, toes, and hips. I could feel the fatigue linger longer and longer than in previous years. No one had to tell me what was pretty obvious to me: I was getting older!

Aside from the physical wear and tear, I was beginning to notice changes mentally, or at least I thought they were mental. I'd had occasional headaches, but I was beginning to experience them more frequently with additional subtle symptoms. I was a team captain and media friendly when it came to a microphone and camera. I began to notice that I was having problems expressing myself succinctly. I'd do an interview, and when asked a question, I had to take my time looking for the exact words I wanted to use. I began to stumble verbally and use *you know* and *umm* as fillers more often. The average person around me wouldn't notice anything, but I knew something was going on. I just couldn't quite put my finger on what was happening.

I had come to terms with the problems I was having with my knees and ankles. Anyone who played the way I played was going to get hurt and have aches and pains. All players have aches and pains! It's a case of who can physically rise to the occasion when they need to. Despite all of the aches in my knees, ankles, fingers, and right shoulder, I could still will myself to play when necessary. I could always spend extra time in the weight room increasing the strength and flexibility of my muscles and joints. But for the problems I thought

I was having mentally, I had to find a way to deal with them. When I was having mental problems with my performance, I sought out help from Dr. Ladata. When I was having problems physically, I sought out either the trainers or Drs. Warren and Levy, the two primary physicians on staff for the team. With all of the anatomy, kinesiology, and other sciences I studied in college, and with all of the many football injuries I'd sustained to that point, I felt relatively well informed, enough to probably be able to diagnose my and other players' injuries. With this "head thing" that I was starting to experience, I didn't know who to see.

My headaches came and went. I could have one for a few minutes one day, then not have another for four or five days. Because I had developed a pretty high threshold for pain, the headaches became more of an annoyance than anything else. Unless they became more intense, I felt that I could deal with them. The problems with my speech and word choice, however, I needed to address. This was not something I wanted to share with others for fear of what they would think of me. After all, I was supposed to be a bright guy. I'd been told by many people, especially white people who thought it was complimentary, that I was so "articulate." When white people make a statement like that to black people, most black people take that as patronizing. Many black people feel that white folks don't think black people, especially black males, can be articulate. I'd never been offended by the comment; instead I took it with a grain of salt. I was more flattered when I was told the same thing by old black men. Black men don't normally compliment one another, so to have an older, wiser black man tell me, "Son, you handle yourself well," and then to hear something like "You make me proud to be a black man" spoke volumes to me. I had always had a fear of being categorized as a dumb jock and a "big moose" even when I was in high school. Perhaps in high school and college football most things intellectual are kept pretty basic. But in the NFL, you can have all of the ability in the world, but if you're not smart enough to comprehend schemes and tendencies and be able to make adjustments quickly, the league will be but a pit stop for you. I had seen many guys who could run fast and were built like a fucking Adonis get shown the door because they were dumb with a capital *D*.

I sought help on my own to relieve the problems I was experiencing. I came across an ad for words on tape that was in some book or magazine I was reading. I think it was called Verbal Advantage. I looked into it to see if I might benefit from it. I ordered a series of audiotapes that I could play in my car's cassette player going to and from practice or whenever I was in my car alone. I was accustomed to exercising my muscles and my body, but I had to learn to exercise my brain again. As the tapes played, a word would be pronounced, after which the definition was given, then the word was used in a sentence. I would repeat the word aloud to refamiliarize myself with a vocabulary that I knew but had lost somewhere along the way. As I listened to these words on tape, I felt as if I were back in Mr. Skoko's literature class in high school. Many of these words were the same ones he used in his classes at McClenaghan to help expand our minds as students. As time passed, I could see that I was able to speak more effectively and with more confidence in general conversations and in media interviews.

Another subtle thing I felt was a general fuzzy-headedness. The ability to effectively communicate was a major concern, but my head also seemed to be in the clouds and I couldn't focus the way I was normally able to. I didn't look at this as anything major, but it was strange. Along with this head-in-the-clouds feeling I noticed the headaches, occasional mood swings, slight bouts of depression, and sensitivity to bright lights and noise. I believe these things were with me for a while, but not until I stepped away from playing during my off-season and I seriously took inventory did I realize what was going on. Doug Kotar had had a brain tumor; deep down inside I thought the same could happen to me. My need to examine those "little things" that I might not normally have noticed may in part have been prompted by the passing of Doug Kotar, which made me much more aware of my body and my environment. While I was playing football during the season, I was usually able to focus my attention on the game or on preparing to play the game, but now I had to be concerned about myself on and off the field.

I became more sensitive and attentive to everything I felt and tried to keep mental notes for myself. I noticed that at times I experienced bouts of depression, which seemed odd to me. I had always been pretty upbeat with few cares or worries. From my playing experience I'd learned to take things in stride, especially off the field, but I noticed that every so often, maybe once every other month, I would begin to sink into what I called "blue moods." I could actually feel them coming on much like a cold. At those times I didn't want to be around anyone. I wanted to be quiet and left alone. I used to hear people talk about being depressed with feelings of hopelessness and despair. I didn't think a lot about it because I figured those people were mentally ill. But now when people talked about their symptoms of depression, I could very much relate to them. Again, I kept these feelings to myself, especially my depression.

Athletes are trained to be of strong mind and body, but I was getting weak in all the areas where I used to be strong. I did not want to be thought of as being a little mentally off-balance and having communication problems. These issues were a bit much to reveal to anyone. I had seen the way even some of Doug's old teammates and coaches had shunned him when he had his tumor, so any revelations about the brain, anything about being mentally not fully there or depression were off-limits for me to reveal to people. Whatever I was dealing with, I was going to handle it myself. While I played the ultimate team sport, my personal experience was to never, ever, share a weakness with anyone because it would always come back to bite you in the ass. The best way for me to keep up with what was going on with me was to keep a journal. The first item I entered simply stated, "I don't think as clearly as I used to, nor is my speech, diction, or vocabulary as good as it used to be and I don't know why!" That journal was for me to refer to as needed, but it was also meant for someone to read if something happened to me and I had no way of communicating with anyone else.

When I took the time to think about things, one thought came back clearly. A couple of years earlier I remembered feeling so down that I actually thought of driving my car off the Tappan Zee Bridge. Nothing so traumatic was going on in my world to make me want to do something like that; it was just where I was at the time. I clearly remembered feeling so down and depressed but then thinking, "If I did that, who would take care of Aja?" Having something positive to live for such as my daughter was ultimately what kept me from self-destruction. I knew then that whether we understand it or not, God places people and things in our lives for many reasons. That was my reason for living and for not veering off the bridge when I had so many chances to do so. From that experience I learned that if I'm ever in a blue mood, I need to put myself in either a physical, mental, or emotional place where I can be still, relax, and think of positive things to offset the doom or gloom that can be overwhelming at times.

When the 1985 training camp rolled around, I was ready and eager to begin. I used to dread the monotony of training camp, but I was in really good shape from working out during the off-season. I also think I was awake to my own football mortality. This was my tenth season in the league, and I was still pretty damn good at what I did. If anyone had asked me when I first entered the league how long I would be playing, I would never have given myself ten seasons. I realized early in my career that football was much too violent and the position I played too tough to physically survive that long. I approached training camp with a fresh attitude and a sense that I was now one of those wise older vets that we'd had when I was first drafted. The high ankle sprain had healed during the off-season so I had my speed, quickness, and explosiveness, but I also had years of experience that I could rely on to play a smarter game.

Parcells had a little more relaxed attitude having gone to the play-offs, with higher expectations now. To assist with his coaching, Bill started to make some of his senior players more responsible for the play of the younger guys. Before practice he might come to me or any of the other older guys and say that a particular player wasn't getting something done in practice. He would say, "I want you to take care of that by seeing that the situation is handled," and then he would add, "If it's not taken care of, I'm going to hold you personally responsible!" My thought was "Damn, Bill, why do you wanna fuck with me? I have enough shit to take care of myself!" That was the way he was, and it was the way he kept his fingers on the pulse of the team. He knew how to work us, and he knew how to push our buttons to get the best out of us.

We worked hard when it was time to work, but we also made time to play. Most of the other players were apprehensive about approaching Parcells with some kind of request, but I wasn't. Call it having balls or just not giving a fuck, but if I thought something would help us come together and feel better as a team, I had no problem opening my mouth and asking or just going ahead and doing it. If we were going to work hard, then we needed to be able to play hard.

Parcells worked us hard during training camp, so toward the end of camp I approached him about allowing the guys an opportunity to celebrate and relax. He asked me, "How?" I told him that I wanted to invite some "entertainers" up and have a beer bash in the dorm where we all stayed. Obviously he wanted to know and asked, "What kind of entertainers?" I said, "Well, the entertainers are actually dancers." "What kind of dancers?" he asked. I told him, "Exotic dancers!" He had been standing with his arms folded but did a double take when I said that and looked at me as if I were crazy! Maybe I was, but I wanted to do something that was a bit unusual. I'd seen ads in the back of *New York* magazine for exotic dancers so I thought it must be legitimate. Parcells thought for a second, then looked away from me and said, "If there's any damage to the dorm, I'm going to hold you personally responsible." I thought to myself, "So what else is new?" When I got the okay, I called the number in the magazine and scheduled three dancers to perform. When I told some of the guys what I had planned, I could see the disbelief and excitement in their faces. I knew some of the guys were not going to embrace this because some were devout Christians, but I knew most of the guys would love to have some "extracurricular" activities. This was certainly going to be a welcome departure from any other training camp any of us had ever had.

I thought one of the true characteristics of a good leader was the ability to go to bat for his guys. All the players were giving Parcells and the other coaches all they had in practice. Most days in July and August were hot and sticky, and to keep spirits up and to just have fun you had to do things that weren't football-related. Inviting the strippers up to training camp was definitely something different for everyone. I felt good knowing that Bill trusted me that much as a leader to allow me to do something so different. I knew the onus was on my ass to make sure nothing got out of hand, and I knew several guys who, if given the opportunity, would find a way to screw things up. I went to a couple of those guys and told them point-blank that I wanted them to be on their absolute best behavior that evening, and that if something bad happened, the shit would be on my shoulders. They gave me their word that they would be on their best behavior.

On our only night off that week, we ordered a keg of beer (and I didn't even drink) with pizzas and enjoyed the dancers. It wasn't so much about having "almost" naked women dancing before us. It was more about the bonding that took place when we were together. Even some of the guys who were solid Christian citizens who snuck in a peek here and there understood the evening of camaraderie and enjoyed being together. The evening went off without a problem and without any snide comments from Parcells the next morning. One of the things I loved was that everybody showed up for practice the next morning *on time* with a smile and with a renewed sense of vitality.

I had done other things like this in years prior, such as having an exotic dancer perform in the dining hall for my trainer John Dziegel when he was getting married for the second time. John was a great guy and a widower in his seventies. After years of being alone he was getting married again. I thought having the dancer show up at dinner was a great way to have a little fun and recognize a truly good man. He was totally surprised when the dancer confronted him, then realized what was going on. I could see that he appreciated the gesture and had fun with it. I remember that Mr. Mara, the Giants owner, was forewarned that the dancer was coming, so as she was walking into the dining hall, Mr. Mara was making a hasty exit so as not to be a witness.

I also instituted Beefsteak Charlie's dinners for my teammates and brought hot, freshly made doughnuts to my teammates on Saturday mornings prior to practice. The Beefsteak Charlie's events usually took place at times when the team was not doing well on the field. After losing four, five, or six games in a row and when we had no one to count on except ourselves, we would go as a team to a local restaurant in a nearby town to have a meal. When we got together, we ate and drank as much as we wanted and just talked. It might not seem like anything major, but surprisingly enough the experiences brought us together as a team. As a player and a leader, I found we played together on the football field but we didn't know one another. That time spent at our dinners was an opportunity for guys to get to know one another, not as football players but as men.

As I got older, I wanted to find ways to keep things fresh and interesting. While I was having fun as a captain for my guys, I rarely focused on me. As a ten-year veteran I began to understand that it was no longer about me. I was still a good player, but the best of what my body could give to the team was behind me. I was not asked to be a star on the field; instead I evolved more into the leader that the younger guys needed on the field and in the locker room.

One characteristic of Bill Parcells's coaching style that I grew to understand was that everyone had a role to play within the team. Our quarterback, Phil Simms, knew that his role was to manage the game, put the ball in the hands of the weapons he had on offense, and not turn the ball over. Lawrence Taylor knew his role was to get to the quarterback or to disrupt the offense enough to allow the rest of the defense to make good plays. The offensive and defensive linemen knew their role was to make each other's unit better in practice. My role was to be the "inside force," shutting down the inside running game, and a strong goal-line defender. An unspoken role I was charged with was to be a solid team leader. As a leader, as long as I maintained a good working relationship with Bill and I was allowed to do even unorthodox things to help bring the players together as a team, I was all good.

As we opened the 1985 season, we continued to make strides as a team, but the most important thing that was different with the team was a new winning attitude among our players. Making the play-offs the previous years showed us that we could be as good as we wanted to be, but we had to seal the deal when we got the opportunity in games. Generally we played well during that season, but we lost a couple of games that we should have won. Four items stand out about that season.

I've been asked so many times how the whole Gatorade bit began. It started as Parcells, in his unique way of pushing motivational buttons, approached our nose tackle Jim Burt to discuss our next opponents after a loss to the Bengals. Bill told Burt that Washington Redskins center Jeff Bostic had a great game against whomever they played the week before. Bill told Burt that if he wasn't ready to play, Bostic was going to embarrass him on the field. Burt being Burt knew what Bostic brought to the table and just blew Parcells off. But Parcells being Parcells was not going to let the moment just slide. He went to other players in the locker room and within hearing range told various players that Bostic was going to embarrass Burt if he was not ready on Sunday afternoon. This back-and-forth went on all week. While Jim tried to play it off, I could tell that Parcells's ribbing was getting to him. At one point Jim was coming out of his down stance using dumbbells to improve his quickness on the snap. Parcells was getting into Burt's head and Bill knew it.

We went into the game and Jim appeared to be more intense and focused than usual. During the game Jim would ask me if I was having any problems with the Redskins linemen getting to me. I told him that he was doing a great job keeping the offensive lineman away from me and giving me the opportunity to stop the runs. As the game was winding down, we were ahead 17–3 and Burt came up to me and said, "That Parcells is such a fucking prick!" Parcells rode Jim's ass all week but got the result he wanted out of him. We were happy with the win but Burt wanted the last laugh! He said, "We should get him!" I said, "What do you mean *we*?" Jim said, "C'mon, Harry-O, you know you're one of Parcells's guys. If I did something by myself, he would have my ass! But if you did it with me, he wouldn't do anything to us." Jim was somewhat right, but I was hesitant to commit to the unknown, so I asked him what he wanted to do. He hesitated for a second, then said, "Let's get him with the Gatorade!" "The Gatorade?" I asked. Jim said, "Yeah, let's douse him with the bucket of Gatorade." I thought to myself, "Damn good win against the Skins. What the fuck?" and then agreed to join Burt.

I looked at Parcells and thought to myself that whatever we did, we had to wait until he took his headphones off, otherwise he might be electrocuted. Burt and I grabbed a bucket of Gatorade and stood behind him as the clock was winding down to zero. As he began to take his headphones off to head to the center of the field to shake hands with Joe Gibbs, Burt and I raised the bucket and splashed him. Parcells was totally unaware of what was coming and was probably shocked to feel the icy-cold liquid running down his back. When Parcells turned around and saw who got him, he couldn't do anything but smile and enjoy the win.

Playing in the NFC East in the seventies and eighties was like playing in a regular neighborhood. It was as if the Giants were on one block, the Philadelphia Eagles were on the next block, and the Washington Redskins were on a block below the Eagles. The St. Louis Cardinals were a couple of blocks over, and the Dallas Cowboys were clear across town on the other side of the tracks. Whenever the Giants, Eagles, Redskins, and Cardinals played against one another, we had mutual respect. We prepared and played as hard as we could. Regardless of who won, when the game was over, we shook hands, patted one another on the rear, and walked off the field together without any animosity. But when it came to the Dallas Cowboys, we all had the same mind-set: we wanted to beat the hell out of them. We rooted for one another in the neighborhood to beat the Cowboys. When it came to playing Dallas, we were like one gang wanting the same thing, to knock the blue star off that silver helmet. The Cowboys exuded an arrogance when they stepped on the field. Perhaps we all were envious, but beating the Cowboys was a delight that everyone felt. If there was one team to beat, they were it.

I did not personally dislike any player I competed against, but we as a defense had "issues" with one player. Joe Theismann had gained a reputation as an arrogant asshole as a player. I had gone to a couple of Pro Bowls with Joe in the past but had no issues with him personally until we were preparing to play against the Redskins in our rematch later that 1985 season. To better defend against them, we watched video of some of the games the Skins had played since we'd won the first game at the Meadowlands. Nothing jumped out at us: the Redskins offense was doing its usual things to move the ball and score. But as we watched the video, one play caught our attention. Joe Theismann scored a touchdown by running the ball into the end zone, then he spiked the ball! No, it wasn't just a spike; it was a spike with authority! It was not unusual to see a player spike the ball after scoring, but to see a quarterback spike the ball with such authority was rare. We must have ran that play back twenty times, not looking at the run but focusing solely on the spike. We made it our mission as a defense to not allow that to happen to us when we played them.

With the success we were beginning to experience on the field also came a new tradition of the defensive unit meeting on Fridays after practice to establish goals for the upcoming game. As captain I would list several categories on the board, such as points allowed, turnovers, yards allowed, etc. I would go around to each player in the room and get his commitment on what we would not allow as a defensive unit. Once we agreed, we would shoot for those numbers in the game. But we took it one step further when it came to playing against Theismann. We had played so many games against Joe that we knew almost everything about him. We knew his audibles, his cadence in communicating with his center and offensive line, and we knew his arm strength. When he was younger, he could run effectively outside the pocket, but he was not now the player he once was. One of our primary goals was to make sure Joe stayed in the game, giving us a good chance to shut down the Skins passing game. Usually the defense wants to knock a quarterback out of the game to eliminate his threat. We were taking the opposite approach, which felt odd, but it was the best for us. When you are competing, especially in a sport such as football, you have to seek every advantage.

It was going to be another *Monday Night Football* game with a nationwide audience. I'd had some good Monday-night games but also some stinkers. Which would it be for me this time? When we took the field against the Skins, we were all a little tired from arriving late the night before from New Jersey. We'd had a comedy of transportation errors in getting to D.C. and our hotel. Unfortunately, our coaches did not make any schedule adjustments to give us a little more rest prior to the game. When you have a 9:00 p.m. game it's not always easy to get quality rest because your normal schedule is interrupted and your mind is so focused on playing the game. For me, anticipating what I had to do was exhausting enough, but to have to wait all day to play was draining.

Once the ball was kicked off, we shook off whatever effects we felt, whether it was lack of energy or sleep. During the game, while driving down the field, the Redskins ran a play-action flea-flicker pass. Once I realized that it was a pass, it was too late for me to get back to my zone. Because I was still near the line of scrimmage, I tried to sack Joe. Joe was looking to pass, but when he saw me, he sidestepped me and continued to try to pass downfield.

That is when "It" happened! The It was Lawrence coming in for the sack and landing on Theismann's leg as it was extended. Some people said they heard the snap of the bone upon impact. I did not hear it because when I'm in the midst of a play, I don't hear anything; my focus is entirely visual, seeing where the ball is and then getting to it as quickly as possible to make the play.

When the whistle was blown, I noticed Lawrence's reaction and wondered what was wrong. Then I saw the mangled leg of Joe Theismann. Both Giants and Redskins players stopped to see what had happened. When we all saw the leg, it was amazing that in seconds we went from being combatants to humanitarians. We all talked with Joe to try to make sure he did not go into shock. As the doctors and the medical staff put Joe on the stretcher, I thought of the goal we had established on Friday, to keep Theismann in the game. That fucking Lawrence knocked him out. As they were wheeling Joe off the field, Joe being Joe said, "Don't worry, guys, I'll be back." I replied, "Joe, you might be back, but it won't be tonight!"

Just like that, a career was over! On that play, Theismann's career ended in the blink of an eye. With every game that I've ever played, I have always prayed prior to the game; not for a win but for every player to be able to walk off the field the same way he was able to walk onto it. I had seen a lot of injuries as a football player, but never seen one as graphic as that. When you play, the unspoken understanding is that any given play could be your last. Even if you try to take special precautions, when you play a contact sport such as football, anything can happen.

We lost the game to Jay Schroeder and finished the regular season with a 10-6 record. We made the play-offs as a wild-card team, beating the San Francisco 49ers in the first round. In the second round we had to play against the Chicago Bears in Chicago. The Bears were a team much like ours—a strong, physical team with good coaching and a solid, core group of veteran players. We matched up well, but I think the big difference was being familiar with the playing environment and the weather. We lost the game 21–0, beating ourselves with a couple of blown defensive coverages and a whiff by our punter, Sean Landeta, near our own goal line that resulted in a touchdown by the Bears. When we sat in the visitors' locker room after the game, Parcells told us that the situation we had just gone through would not happen again the following year. He challenged everyone, but especially the older guys such as me and George Martin, to take ownership of the situation because our clocks were ticking and we might not have another shot at getting a championship.

For the second year we made the play-offs but failed to advance to the championship game. We thought we were a pretty good team, but we were not that good, yet!

CHAPTER 12

On a Super Run

During the off-season we had to live with our loss to the Bears and the realization that even if we thought we were good, we had to prove it on the field. Parcells challenged us, and each of us individually had to put our chips on the table and commit to the team. The off-season was uneventful to me except that the team drafted some good players to go with what I thought was a pretty strong group of players already in place. Eric Dorsey was a defensive end from Notre Dame that I knew absolutely nothing about, but the Giants thought highly of him and took him as their number one draft pick. The second-round pick was also a player who commanded the attention of the media, Thomas "Pepper" Johnson, an inside linebacker from Ohio State.

I had noticed Pepper the previous football season while watching an Ohio State–Minnesota game on television. As I watched the game, I kept seeing this one defensive player all over the field making tackles. I thought to myself, "Damn, that guy's going to be a great player for somebody when he gets to the NFL." The Giants thought the same as I did and selected him as one of their second-round draft choices.

The accounts of the draft in the New York newspapers said Pepper was the "heir apparent" to me at inside linebacker. With that addition, the core of linebackers for the Giants was strong. I was the wise old veteran; Lawrence was the Ferrari on the outside; in just two seasons Carl Banks had established himself as a force on the other side opposite Taylor; and Gary Reasons was good against the run and the pass. What I didn't think about was how I was becoming the weak link as the elder statesman of the group. I was no fool; I saw what had happened with Van Pelt and Kelley a couple of years earlier. That many in the media had already put Pepper in the lineup rubbed me the wrong way, but it should not have. The Giants had to prepare the team for the future, whether I was rubbed the wrong way or not. While I was challenged by Parcells to be better the next year, I was also challenged by the team's drafting Pepper Johnson as the "heir apparent" guy who was going to nudge me out the door. What was done in the draft was like a shot across my bow; it reminded me that regardless of how good I thought I was, I could never feel secure in my role as a player or as a leader.

I worked hard during the off-season to be better than I was the year before. I knew I was in good shape in '85, but whatever we had in 1985 had to be better for '86. I also knew that I could not give anyone a reason to doubt me as a player. To show one crack in my conditioning or my play would open the door to Pepper or any other player looking for an opportunity to ease me out of the equation. My mind-set became to work my ass off and make sure that if I was challenged in training camp, I was going to answer the bell every time and come out on top. If I was going to lose my job to anyone, they had better be head and shoulders better than me. I made sure that for everything we had to do, I was going to be better than everyone else.

I got my first glimpse of the 1986 Giants at our minicamp, held in late May, almost two months prior to training camp. I could sense a much different attitude during that minicamp; the players were much more intense and had a different work ethic than I had seen before. I was impressed that guys were looking strong physically and thinking about what we failed to do as a team against the Bears months earlier.

When we arrived for training camp at Pace University, I knew it was going to be grueling. Parcells put his foot on the pedal from the beginning of camp to the end. We worked our asses off and no one complained. In earlier years a few guys might have complained in the locker room or in private, but that was not the case this year. We all knew that camp was going to be tough, but we were ready. I was ready for my own challenges. When I was on the field, I made sure that whatever Pepper did, I did it better. If we had to run sprints, I made sure that I finished before anyone else. I was going to set the pace and lead by example.

When the season opened, we disappointed ourselves by dropping our first game to the Dallas Cowboys on *Monday Night Football*. The following week we prepared for the San Diego Chargers knowing that they had defeated the Miami Dolphins 55–10 in South Florida. That week I received a letter from some guy in Rahway, New Jersey, who said the Giants would never win because we had too many "niggers" on the team. He was an equal-opportunity offender, saying that the white guys were no better because he thought they were a bunch of "fuck offs." The letter was sent to me because I was the captain of the team. I took the liberty of reading it to the team over the intercom system. I wanted guys to understand that even though at times they thought they were hot shit on the football field, in the minds of some people we were all dumb-ass jocks. The letter unified us regardless of color, religion, nationality, or political affiliation. Once we put on those NY Giants uniforms, we were all the same.

We beat the Chargers in a game that many thought we would blow because we had lost to the Cowboys and because of the dominance of the Chargers against the Dolphins the previous week. At the end of that game, I celebrated the victory with my first solo splash of Gatorade on Bill Parcells. That win was huge for the team because it was against a high-powered offensive team and a defense that was pretty damn good. We went on to win games against the Raiders, Saints, Cardinals, and Eagles. Those wins gave us a false sense of security; we got too comfortable because we knew we were good, and we lost to the Seattle Seahawks on the road. Some might say it was a "trap game" for us and that we were looking past the Seahawks to a division opponent, the Redskins. It was not a trap game for us, though; we simply just did not score when we had the opportunity on offense. Losing to Seattle was a reality check for us, and if there was going to be a loss to wake us up, that was the best time to be knocked across our heads.

We did wake up and got on track with our season, beating the Skins the following week, then the Cowboys and the Eagles. The game against the Vikings was a scare for us, but Phil Simms connected with wide receiver Bobby Johnson on a huge and dramatic fourth-and-17-yards pass play. Raul Allegre kicked the winning field goal and turned a potential loss into a win. (I'm not going to go into detail about the play, but it will undoubtedly be one of the top ten plays in Giants history.) The following games set the tone for what I thought was the most dominant span of weeks I had in professional football. We beat the Denver Broncos, the 49ers, and the Redskins. Beating the St. Louis Cardinals at home and then the Packers to finish the season was some of the most physical football I had been a part of during my career with the Giants. We were so physical that we beat teams into submission. Our play reminded me of the same type of power football the Pittsburgh Steelers had exhibited when they beat teams in the seventies. We beat up some teams so badly physically that I actually felt sorry for them. That is something football players almost never feel, but I did. The term *smashmouth* was used to describe our play on both sides of the football. It was appropriate because we didn't care what the opposing teams ran against us. We took great pride in playing hard, tough, physical football against any teams we played against. Toward the end of the season we were able to play loose because we didn't have a lot of pressure on us. We knew that we had sewn up the NFC East title and were in the play-offs, but when we took the field, we were strong and healthy and worked together like a well-tuned machine.

We entered the play-offs with exactly what we wanted: home-field advantage. From the Bears play-off game the previous year, we knew how important it was to be able to play at home. We wanted to play in our house, in front of our fans, and in the weather of New Jersey in January. Any team that we played would have to come through the Meadowlands to get to Super Bowl XXI.

After a bye week, our first team up was the San Francisco 49ers. The Niners always scared me because anytime you had Joe Montana as a quarterback and Bill Walsh as a head coach, you always had a chance to be knocked off. Our routine prior to every home game was to practice the day before the game, then in the evening we all checked into the Hilton Woodcliff Lake Hotel and had a general team meeting, a defensive meeting, and then went off to our rooms to get a good night's sleep. I lay in bed hoping to get to sleep and be alert to do battle against the Niners, but instead I tossed and turned for two to three hours. I realized that I was not going to get any sleep, so I got up, got dressed, and made my way out of the hotel for my home about four miles away. It was after our 11:00 p.m. curfew, but everyone was in bed getting sleep except me. I went home, put a practice VHS tape in my VCR, and watched tape of the 49ers for the rest of the night. At about 8:00 a.m., when I should have been waking up, I was getting sleepy and wanted to take a nap, but I couldn't risk closing my eyes and then perhaps oversleeping and being late for the beginning of such an important game.

We went into the game in cold, but not too bitterly cold, weather. I had gotten into the habit of wearing nothing but a layer of Vaseline under my shoulder pads. In cold weather many of the guys put long sleeves on to stay warm, but I wanted to confront the elements head-on. In the summer I embraced the heat and humidity. I dealt with the heat by thinking of the cold of winter, and in frigid temperatures my thoughts of summer, complete with heat and humidity, always kept me warm. I was tired because of lack of sleep, but the weather was going to keep me awake, and the 49ers were certainly going to keep me alert.

I knew I was exhausted, yet this reserve of energy came out of nowhere. I could tell from the opening kickoff the intensity of the team was jacked up. Everyone seemed to be flying around, hitting anything in the opposite-color jersey that moved. An early turnover by wide receiver Jerry Rice was an omen of things to come. We jumped on them in all three phases and smothered them like a python. We won convincingly, 49–3, and advanced to the next game, which was the NFC Championship game against the Washington Redskins. It was a big win for the team, but I couldn't celebrate; I was wiped out. I only celebrated by going home to bed.

Preparing for the Redskins felt different because they were a division opponent that we had already beaten twice during the season. We knew everything about the Redskins, but then again, you never know when it comes to playing in the NFL. With Joe Gibbs as the head coach, anything can happen! Much like the previous week we prepped all week, and on the evening prior to the game we checked into the Hilton for meetings, a meal, and curfew. I had developed a cold and took NyQuil to manage the symptoms and also to help me get some rest. Around 1:00 a.m. I woke up and couldn't get back to sleep. I finally got up and left the hotel at about 2 a.m. As I was walking to my car, I remember thinking, "Damn, these guys are so lucky to be able to sleep without a problem!" When I arrived home, I did what I did the previous week and fired up my VCR and watched video of the previous Redskins games. This time I took a short nap before heading to the stadium to get dressed for the game. As I was walking through the training room, I heard Phil Simms say, "Man, I was not able to get a lick of sleep last night," and another player agreed with him that it was difficult to get rest. I finally realized that it wasn't just me; other guys were also so wired they could hardly get any quality rest. The play-offs are a different animal from the regular football season. With so much on the line everyone's focus is narrowed and the intensity is much more elevated. Getting to this point of the season was rare for most teams. If we blew it, especially at home, we might never get back to this place again. This was going to be a defining event for us as a team and for me as a player.

We played the Skins tough, scoring two touchdowns and a field goal, but we played the strongest on defensive, holding the Skins to no points. I had a good game, making twelve tackles to help stop the running game. In late December and mid-January everyone in the league knew that if you couldn't run the ball against the Giants defense, you would have a big problem winning because it was always hell to throw against the strong winds in the winter at Giants Stadium. The Redskins couldn't get on track passing against the wind, but even when they had the wind in their favor, it still affected the flight of the passes thrown. When we scored first and went ahead, we knew it was going to be our day. Whatever the Skins tried to do on the ground against our front seven defenders we were able to shut it down. With the ball on the ground and the fans acting as the twelfth man for us, there was no way that we were going to lose, especially this day and in our house. As the minutes and seconds on the game clock were winding down, I saw what I had always wanted to see in Giants Stadium: Giants fans finally had a reason to celebrate. I wanted to savor every moment I could as time wound down. Confetti was being thrown from the upper deck of the stadium and it fell to the lower deck, with shreds of newspaper all over the place. The winds were strong and blew debris all over the place, making the effect even more spectacular. Even rolls of toilet paper were being thrown. But no one cared; it was a time to celebrate.

Everyone in the stadium was elated. Everywhere I looked, smiles were on every face with the exception of some of the Redskins', but most of them were happy for us and wished us good luck in our next game. Though we were competitors on the field, we respected one another. We always played hard every time we squared off on the field, whether it was at RFK Stadium or at Giants Stadium. They knew as well as any other team what we had gone through as an organization, and they knew it was our time! Regardless of who prevails in the NFC or AFC Championship game, the loser always wishes the winner good luck because that winner has to uphold the honor of the conference in the big game. That game was Super Bowl XXI, to be played in Pasadena, California.

Many older Giants fans remember that cold, windy evening at Giants Stadium when the prayers of so many die-hard fans were answered. They remember my nose tackle Jim Burt climbing over the wall and going into the stands to get his son to share in the moment. It took me a while to grasp what was happening. As I began to walk off the field, I was caught by the hordes of cameramen and reporters with microphones wanting a comment on how I felt about going to the Super Bowl. I could hardly believe it because the whole thing seemed so much like a dream. The enormity of beating the Redskins three times in a season and finally earning a shot to go to the Super Bowl was on my mind, but just looking at my life and where I was at that time seemed so huge. How could I, a kid who just wanted to play for the girls, wind up on the center stage of sports for the entire world to see? Just to be in that position was hard to believe having unknowingly at times navigated my way through so many situations on and off the field. My career had more than its share of ups and downs. Despite every injury I sustained in a game or in practice I was able to come back and play. In some instances I was able to come back and play at a higher level than before. I looked at some of the off-the-field decisions I'd made and understood that if I had done some of the things I wanted to do differently when I wanted to do them, there was no way that I would be headed to the Super Bowl. I'd experienced many disappointments in my earlier years playing on shitty teams, and even though I wanted out at times, I was glad I stuck it out and stayed with the Giants.

Our loss to the Bears in Chicago the previous year was fading fast from all of our memories. This was our year and we were going to the Big Dance. In the locker room we all celebrated, but Parcells wanted us to try to keep our emotions in check. With network cameras all over our locker room broadcasting how we responded to winning, and with the challenge that we had before us, Parcells wanted us to act professional. As much as we wanted to show our asses, each of us knew that we still had work to do. We had to keep reminding ourselves and one another that our mission was not over. We still had one more hill to climb: beating John Elway and the Denver Broncos.

We had two weeks to prepare for the game in Pasadena, California. Few people realize the preparations of the team personnel and each player before even getting to the site of a championship game. I was making sure that all of my family members and close friends got tickets to the game. I had to take care of my immediate-family members' travel accommodations and hotel arrangements, and I wanted to make sure that everyone had some spending money as well. Each player on the team was allotted twenty-five tickets. At $250 a ticket, some of the guys thought it was better to tell their family members to stay at home and watch the game on television. Other players sold their tickets to ticket brokers and scalpers, who paid almost double for the seats. There was absolutely no way that I could do that with my tickets. So many people had made sacrifices for me to get to where I was as an athlete. I probably needed more like two hundred tickets and would have paid for them if I could have gotten them. I was thankful to be in the position I was in and I wanted my loved ones, especially my family members, to share in what I was experiencing.

My sisters, Ruth, Loretta, and Louise, were very much like surrogate mothers to me. In the absence of my mother, they'd made my college life more comfortable whenever I needed something. My brothers had to be there because, without their knowing it directly, they had been influential in their own way. My kids, Aja and Donald, well, let's just say that if anyone was going to be there, it would be them, even if I had to keep them on the bench with me during the game. My best friend, Steve Parks, had to be there to represent those guys I played with in high school. While I knew my responsibility as a player on the field, I also knew my responsibility to show my gratitude to all of those folks who supported me from day one. I had to share the experience with as many family members and friends as I could.

As a team we were pretty healthy, but for some guys who had nagging injuries, the two-week spread between the NFC Championship game and the Super Bowl was a welcomed opportunity to get better. Other players were either on the injured reserve or would not play at all because of their ailments. They traveled with the team and attended practice, but instead of participating on the field they spent time getting treatment from the training staff. I knew it was hard for them, but there was no fucking way that I was going to miss out on this experience. My attitude was, even if my leg was being held on by a thin piece of skin, I was going to play! I probably shouldn't have been so concerned about so many other things, but I felt bad for those guys who had gotten to this point only to not be able to dress for the game and play. Those guys were my teammates, and I knew the euphoria I was feeling and I wanted them to feel the same way I felt.

During those two weeks I remembered what I went through in preparing to play against the 49ers and the Redskins. I couldn't sleep the night before playing those teams. This time, knowing that I was going to be playing in the absolutely most important game of my life, I had to take a different approach to getting ready to play. The only thing I knew to do was to downplay the significance of the game by telling myself that it was just another game. I knew that if you kept telling yourself something enough times, you started to believe what you were saying. It was the only way I knew to keep myself from becoming anxious and nervous. The New York market always had more reporters and cameras than most other NFL cities, but because of where we were going, the number of reporters and cameras seemed to quadruple in our locker room after practices. While I downplayed the excitement of playing in the Super Bowl in the media, privately I was about to burst open with anticipation.

We spent a week getting ready for the Broncos in New Jersey, where the weather was cold, but for once nobody minded the frigid temperatures. As we prepared to leave for the West Coast, every person I met seemed be a Giants fan. Everyone who knew I was a player offered good-luck wishes. One of my neighbors in the condominium development I lived in left me a bottle of Dom Pérignon champagne with a message written on the bottle in silver ink: "To Harry, Good luck in SBXXI." I'd seen fans' disappointment and anger for years; now I was feeling nothing but love from them. I'd always known my responsibility to represent my home folks from Carolina and to some degree the Giants fans. But what I was feeling was a true responsibility to represent the whole New York/New Jersey area. Even New York Jets fans became Giants fans, if only temporarily; we were all in this thing together as a region of the country. From the oldest fans who constantly reminded us that they were Giants season-ticket holders or they were "fans since the Polo Grounds," to babies who were dressed in Giants jerseys, everyone was a Giants fan and was rooting for the team to bring home the Lombardi Trophy.

We flew to California a week before the game with a special United Airlines crew that we had been using for much of the season. Another of Bill Parcells's superstitions was to stick with what got you to the dance. Once we arrived, we all knew that we had to put on our game faces because it was all about business. We listened to some of the Broncos players give radio and television interviews where they said, "We're just happy to be here!" For us, that was bullshit; we weren't just happy to be there. We were there to finish the job we knew we had to accomplish. We wanted everybody to be on the same page when it came to talking to the media. Yeah, being there to play in the Super Bowl was good, but it would mean nothing if we didn't win the game. I knew I didn't want to become a trivia question for fans: "What team played against the Denver Broncos in Super Bowl XXI and lost?" We were there to win!

The other thing we had to be conscious of was not screwing up off the field. While I had never been to a Super Bowl before, the tales of players screwing up during that week were well documented. I had heard stories of problems players could encounter off the field or of guys making bonehead choices only to have their decisions come back to haunt them and their team in the media later in the week. Shit, I was from New York, where you could get anything you wanted for a price. Where we were, you could get whatever you wanted free of charge. As a captain, I knew that if one of our players got into trouble, it would not just reflect on him but the entire Giants organization. One of the things Bill instilled in his older core players such as George and myself was that we would be held accountable for our players who looked to us for guidance. Most of the guys understood what their position was as a Giants player about to play in the biggest game of their lives. Most knew to stay away from trouble, but in every group you have one or two guys that think out of their ass and not their head. So, whenever we got even a hint that one of the guys was thinking about doing something that would negatively reflect on the team, we were all over him before he could fuck up.

We had a few days of practice at the Los Angeles Rams training facility near Costa Mesa, California. There we enjoyed what was more like an extended road trip. We had our daily practice and meetings, but we also had time to spend with our families, who were in other hotels near ours. Each of us was given a complimentary car by Hertz to drive while there. We were eventually moved to a hotel in Pasadena two evenings before the game. There, all family time, interviews, and press obligations ceased. Our only focus from that point was playing the game.

I continued telling myself that it was just another game, even on the night before. When I woke up in the early hours of the morning of the game, I lay in bed and took an inventory of my life. How did I get there? Who made it possible for me to be there? And most important, why me? I thought of every player I had played with and against on every level of competition. In my mind I could almost see every play that I'd made on the football field from the beginning. I remembered every sprint I ran, every weight I lifted. I remembered every ache and pain I'd felt as I lay there. I'd made it there, but I knew it wasn't because I was the best. It wasn't because I was the fastest, the strongest, or the brightest. So many others had me beat hands down in those areas. Things happen for a reason, but oftentimes we don't fully know why, they just do!

I wondered why I was born when I was and missed possibly having to serve in Vietnam like my brother and some of his friends who died in war. Why did I pick football over band? Why did I have a girlfriend who influenced me to get my work done in school to help make it possible for me to earn a scholarship? Why did I walk away from football when I first tried out for the game only to find my way back and then walk away again at the end of high school? Why was I given a second shot at playing on the next level through getting into a black college? How was I able to make it to the NFL instead of all of those talented guys I played with at South Carolina State? How was I able to learn and master a position at the highest level of competition that I had never played before? Why? How? I was full of questions, but the only answer I came up with was that, for whatever reason, I was placed in the position I was in to do what I was supposed to do. As much as I thought it should have been Brian Kelley, Brad Van Pelt, or even Pat Hughes, the linebacker I replaced in my early years with the Giants, or Thomas Holliday, or Razzie Smith from South Carolina State, or Junebug, Bubble Gum, or even my best friend, Steve Parks, from high school, it was for me to do. While it was me and my body that I was taking onto the field, I was carrying all of them and so many others with me into the game. I knew that the wish of every player who plays football was to be where I was, at the apex of a career playing in the biggest game of any player's life.

At that point I allowed myself to believe that it wasn't just another game but the biggest game that any player could ever play in, the Super Bowl! I remember the chill I felt that resonated throughout my body as I got up to take a shower and got dressed. The adrenaline was starting to flow through me, making me a little weak-legged. When I went to our pregame breakfast that morning, I sat with some of my teammates, who talked of their nervousness. There's always some anxiety when you play in a game of this magnitude. The nervousness was not about playing against the Broncos. Hell, we played against them weeks earlier and beat them. Most of the guys talked about the one thing they feared about the game: tripping upon being introduced, with millions watching around the world. Amazing as that might sound, it's true. Many players who've played in Super Bowls acknowledged that was probably the most nerve-racking thing about playing in the game. I didn't know if that would happen to me, but I wasn't going to think about it on my way to the Rose Bowl on the team bus. I was busy trying to remember all of the things we'd gone over during our two weeks of preparation for the Broncos.

When we arrived at the Rose Bowl, I was impressed with the festive decoration of the venue, but what stands out in my mind was seeing the Giants and Bronco fans outside the stadium. Most of the players wore headphones and listened to their favorite music to soothe them. While we could not hear anything from the outside, we saw thousands of football fans cheering our arrival. When we got off the buses, each player's focus was solely on getting ready to play. As our players dressed, I could sense tightness in the room from some of the guys. There wasn't the normal chatter that you'd get before a game. Everybody was in his own deep thoughts handling the situation as best he could. We had gotten advice from players and coaches who had been there before, but no book was ever written to tell players what they would experience in this situation. We all had our own individual ways to get ready for this game. Just as there were fifty-three players on the team, there were fifty-three different modes of readiness.

Prior to the team stretching period, I walked out on the field in my game pants and T-shirt to get a feel for the playing surface to be certain of the right shoes for me. I wish I could have bottled and saved that time forever. The pre-game excitement and the reception given to me by Giants fans were great. What made that time most special was seeing my family members. I motioned to my daughter, Aja, to come down to the field level. She came down and jumped into my arms and gave me a great big hug. That hug from Aja made me know that everything was going to be okay. I had no reason to be nervous or uptight. That hug from Aja was just like getting a hug from my mother. Holding her and feeling her energy helped me to understand that I was doing something that was bigger than me. For the rest of her life she would always remember that hug, and I was glad she was able to share it with her daddy and her family. After a few smooches, I gave Aja to my sister Ruth, who came down to the field level to get her. As they headed back to their seats, I returned to the locker room to get ready to play the game.

After our last bathroom breaks and uniform adjustments, we prepared to take the field. Bill Parcells gave us our final instructions. He told us that we might never get here again so we should enjoy the experience and then said, "We're introducing the defense." With that, I knew we were on and ready to go! I wasn't nervous but I got chills knowing I was going to play in the biggest game with my guys, my teammates. As the offense and the rest of the defensive nonstarters began to head out to the field, the starting defensive unit stayed in the locker room a little longer. We looked at one another but said little; we all knew the time for talking was over. If one sentiment was central to all of us, it was that we wished one another good luck. As we made our way to the field as a defensive unit, we were as ready as we could ever be, and I felt blessed to be a part of this mission.

I don't recall which team was introduced first or last, but I knew that as we were being introduced, it was not just to the 104,000 people in the Rose Bowl, but to the millions of people watching around the world. I knew that for the few seconds after my name was called until I reached the part of the field where my teammates were waiting for me, that was going to be my time, my five to ten seconds of fame. Our defensive-line unit was introduced first: Martin, Burt, and Marshall, then the linebackers Banks, Reasons, and Taylor. Upon hearing my name being called over the public address system, I didn't want to jog as I probably should have. I had a mind to extend and savor the seconds of being introduced, but instead, because I was so pumped up, I sprinted out through the cheerleaders to my teammates waiting to greet me. Once I made it through my teammates, the scary part was over; my legs felt rubbery but I made it. Then I headed over to the sideline to get ready for the national anthem and the coin toss.

I had always been inspired by the playing of the national anthem. I think that started when I was at South Carolina State. There they played it with spirit and with feelings from deep inside their souls. When I stood on the field in college getting ready to play, I could feel the power of the band's horn section penetrate through my being. That might have been because as I stood on the sideline, the band was right in front of me and I got the full effect of the sounds. Prior to college I had never heard the national anthem played that way on television; it was usually that "milk toast" version that never deviated from the way it was written. Once I was in the NFL, regardless of who was singing or playing the anthem, I always heard the SC State Marching 101 band's version in my mind. That anthem the way I remembered its being played by SC State always signaled to me, "Game time!"

No band like State's was playing; it was Neil Diamond singing. I'd loved several of his songs, but with the anthem I reflected back to Orangeburg on a nice fall Saturday afternoon to really get into that playing mode I wanted to be in. Once Diamond finished, I got another thrill, a flyover by the Blue Angels. I was already pumped with the crowds in the stands. Then the flyover by those jets—damn, what could be better than that?

I always spoke with Parcells prior to going out to the center of the field for the coin toss. I could see in his eyes that he was also pumped and ready for the most important game of his life. We players were all getting ready in our own way, hitting each other's shoulder pads and slapping helmets. Coaches ready themselves once they are on the sideline by making sure they have all of their notes and reminders and that they are all strapped up with their headsets to communicate with one another and the coaching booth upstairs. Parcells told me that if we won the toss, then we wanted to receive the ball, which I knew was a given. He then said, "Go ahead!" I thought, "By myself? What in the fuck is he talking about?" Normally George Martin, Phil Simms, or another appointed captain of the week might go out with me for the coin toss, but I had never thought that in a game of this stature I would be the lone captain representing my team. I didn't argue with him and assumed my position on the sideline with the officials waiting to escort me out to the center of the field.

As I began to walk, I saw the Broncos captains walking from their sideline. I thought they would be sending two or three players, but instead I saw seven or eight guys walking toward me. For a moment it looked like one of those westerns where the lone hero gunslinger is about to take on a whole gang.

I got the feeling that Parcells wanted this image of one man taking on a gang. On that short walk to the center of the field, I also thought about how I was the lone guy chosen to represent the other fifty-two players and the entire Giants organization. My heart was heavy but I beamed with pride in that role as leader. It was the most awesome feeling I had ever felt on any football field. In later years Giants fans told me how "cool" that was to see either in person or on television. Some have also told me that when they saw me walk out against seven Broncos players, they knew it was over.

At center field one of my favorite officials, Jerry Markbreit, told the captains to shake hands and introduce ourselves, but, hell, I knew all of those guys, such as John Elway, Tom Jackson, and Karl Mecklenberg. Then he introduced Willie Davis, the former Green Bay Packers great that I'd admired as a young kid when watching the early Super Bowls. Willie was one of the players whom I tried to emulate as a kid, wearing his number 87 on my T-shirt. Willie was the honorary captain and did the ceremonial coin toss. By this time I was on such a high that I could hardly stand myself. Normally, this stuff happens on television and to other people. But this stuff was happening to me at that moment. Never in my wildest dreams as a little black kid growing up in South Carolina could I have imagined being where I was and going through what I was going through for all the world to see.

The teams went on to play the game and the Giants eventually won it 39–20. We got a tremendous effort from our quarterback, Phil Simms, who was named MVP and went to Disney World, as well as George Martin, who sacked Elway in the end zone for a safety to end the first half with us trailing 10–9. My linebacker mates Carl Banks, Gary Reasons, and Lawrence Taylor all had good production in the game, and at the end there was the anticipated Gatorade splash of Parcells and defensive coordinator Bill Belichick.

As the game ended, I got to see what few players could. In the stands I saw fans that lived and died with us as a team, not just that season, but for many, many years. They booed us and sometimes showed their displeasure with our performances on the field and for the outcome of games, but they always hung in there with us. I saw their smiles and watched them celebrate in the stands. I saw the happiness on the faces of coaches who worked their asses off to get the job done. And I could feel the joy of each of my teammates as we walked off the field and entered the locker room. Those guys did it; those guys prepared, took on the challenge as a team, and would not be denied. I had been associated with many players on many teams, but these were the best damn group of guys to work and play with.

I was ecstatic for my partner George Martin. He and I were the ones that most fans felt happiest for as Giants players, and we were the ones that most fans could identify with. We were the lone holdovers from those dark and lean years when the team sucked. The fans knew of the many ups and downs that we'd had to endure as players. This was a time for joy but also a time for tears. Never in my dreams could I have known the feelings I felt immediately after that game. We did it! We were world champions! No fan could really understand the heart and courage George and I had had to muster up. Nor could anyone understand the aches and pains we individually had to endure to get there. Playing in the Super Bowl and winning it all is the culmination of a journey that every player who is dedicated and committed to his team should experience. I was lucky to have had the opportunity to be in that locker room with my guys and my coaches. I wish I could have bottled that time and saved it or at least been able to share it with many others. I've been asked by many what winning the Super Bowl feels like, and I can only say it probably feels the same as walking on the moon for an astronaut. Only those who've experienced those feats can fully understand and appreciate what they feel like. I know for myself words cannot express the euphoria of the accomplishment.

After that game, I pulled one of our owners, Wellington Mara, into the shower to get him wet. We didn't use champagne like baseball or basketball teams did. I don't know if that was because of Mr. Mara's staunch Catholic religion or because of the cost of the stuff, but if we were going to celebrate with anything, it was going to be with a can of ginger ale or Pepsi. Pulling Mr. Mara into the shower was hokey, but I felt it needed to be done, especially for a man who gave a lot but got much of the blame when the team didn't produce for years. My relationship with him wasn't the greatest, but if somebody was going to celebrate with him, I knew it had to be me. Nobody else had the balls to do something to a man so dignified as Wellington Mara. Why not treat him like one of the guys for a moment on a special day?

After the game we partied with our families back at our hotel. The next day, after conducting several national morning-show interviews, I prepared to make another trip to Hawaii for the Pro Bowl. This time I was taking about eight of my teammates with me on what was becoming an annual trip after the football season. The rest of the team and coaching staff went back to New Jersey for a huge public celebration at Giants Stadium.

Several weeks after returning from Hawaii the team made its obligatory trip to the White House to be honored by President Ronald Reagan. When I started playing football, I never thought that I would wind up in the presence of the president of the United States, but there I was, front and center. Standing in the East Wing of the White House, captains George Martin, Phil Simms, and I made a formal jersey presentation to Mr. Reagan on behalf of the team. That was about as nerve-racking as defending an offensive team that's first-and-goal on your 5-yard line, threatening to take the lead. Most of the team and team officials attended the event. But the highlight for me was toward the end of the day when several Secret Service agents came looking for Harry Carson. One of my teammates pointed me out, and the agents told me that the president wanted to speak with me at the end of the event. I was surprised that the president would want to see me before he departed for Camp David for the weekend. My teammates wondered what was up, and I didn't have a clue.

When the event ended, two agents asked me to follow them. For a second I thought perhaps the president wanted to get my input on creating lasting world peace or something like that. Ha-ha. I was taken outside to where my teammates were, but I was positioned about twenty to thirty feet from them. I was facing them with my back to a set of stairs. Then I heard the president and Mrs. Reagan coming down the stairs at my back. Just as I turned to see Mr. Reagan, he hoisted an orange bucket over his head. The president, getting into the whole Gatorade splashing act that represented our season, poured popcorn over my head. When he brought the bucket down, he was laughing and had a big smile. Mrs. Reagan was also getting a big kick out of the gag. I smiled and thought, "Okay, you got me. That was why the president wanted to see me." I looked down and saw the bucket was still half-filled with popcorn and thought, "I should get him back!" For a moment I thought I'd better not, especially when I knew that Secret Service personnel were all around me with big guns under their jackets. Then I thought, "Fuck it. I'm going to do it." So I grabbed the Gatorade bucket from President Reagan and drenched him with popcorn. That got an even bigger laugh from him and Mrs. Reagan, and I didn't get blown away the way I'd feared. That night all the evening television sports programs around the country covered the back-and-forth Gatorade popcorn showers between the president and me. Since then I've realized that I'm the only person (once again) to have had the balls to do something like that to any president.

I remained on a high from the whole Super Bowl experience for a couple of months. I had so many requests to appear here and there for all kinds of reasons. Television and radio interviews, banquets, commercials, you name it, I did it. When things started to calm down for me, I realized that I needed to begin to focus on getting ready for the next season and defending the crown we'd won, but not just yet. The people in my hometown had made preparations to honor me with a Harry Carson Day. I didn't want it because I felt uncomfortable being the center of attention, but my sister Ruth convinced me to allow the many people of Florence to show how proud they were of me and what I had accomplished with the Giants.

When Harry Carson Day came in mid-April, it appeared to be a special event for all involved. Many people who had a long-standing relationship with my family stepped in to help make it a successful and memorable event. I was driven around by limousine, given the key to the city, and had it proclaimed my day by the mayor of Florence. A program was held for the public at Memorial Stadium, where I'd played many of my high school games. Most of the kids and adults wore Harry Carson #53 T-shirts. Many of the folks in attendance were people I knew, but so many others knew me that I didn't know at all. They had seen me on television or read about me in the newspapers and just wanted to come out and say, "Congratulations! We're proud of you!" I was so honored with the outpouring of love from everyone. That so many people would take the time to come see me meant the world to me and made me proud of whatever sacrifices I'd had to make to get to that point. To see the looks on the faces of the kids who had only heard about me from their parents was worth whatever I'd had to go through, both personally and professionally. Those moments on that day once again made me realize that it wasn't about me, it was about them. Later that evening a more formal program honored me. Many of my more immediate family members, friends, close family friends, and others attended that one. One surprise was that George Young, our general manager, who had attended the earlier event, stayed to attend the later event as well. George was in the midst of scouting and getting ready for the upcoming draft, but he stayed and helped many of my hometown people honor me. The whole thing was moving and touching, a tremendous tribute to me, one that I will always remember. George Young and I had been adversaries in contract negotiations, but I genuinely liked the guy and respected him so much more when he stayed.

Several of my teammates wrote books after that Super Bowl win. Jim Burt, Lawrence Taylor, Phil Simms, and Leonard Marshall, among others, put their experiences in print. I'm glad my book, *Point of Attack,* came out before our team played in the Super Bowl. That way my story wasn't in competition with what they had to say in their books. The only other significant thing left to do after winning the Super Bowl was to get our Super Bowl rings. We got ours during a minicamp session at Giants Stadium in late May of 1987. When they were presented to us, we all felt like little kids opening our gifts on Christmas morning. I wasn't a jewelry person, but I knew I was gonna wear the hell out of that ring! It was a symbol of the season in which fifty-three guys suited up, put all of our differences aside, including our egos, and worked our asses off together to achieve that one goal of being the best. From the moment I placed the ring on my finger, I knew it was something special. Much like getting my high school diploma and college degree, I earned it and nobody could take it from me. It dawned on me that I had something that few other people in the world had, an NFL championship ring. Owning one put my teammates and me in a special class of individuals, and the uniqueness is you can't buy your way in, you have to earn it! Bill Gates with his billions of dollars could not go to Tiffany's or Harry Winston to buy one. I had heard players talk about the ring, but not until I got mine did I truly understand what it meant to be able to wear one.

CHAPTER 13

You Know When It's Time to Go!

My plans to start the 1987 season were much like those for any other season except that I knew that I was physically getting older. I did more than my share of conditioning with lots of running and weight lifting. One of the key reasons for our success the last two seasons was that the entire team was in shape, healthy, and ready to go from the first day of training camp. As we reported for training camp and prepared to defend our title, all was well until we received news that our starting tackle, Karl Nelson, had been diagnosed with a form of cancer, hodgkin's lymphoma, and would not be able to play that season. We were conditioned as athletes to not let external factors have a major effect on our play, but I didn't give a shit about his not playing; I was most concerned about Karl's living. I had gone through similar situations with Doug Kotar, John Tuggle, and Dan Lloyd, who all were diagnosed with some form of cancer. Doug and John lost their battles with the disease, but Dan survived. One of our assistant coaches, Bob Ledbetter, tragically passed away in '83 from a stroke, so when I first heard that Karl had been diagnosed, I immediately started to assume the worst. I knew that Karl's life would forever be changed as result of his diagnosis. He was not going to play, but he was going to be around during the periods of treatment he'd have to endure. I also knew that when you go on injured reserve and are not able to participate, people, even your own teammates at times, tend to just tolerate your being there but don't give you a lot of attention because you're not in the mix playing and contributing.

One day as we were getting ready to practice, I noticed that Karl was doing his therapy alone in the training room. Most of the players and the coaches basically ignored Karl. After getting my ankle taped by the trainer, I walked over to him and jokingly told him, "Don't worry, Karl, I'll be your buddy." I did that in a laughing way, but I was serious. I remembered feeling like an outsider when I was injured and couldn't practice or play even though I was the captain of the team. Most fans have no clue that when you are a football player and you're not able to contribute, you feel worthless. I had gone through that experience several times and had seen other guys go through it, so I didn't want Karl to feel alone when he really needed the support of his team. Other guys felt the same way, and while they might not have verbalized it, I knew as a group we were going to have to do whatever we could to support Karl through that period.

Karl's illness hit us right in the face; the reality of life for some of us was that the "game" of football was irrelevant at that time. When it came to living or playing a game, living won hands down. It was not that playing football wasn't important, it was, but our priorities changed to more important things, our teammate! Ultimately, football was just a game!

The business of football entered the picture for us as a team and as a league. When the NFL Players Association and the NFL failed to reach a deal on a new collective bargaining agreement, we as players were faced with a potential strike against the owners and the NFL. With these things on our minds I didn't think we had the same hunger we had the year before. We'd climbed the mountain and gotten to the top and realized that once you're at the top, there's no place to go but down. Winning a championship was a great experience and it took a lot for all the pieces to fall into place, but that year it seemed that we lacked the same spark and drive to get there again.

We started the season on a down note, losing a couple of games before we went on strike. Once we went on strike, the NFL owners continued the season using "replacement players." We called them scabs because they were there to take our jobs and earn a couple of bucks and live the "NFL experience." I could have hated those guys, but if I were in their position, I might have done the same thing. What did disappoint me, though, were those Giants fans who had always proclaimed themselves to be such "loyal and die-hard fans" but crossed the picket lines or bothered to watch such inferior football. Some of those "loyal" fans cursed the regular players for taking away "their game." I heard some of those fans say on sports talk radio that they were pissed, all because the players wanted to make things better for all players by gaining free agency, better pensions, and better health benefits. I got a feeling that these fans thought it was their right to have football every Sunday and that the players shouldn't deny them their pastime. I had gotten that feeling numerous times before, and I felt that some fans thought we were just pieces of meat with no other purpose but to please their desires on Sunday afternoons. I know most fans, especially most Giants fans, are really great. But we could probably never please some hater fans because they'd placed bets on games and we'd failed them at some point. Those fans I always tried to stay clear of.

The strike ended after three or four weeks and we returned for the remainder of the season. We would be unable to defend our title since the season had got off to a bad start and the scabs had failed to win a game. With all that I'd been through on and off the field, I began to think toward the end of the season that it might be a good time for me to move on. I had played for twelve years. When I'd first entered the league, I didn't know if I could make it in the NFL, but I knew I would give it my best shot. I enjoyed playing but didn't necessarily like practice, especially practice sessions on artificial turf. My knees, ankles, and legs were always achy after playing or practicing on artificial turf, and I was beginning to slow down on the field. I could still get the job done when I needed to, but it took more effort than previously.

Every so often when I spoke with Parcells on the field before practice, he would say something that would resonate with me and give me something to think about. We were talking about how a player knows when to hang his cleats up. I remember Bill saying, "You know, Carson . . . if a player is honest with himself, he'll know before anyone else when it's time to go! When he can't quite get to the point of attack like he used to, when he doesn't tackle the running back the way he was able to tackle a year before, or he's not able to get to an area in zone coverage as quickly as he used to, he knows before anyone else that it's time to go. Unfortunately, too many players ignore the signs and try to play much longer than they know they should." I could see things in myself that no one could see. Everyone looked at me as a stud player on the field, but no one knew the pain that I had to deal with at times to stay on the field. I had a bum right shoulder, bad knees, and a bad back, just to name a few ailments, but I pushed myself to compete and stay on the field because I looked at myself as being the leader on defense. The guys on my side of the ball were "my guys," I took pride in that. It was one thing to be a player for the world champion New York Giants; it was another thing to be the leader and the captain of a pretty damn good group of players and a strong, dominant linebacker core.

Those physical ailments were not the only things that I had to contend with. I began to notice that I was having more and more headaches that would come and go for no apparent reason. Along with those headaches I would find myself in blue moods, feeling down or depressed, more. Several of my teammates had observed during my career that I was moody. I usually stayed so busy that I didn't always see it the way they did. My old teammate Gary Jeter jokingly told me that my initials fit me well because I was "hot and cold." I was a little pissed that he would even insinuate something like that. But in time, I noticed that he was right. At times if I was up, I really was up and on. But when I was down, I was really down!

One Monday illustrated for me where I was at the time. We had just won a game the day before and had to come in to lift weights and stretch to get ready for the following week. As I was traveling to the stadium from my home, I had a banging headache and felt blah and down for no apparent reason. When I arrived at the stadium and entered the locker room, most of the guys were talkative and joked around with one another. They were feeling good since they had just won a game. I didn't feel the same and didn't feel like talking to anyone, so I went to the trainers' room to tell trainer Ronnie Barnes that I had a severe headache and was also feeling depressed. He told me to take some Tylenol for the headache, but when I told him of the depression, he looked at me with a puzzled look as if to say, "What can I do about that?" I think he might have thought I wanted to get out of practicing by telling him that. There was nothing that I wanted him to do. All I wanted was to alert him about what I was experiencing. I had been depressed before, but usually the depression occurred during the off-season or away from the stadium. This was one of the few times that I had ever acknowledged to anyone that I was depressed.

I had never then heard of a player being diagnosed or even admitting that he was depressed. Depression was for "sick" people, not for big, strong football players who made hundreds of thousands of dollars. The average person, especially those "fans" I didn't care for, would probably ask, "What in the hell are you depressed about? You've got it made playing a kid's game!" At other points in my career I had even thought that way, and these feelings had led me to keep my depression to myself. I had rarely been in such a low place before, but this time I was in full swing and I felt I needed to get it documented. Whenever I had been like this before, I played upbeat, inspirational music to try to snap me out of it or I'd read one of the many inspirational books I had purchased to find some passage that hit home to make me feel thankful. The key for me in dealing with my little bouts of depression was to be aware of what was happening as it was happening. Sometimes the remedy was to just sit still and be alone or to do something constructive to help me know that *I* controlled whether I was going to be happy.

As the football season ended, I felt as if the entire season were a waste of time. Karl's situation hit home for all of us, but the strike affected all of the teams in the league equally. One of the more valuable lessons I took away from that season was that when you are the champions, there are no "regular" season games for you; everybody plays you as if it's a play-off game. So if you've won a championship and think defending that crown is going to be easy, you'd better fucking think again because everybody, even the lowest teams, will bring their A game when they compete against you. As a team, we had our asses handed to us royally several times that season by teams we were superior to talent-wise, but talent doesn't mean shit if you just show up and aren't ready to play.

By the end of the season, I knew it was about time for me to go. Playing the game was still fun at times, but at other times it became a chore and was more like work. I had to start seriously considering what I was going to do once I stopped playing football. I knew I didn't want to coach. That decision was made when I casually asked two of our defensive coaches, Romeo Crennel and Lenny Fontes, when they started their workday. They told me it was usually around 7:00 a.m. I thought, "Damn, that sure is early," but then I asked when they left to go home, and they both told me that they left at nine or ten at night. I wondered aloud, "Well, damn, when do you get to see your children?" They said that being away from their families was one of the toughest parts of coaching. They told me that they didn't get to see their children until Saturday afternoons when we had a home game. Those thoughts, along with the common knowledge that coaches are hired to be fired or that they had to constantly move to advance to a higher position, sort of sealed the deal for me. I had two kids, Aja and Donald, whom I wanted to be able to spend quality time with. I knew I had to come up with some kind of transition plan for what to do with the next phase of my life.

Ironically, during my off-season I received a letter from a broadcasting agent who suggested that if I was interested in doing television, some projects might be available to me. I was impressed that someone would reach out to me with such an offer. It also made me realize that others were thinking about my leaving the game. I eventually contacted the agent, Michael Glantz of International Management Group, and he referred me to CBS Sports for a possible audition to cover NFL games. I had already been doing some coverage of the team with the local WCBS affiliate that season, but this opportunity was more than a two-minute commentary during the sports report once a week.

When I eventually auditioned with CBS, the results were less than spectacular. The decision makers at CBS didn't think I was at a point where I could unseat any of their analysts. The situation was interesting but humbling because for the first time in a long time I failed on a personal level. One problem I had during the audition was watching actual game footage and providing analysis. I found it difficult to translate what I saw with my eyes into words. When I was on the football field or in defensive meetings, I could do so with no problems, but being outside my comfort zone in a cold, generic studio did a number on me. Oh, well, while some people thought I might retire right then and there after finally winning a championship, I knew I wanted to leave the game on my own terms and not because of an opportunity.

During that off-season my right knee had been aching quite a bit. I think it was a result of the constant pounding in the trenches during games and sometimes unnecessarily practicing on the artificial surface at Giants Stadium. After complaining several times and then talking with the Giants medical staff, I opted to have the knee cleaned out. The belief was that cartilage particles were floating around in the knee irritating it and causing the knee to become tender and sore after workouts. After Dr. Warren performed the surgery, he told me that I had little cartilage left in my knee. From that point on, any pounding on that knee would be bone-on-bone without much of a cushion. I already knew what playing without a posterior deltoid muscle in my right shoulder was all about. I had pretty good range of motion in the shoulder, but no muscle there to absorb blows. I had to wear a hard-shell cover with cushion around it to protect from being hit on the bones. I knew what playing with mangled fingers was about, too. I took what Dr. Warren told me as yet another inconvenience I would have to adjust to.

In June 1988, prior to that season, I was dealing with several personal issues. Most important, I was getting married later in the month. But before that, I felt I needed to do something on a smaller scale. I contacted our general manager, George Young, and invited him to have lunch at the Sheraton Hotel in Hasbrouck Heights, New Jersey. I think George was taken aback that I would even invite him to lunch, but he accepted. When George and I met, I thanked him for joining me, then said, "George, I have two things I want to say before we eat. First, this is going to be my last year as a player, and second, I want more money!" George looked at me calmly through his thick bifocals and said, "Okay and no!" I formally announced my intentions to retire to George before anyone else. I anticipated his response to my retiring, but asking for a few more bucks? What harm could it do? I accepted his refusal and knew that the only thing I could do was move forward.

I had done my share of bitching and complaining about not being paid what I thought I was worth, but nobody forced me to sign any contracts, and when I signed my last contract, it was a good deal. Unfortunately once a deal is signed, it becomes obsolete as the next quality player in the same position will surpass that. I was scheduled to make $550,000 that year along with some incentives that could push my salary a little higher. I would never again be in a position to gripe about dollars with George, so at least I wasn't going to have to concern myself with that again.

I'd considered retiring on my own terms for several years. Every year I saw players unceremoniously shown the door, leaving the game with all their possessions in a garbage bag. I certainly did not want that to be the way I left football. When I looked at my career, I didn't think I had anything else to play for. I had my championship ring. I had been captain for many years and had played in nine Pro Bowls in twelve seasons. Money was the only reason I had to continue to play, and that didn't interest me. I sensed that both Pepper Johnson and Gary Reasons, the other inside linebackers, were growing impatient with my sticking around. I knew they respected me as a player and as a leader, but like any players in their position, they wondered when they would get their turn to play regularly. I would also meet people in everyday life who would ask over and over, "So, Harry, how much longer are you going to play?" Whenever I heard that question, I knew it was not being asked in a mean-spirited way to imply that I could no longer play; it was often asked of me just to make conversation. It was another of those little annoyances that would get under my skin and bug the hell out of me. As long as I allowed myself to be accessible to fans and the media, I knew I would continue to get questions like that, so I would just have to deal with it until I went public with my intention to retire at the end of the season.

After getting married in June and spending some quality time on my honeymoon with my wife, Shari, I had to prepare for what I knew would be my last year playing if I was lucky enough to survive training camp. I say "survive training camp" because I never knew from year to year what to expect in training camp. If a player pulls a hamstring, tears a muscle, or sustains any other injury that prohibits him from practicing, it can open the door for others to show the coaches that they can do the job for less money. When I arrived at our new training facility at Fairleigh Dickinson University in Madison, New

Jersey, I had to make a quick adjustment to the new surroundings. I had grown so accustomed to training at Pace University in Pleasantville, New York. Not only did I have to get ready for FDU, but I also needed to get ready for some new players who were coming on board as a result of our lousy previous season. I was still the starting weak inside linebacker, but I could just sense that Pepper Johnson was getting impatient. I also thought the coaches were finally ready to infuse some youth into the defense. I continued to elevate my game practice after practice, whether it was on hot, muggy days in late July and in August or on those pleasant days that we didn't see a lot of at that time of year. I worked hard to maintain my competitive edge on the field, but I knew my body was getting tired. With every practice and with every drill, I knew it was going to be the last time in my life doing those things. That knowledge made those experiences more tolerable and even made them more fun than they ever were in previous training camps.

Our last game in the exhibition schedule was against the Cleveland Browns, and we lost. After the game we had a few days off until we had to report back to practice. I traveled to my home in South Carolina to spend a couple of days with my family while the coaches trimmed the roster and prepared for the opener against the Washington Redskins. While I was in Carolina, I received a call at my home from Bill Parcells. Parcells didn't reach me initially, but he left a message with my sister. When she told me that Bill had called, I thought it couldn't be good news. The end of the exhibition season is when coaches have to cut down their rosters. For a moment I thought, "Well, it's finally my time to be either traded or released by the organization." I began to question my decision to tell George Young that I was retiring after the season. I thought perhaps the coaches were looking to preempt my decision and make a statement to the team by getting rid of me.

When Parcells finally called again and we to connected, I braced myself for the news. But there was no way I could have prepared myself for what he told me. Right off the bat Bill said, "I'm very disappointed in you, Carson." That statement didn't sound like what you'd imagine a coach would say when he wants to make a move, especially with an older veteran player. I expected to hear something like "Sorry, but we're going in a different direction." I asked, "Bill, what are you talking about? What do you mean I've disappointed you?" Parcells told me that I tested "dirty" in a recent random drug test during training camp. He said that I'd had cocaine in my system. I let out a hearty laugh thinking that he was pulling a bad joke on me. After all, Bill and I had a pretty good relationship because he was my position coach before he became the Giants head coach. After a minute and not detecting a change in his tone, I realized that Bill wasn't joking; he was serious. During our brief conversation I rode an emotional roller coaster in only a minute. I went from accepting a possible release from the team to feeling as if I had been hit in the gut with a baseball bat with accusations of involvement with drugs. No words can adequately express how hurt I was. Parcells told me to see our trainer Ronnie Barnes when I returned to practice and that I would have to submit to NFL drug monitoring for the season.

I could have been called many things, but a drug abuser was not one of them. Before I got married, I screwed around . . . a lot! Many of my teammates and close friends knew that, but no one could ever say that I smoked anything, drank alcohol, or even dabbled with any kind of drugs. I steered clear of those things. I took pride in being an athlete and not just another dope-addicted football player. I knew that I may at times have been so overwhelmed that I would forget some minor things such as birthdays, paying a credit card bill on time, or picking up everything I wanted at the grocery store, but I sure wasn't that forgetful about using drugs.

When I returned to New York, I was incensed, pissed, and seething but couldn't say a word of what I was going through to anyone, not to my family, certainly not to any of my teammates, and not even to my wife. My agent, Craig Kelly, traveled to New York to hold a meeting with me and several other attorneys to explore my options. Ultimately, I had no options and no recourse except to subject myself to testing by the NFL. Any failure to go along with the monitoring would basically be an admission of guilt and would be made public to the media. After the meeting I arrived at the stadium to take part in practice. Because I was late getting on the field, many of my teammates and some of the Giants beat writers thought I was staging a one-day protest for a new contract. I wish they had been right about that, but it wasn't the case. At this same time, my teammate Lawrence Taylor also tested positive for cocaine. Because this was his second offense, he was suspended for four games by the NFL. Most of the media attention was on Lawrence, and no one except the Giants medical staff and Parcells knew that I was also implicated in drug use. Because of Lawrence's situation, I knew that anyone who didn't know me and became aware of the drug allegations against me would most likely think that I was guilty. Call it guilt by association; many fans thought that all players were alike anyway. To be more direct, because Lawrence and I were black pro football players, I'm sure some would have said, "They're all alike." That we were both linebackers and he and I had been suite mates during training camp at FDU was perhaps the biggest reason for people to assume I was guilty.

My only option was to quietly subject myself to testing two to three times a week by the NFL. A failure to do so would basically be an acknowledgment of guilt. I had always been one of those holier-than-thou, goody-two-shoes players when it came to illegal drug use and would say shit like "You shouldn't have a problem with random testing if you don't have anything to hide." The situation I was in was pure bullshit! For the first time I realized how so many innocent people could falsely be accused of something and then jailed or even executed. I didn't understand why this was happening to me, but I did know I could not trust others, especially anyone within the New York Giants organization.

I decided to go to my personal physician, explain what was going on, and have myself monitored. If my situation became publicly known, I didn't want it to be my word against that of the Giants and the NFL without anything to back me up. That personal monitoring lasted for a couple of weeks and never once showed anything in my system. I've always assumed that when we were tested in training camp, my urine specimen was accidentally switched with someone else's. A situation like that should never happen to anyone, but it happened to me!

It was not a rosy picture. I was starting my last season playing in the NFL with a huge dark cloud hanging over my head. I had been a good and loyal soldier disregarding hurts and pain to lay my body on the line for my team. I felt betrayed by someone, I just didn't know whom. When Ronnie instructed me on how the testing would take place, even at the age of thirty-four I felt like a kid being unfairly punished. No one except Ronnie and the doctors were to know what player or players were being monitored for drugs. I was instructed to go to a vacant locker room down the tunnel from where the Giants locker room was to meet a man the NFL employed to take urine samples from players. The samples would then be submitted to a lab, tested, and the results shared between the NFL and the team.

It's hard for me to find words to describe how I felt the first time I walked into that room and told the man who did the monitoring my name. He checked my name off his list, wrote my name down on a strip of tape to act as a label, handed me a small bottle, then instructed me to urinate in that bottle. I had been in uncomfortable situations before, but never to this extent. I was expected to piss in a bottle while this person, who, incidentally, was white, watched me to be completely sure it was my urine. Apparently, other players around the league had found ways to trick the monitors by using other people's urine that they hid on themselves. Those individuals definitely had drug issues. I had nothing to hide. My problem was that, because the NFL said I tested positive, Parcells, the team doctors, and the Giants believed them. As I urinated in that bottle, I felt as low as I have ever felt as a human being. As a black man, that was the most degrading thing I ever had to do. To have a white person watch me do what is one of the most personal and private things anyone does took my inner spirit back to my forefathers being sold, beaten, and lynched during slavery. To me this was no different from being a slave.

When I finished and handed the man the bottle, he placed a cap on it, then put the tape with my name over the cap to label it as my specimen. While he did that, I could clearly see his list of players to be tested. What was supposed to be confidential wasn't. If I could see the names of those other players, I'm sure they could see my name when they came in. But I wasn't just "another player," I was the captain, their captain. I was their leader. I was hurt, embarrassed, and in the most painful period I could remember being in. If I had been guilty of using drugs, it would have been a different story. I would have owned up to it, but I found myself in a place that I never thought I could ever be. Me? Drugs? No fucking way! I stayed away from beer and alcohol in high school.

I stayed away from grass, wine, and beer in college and definitely wasn't about to go down those roads as my career was winding down in the NFL.

I was always learning as a football player from my experiences on and off the field. I took pride in learning lessons from the mistakes others made. My father was one of my true role models, although he never knew how much of an impact he had on my life. My dad drank a lot, as did many of his friends. While I only saw him drunk two or three times, I swore I never wanted to be like him. In spite of how he at times neglected our family, I loved him, but I didn't want to inherit actions such as his drinking.

I also learned from Lawrence Taylor's experiences. When Lawrence arrived from the University of North Carolina, I saw him as one of the most talented athletes I had ever seen. He was, in my opinion, a good country kid from Williamsburg, Virginia. I thought he was very much about home and family, but as the years went by and his fame and notoriety grew, I began to see a different person. Lawrence wrestled with some issues. Most of the team knew something was going on with him, but for the most part everyone kept his mouth shut. I had the locker next to his, but we never talked about his problems. I just knew that he wrestled with those issues occasionally. I asked myself why Lawrence, in all his greatness—who could will himself to do whatever he wanted on the football field—couldn't will himself off the substances he was having problems with. I wasn't the smartest person in the world, but I knew myself well enough to know that if I tried something one time and I liked it, I was going to try it again and again. So, I realized it was better for me to adopt the attitude of "You can't miss what you've never had." When it came to drugs and alcohol, everyone who knows me knew where I stood. They also knew that I was just like almost every other man: before I married, I was more into women than getting high on something!

Pissing in a bottle in front of that man was the ultimate humiliation. If I had allowed it to happen, it could easily have stripped me of my dignity. As the season progressed, the testing went from three times a week to twice a week to once a week. Eventually I had to share this with my wife. She found it hard to believe that the team would even suspect me of using drugs. While I didn't talk about the subject, one of my doctors approached me with it. Russ

Warren thought there had to have been a mistake with the initial result and suggested my original specimen be retested by the league. Unfortunately, by that time my specimen had been discarded by the testing laboratory.

Knowing that Dr. Warren believed in my innocence gave me a reason not to think that the entire organization had conspired to tarnish me. In my meeting with my team of attorneys, it was suggested that the team might have wanted to tarnish me because they thought that after I retired from football, I would go into broadcasting and trash the team because of the always ongoing contract disputes between the Giants and me. One of my attorneys felt that the team could always hold the "drug rap" over my head as a hammer should if I ever get out of line as a broadcaster. I found it hard to believe that the team would do that, but then again, you never know. I had heard stories of other players ending their relationship with their club on not so friendly terms, so this could have been someone in the organization's idea of sending me a message.

As bad as it was enduring those drug allegations for an entire season, I did get to play some football. Several things stand out from that last season in the league. In the third game of the season, in my last trip to Texas Stadium to play against the Dallas Cowboys, we were in the lead but the Cowboys were threatening another of their infamous comebacks. During my career, the Cowboys, with players such as Roger Staubach, whom I competed against in my first year, had proven they were able to come back in the closing minutes of games. It was not going to happen in my last game at Texas Stadium. With the Cowboys threatening to score and go ahead, I intercepted a pass inside our 5-yard line and returned it sixty-five yards to help seal our second victory. That play was another reason why I knew it was time to go because I was chased down from behind by a wide receiver, which should never have happened. It was all I could do to lumber those sixty-five yards, but I should have been able to get at least another twenty yards before being caught.

Another lasting memory was in my final home game against the Cowboys at Giants Stadium. Eighty thousand people in the stands screaming for the Giants to kick the Cowboys' asses. In that game, I came to terms with leaving football. In the fourth quarter, while our offense was on the field, I was on the sideline and took a moment to look into the stands at the crowds of Giants fans. I took it all in: the sights, the sounds, and the reality of being there at that moment. I remember thinking that experience would never happen again for me after that year. I had been a professional football player for almost thirteen seasons, and I had never really thought about the awesomeness of it all until then. I think most players miss the game because while they're playing, they never stop to take in the experience. At that moment, during the biggest Giants game of the season, I captured that experience and put it right next to my heart. That way it can never be taken from me.

The best football highlight of my last season was something that didn't happen on the field. Only my coaches and teammates know about it. During the middle of the season we were playing the Detroit Lions at Giants Stadium. The Lions weren't that good at that time, and we played (as we tended to do) down to the level of the competition. Detroit had a 10–9 lead on us as the first half ended. As we were walking in for halftime, the Giants fans booed us. I was embarrassed, and hearing those boos took me back to those early years I spent with the team. Once we got to the locker room, players went to the restroom, to see the trainers, or did whatever they needed to do at their lockers before going into our halftime adjustments meeting. We then gathered in our meeting rooms, which were separated by partitions or movable walls. I sat in my chair in the front of the room, waiting as our defensive coordinator, Bill Belichick, conferred with our other defensive coaches, Romeo Crennel, Lenny Fontes, and Lamar Leachman before addressing the defensive unit.

I always tried to keep my poise in meetings, but this time I lost it. I began to tell my teammates that I had been in that place before as a player and it wasn't a good place to be, especially after winning a Super Bowl two years earlier. I began to yell at the top of my lungs that we were a better team than we showed in the first half. Then I got grungy with them by challenging their manhood and their playing abilities. I began using a lot of four-letter words, but the floor was clearly mine. No one said a word and no one made a move while I had the floor, yelling and foaming at the mouth. I told my guys that if they didn't want to play, then they should "stay the fuck in the locker room!" I was going to go back out with or without them and kick ass! I didn't realize that I was keeping the coaches from making their adjustments for the second half. By the time I finished, Belichick said there was no need to make any adjustments, it was about playing the way we as a team were capable of playing. While I thought I was preaching to my defensive unit, apparently the offense on the other side of the partition got the same message as well, and they didn't make any adjustments either. We went back out onto the field and beat the Lions 30–10.

I was proud of how my guys responded to the challenge I presented to them. I had always known in playing football that different things motivate different people in different ways. When it comes to the male athlete, challenging his manhood or his ability does it almost every time. That situation was also important to me because, as a result of their response, I knew their respect for me was still intact. During the season so many things were going on and I didn't know who exactly knew what about my being monitored. As much as I hated that "situation," I still enjoyed going to battle on Sunday afternoons with the guys.

As the season progressed, we were in position to possibly make the playoffs if we could win a few games down the stretch. We went to Phoenix in mid-November to play against the Cardinals. It was that team's first year playing in the desert, having moved from St. Louis in the off-season. Prior to the season the greatest concern about playing there was the heat. Because it was November, the weather wasn't that great of a challenge for us. Unfortunately, in that game I experienced problems with my right knee again. It didn't hurt, but for some reason when I was on the ground after making a tackle, I had problems getting up. When I went to the sidelines and had my knee examined by the doctors, I was told that the knee was structurally sound but that I probably had some loose tissue getting caught in the joint that created the problem. Dr. Warren told me that it was up to me whether I had it removed. I wanted to think about it since I was hoping the knee would eventually heal. During the week it didn't get better, so I opted to have the surgery. I asked Dr. Warren how long it would be before I could play again. He told me that it was up to me and my pain threshold. He wouldn't have to do any major work, so I would have to be more concerned about the small incisions made during surgery than removal of the loose tissue.

I checked into the Hospital for Special Surgery thinking that I could come out after the surgery and play a couple of days later. When the surgery was over and I was out of recovery, I was immediately sent to the rehabilitation area to work on my flexibility. The effects of the anesthesia were still in my system and I was feeling a bit groggy, but I did everything the physical therapist asked me to do in the hope of getting back on the field as soon as possible. I went home that evening and went to Giants Stadium early the next morning to get treatment and therapy. While I was riding the stationary bike and watching the local sports on television, I heard my name mentioned. The Giants had placed me on the injured reserve list. I thought, "What the fuck?" Nobody told me that I had been placed on IR! Being placed on injured reserved meant I would have to miss the next four games, including my last home game. Once again, I felt as if a dagger were being thrust into my heart. I felt betrayed because I had spoken with Parcells prior to the surgery. It was understood that if the procedure could be done through the scope, I would not miss any playing time, but if Dr. Warren had to actually cut me and had to go into the knee, I would have to sit out for a few weeks. When I awoke from surgery, the number one thing on my mind was getting back on the field. I'd had more than my share of disappointments that season, and it seemed that this was yet another one, except I thought this was no mistake, it was intentional.

Prior to the first game I was missing, which was against the Philadelphia Eagles, I arrived at the stadium to get my rehab. When I walked into the locker room, I once again felt insignificant since I was on injured reserve. Everyone was getting dressed to go out and stretch while I got my physical therapy. I could sense that things were not right in the air. Perhaps it was my own bitterness for having been placed on IR, but as I was standing in the tunnel prior to the game, I remember my partner George Martin stopping to tell me something before going out on the field. As I looked into George's eyes, I could sense a pain that he did not want to share with me. George never wanted to get caught up in any kind of drama. After all, he had a game to play. But he also felt I needed to know what was going on in the locker room. Simply, he said our trainer John Dziegel wanted me to "watch my back" because he was concerned the Giants might try to fuck me before I had an opportunity to fuck them! Initially I didn't know what this whole thing was about. Why would I need to guard my back now? I was the captain; I prided myself on giving my all on the football field and in the locker room. Why in my final year when I should have felt positive about ending my career did I feel like an outcast?

I kept George's comment to myself, but internally I began to fume. Like a computer in search mode, I began to replay in my mind who and why anyone would have an issue with me, especially with my pending exit from football. As I began to mentally scroll through my history with the team, I began to understand why I needed to be "kept in check" or "fucked" before I could fuck the Giants organization. From the time I entered the league, I never felt that great about my contracts with the team. After my rookie season ended, I remember our then general manager, Andy Robustelli, wanting to make changes in my deal, but it never happened. I remembered being so unhappy later with my contract that I gave George Young a tube of Vaseline, telling him that if the team was going to screw me contractually, I didn't want it to hurt too badly. I liked George personally, but I remembered how he seemed embarrassed by the whole thing, telling me, "I know how you might feel and I wish I could do something, but my hands are tied." Gathering these separate incidences, along with a final comment shared with me by a female acquaintance, gave me all of the information I needed to come to some kind of conclusion.

As a quartet of linebackers, Brad, Brian, Lawrence, and I did some work with a marketing guy named Alan Deitz in the early eighties in regard to the Crunch Bunch theme. Alan had an attractive female assistant named Marie, who worked with us on the project. Quite by accident while in Hawaii for a Pro Bowl perhaps in 1981 or 1983, I ran into Marie on the beach with our co-owner at the time Tim Mara. At the time I didn't see Marie's being with Tim as anything scandalous. He was single, she was single, and with the exception of the twenty-to-thirty-plus year age difference, it didn't bother me. That chance encounter meant nothing to me until I eventually saw her when we were both back in New Jersey. Marie shared with me parts of a conversation she had had with Tim after our brief meeting on the beach. She told me that my name came up in their conversation later. Marie knew I had issues with the team regarding my contract. She told me that Tim said there was no reason to pay me more because "they expected with the way you played you would eventually get hurt and not be able to play." I did not solicit this information from Marie. She felt it was something I needed to know and be aware of with Tim.

What most fans did not know about the Giants organization at that time was that although the team was owned by the Mara family, 50 percent of the team was owned by Wellington Mara's side of the family, and 50 percent by Tim Mara's side. I was not privy to everything that transpired within the front office, but I could sense distrust on both sides. Any decision that needed to be made had to be approved by *both* sides of the family.

The more I thought about it, the more it made sense to me. Most players respected and adored Wellington Mara. To that point, I could not say anything negative about the man. Conversely, I had never heard any player say anything even remotely complimentary about Tim Mara or his side of the family. I could not definitely point to any one individual who could have been pulling the strings, but I feel that Tim Mara in all probability had something to do with the fucking I was getting.

The team lost to the Eagles in overtime. The next week the Giants played against the Saints in New Orleans. The game was played around my birthday in November. To celebrate, my wife and I spent time in the city enjoying dinner and getting away from football. That was a significant weekend for me because while the Giants played without me, I went on with my life without the team. I did not miss football or the team as I thought I might have. That weekend without football was to be a preview of my life after the game. As much as I had enjoyed playing football and thought I had paid my dues being on some really shitty teams, I felt I was being unceremoniously dumped by the team. I went through my rehabilitation period without complaining much. I sat out the four games that I needed to sit out as a result of being on the injured reserve list. The last of the four games was our final home game, against the Kansas City Chiefs. At that game George Martin and I were introduced to the Giants fans and recognized for having played our last home game at Giants Stadium. George was in his uniform and I was in my jeans and my game jersey. I was appreciative of the recognition, but no one could feel the deep hurt I felt at that time. I wasn't supposed to go out like this, but after playing thirteen seasons

I still considered myself the exception rather than the rule because few play-ers had the opportunity to call their own shots and leave when they wanted to leave. Most players are shown the door or are injured in one season and can-not make the club the next. In many ways I was lucky, even with the bitter-ness I carried with me.

Fortunately, I had one last game I could play after coming off the injured reserve list. The Giants were to play the New York Jets at Giants Stadium, but it was a Jets home game. I wondered if I still had a starting position on the defense or if I had to work my way back to the starting rotation to play in my last game. On our first day of practice for the Jets, I was dressed in my practice gear. After our warm-ups, stretching, and agility drills, I waited to see if I was going to be a starter or on the second-team defense. When we began to run plays for the defense, Belichick called my name and told me to get in at signal caller. I was relieved because I didn't want to have to go through one last indignity before calling it quits. Lawrence Taylor had been playing inside linebacker for several games while I was out, and he did a great job, but it felt good to be back in my old spot, and I'm sure Lawrence felt the same about going back to his outside linebacker position.

With a record of 10–5 we still had a chance to make the play-offs if we beat the Jets. The Giants had won the last three games before that Jets game. We were accustomed to playing against the Jets every year during the exhibi-tion season, but we rarely played them during the season, and we had never played them with a potential play-off spot on the line. Three things stand out in my mind about that game. First, because we were the visiting team, our sideline was on the opposite side of the field from what we would normally be on. Second, the offense was introduced prior to the game. That eliminated any thought of my being introduced one last time at Giants Stadium. And finally, our team must have been overconfident because we struggled against the Jets. The Jets played as if they were looking to go the play-offs. They won the game in the final seconds, knocking us out of contention for the play-offs.

When the gun sounded to end the game, I walked off the field with mixed emotions. I felt bad that we lost and the season was over for the guys. On the other hand, I was as happy as a pig in shit that the game was over, the season was over, and my career was over. As I exited the field and began to unbuckle my shoulder pads for the last time, I felt like a marathoner who had just given my all in a race that lasted thirteen years with the last mile being the worst part. No one could have known the happiness I felt deep inside. It seemed that the weight of the world was finally lifted off me. No more sprints, no more having to lift weights unless I wanted to lift, and, as simple as it might sound, no more having coaches barge into my room the night before games to see if I was there after curfew. At that point I was a thirty-five-year-old grown-ass man who had children of his own. For me to act as a man and play a man's game and then be treated as a child was beneath me. All of those things paled in comparison to my being subjected to the nightmare I found myself in that season. I felt a relief that I never thought I would feel when it came time to leave football. I thought I would feel sad walking off the field for the last time and hanging up my shoulder pads and helmet to be worn no more. I recognized that a large and important part of my life was over, but most important for me, pissing in the cup week after week to prove my innocence was over.

After that game my wife and I had dinner at one of my favorite restaurants. Even though we'd lost the game and my career was over, I was happy to bid it good-bye. I never thought I would play for thirteen years, but just as I knew when I was drafted, for every beginning there is an end. The dinner was a celebration of my career, but it was also about putting my final year behind me; it was my way of turning the page to a new chapter of my life.

CHAPTER 14

After the Cheering Stops

At the start of this book I noted that every player's football experience has a unique beginning. Likewise, in leaving the game, every player's ending is different after the cheering stops.

With my football career firmly behind me (or so I thought), I looked forward to the unknown of my future. I left the game when I wanted to leave. It was important not to be shown the door like so many other players or to overstay my welcome like a relative who doesn't know when it is time to leave. You can call it having a degree of integrity as an athlete, but from what I saw with other players, that exit was difficult for most, especially if they were not able to attain their individual goals such as winning a Super Bowl or making the Pro Bowl. Strange, but I never loved the game like so many other guys. I liked it and wanted to give my best in playing it. But love was a bit too much to say. It was a relief to be out of the game and actively away from the game as a player. It was also a relief not to be in a football mode either thinking about the game or training for the game.

In mid-February just two months after the season ended, I received a call from my former position coach, Bill Belichick. I was a little surprised—why would he be calling me? After a bit of small talk he said, "We're putting you on the list to become a Plan B free agent." Plan B free agent? What in the hell was that? Apparently, it was a new concept in the league to protect a certain number of players while giving others an opportunity to be exposed as free agents and be signed by other teams. When he told me I was going on the list, it just went right over my head because the NFL was going to stay in my rearview mirror.

A couple of days later I received a phone call from my old coach John McVay, who was an executive in the San Francisco 49ers organization. I had always liked and respected John personally and as a head coach and was pleased to hear from him. I always thought John was a decent guy who was done in by the Fumble in 1978. But why was John calling me just out of the blue? First Belichick and then McVay, something was up! Because I was listed as a free agent available to be signed by any team, John was reaching out to see if I was interested in coming back to play. The 49ers needed a run-stopping guy in the middle to bolster their defense. John wanted to know what I was paid my last season. He said whatever it was, the 49ers were willing to offer a 50 percent raise. I was surprised by the call and very surprised by the offer. I told John I was recently married and needed a few days to digest everything. He understood and agreed to speak with me again soon.

Over the next few days I spoke with my attorney and agent, Craig Kelly, who told me that three other teams (Denver, Miami, and Washington) had inquired about my availability and interest in playing again. I was surprised by the interest from San Francisco and the other teams because I thought I had made it clear that I was done, but those teams wanted to know if I was done for good! The teams that had contacted Craig never made the offer that McVay made to me, they just inquired. I felt flattered by the attention and happy to know that some teams still wanted me even after a long career with the Giants.

Eventually John and I did reconnect and we talked again about the offer, which was generous and almost too good to pass up. I shared with John that as much as I appreciated the interest and the offer, I was unwilling to uproot my family and move clear across the country. At any other time I would have given serious consideration to taking the money and continuing my career. Hell, all I had to do was stop the run on first down and on grass. I could probably have played for another five years if I really wanted to in that scenario. Players from some of those black universities such as Jackie Slater were built to play for an extended time. The San Francisco situation could have been a sweet deal for me, but I played my thirteen seasons with the Giants and wanted to be remembered as a Giant. Physically I could have played, but mentally and emotionally I just wanted to move on with my life. When I spoke with John, he understood my position and respected it, but his job was to look for talent regardless of the circumstances. Before long I learned that the 49ers had named Matt Millen as their free agent addition to their linebacker corp.

I think Matt and other middle/inside linebackers during that time were pissed with me because they didn't think I fought hard enough to get more money from the Giants. I say this because in my last couple of years with the Giants, I was considered by many to be the top inside linebacker in the NFL. The problem for other inside linebackers was that if they wanted their contracts renegotiated or restructured, most general managers would use the line "Well, we can't pay you more than Harry Carson. He's the top guy in the league and he's making $550,000." As a fellow linebacker I was happy for Matt, but I was also happy that I chose what I knew was the best thing for me since it was never about the money.

For the first time in thirteen years there were many firsts; most notably it was my first time not going to a minicamp to get ready for another football season. The Giants always held their major minicamp with all the rookies and veterans around Memorial Day. I was aware that the team was holding camp at Giants Stadium, but I had no interest in attending, not even as a spectator. I felt that I was able to make a clean break from the game and not be one of those guys who could not let it go. Instead, it seemed as if the game would not let me go. First I got the call from Belichick, then the call from John McVay, but the next call really surprised me.

Right after the Giants minicamp I received a call from Bill Parcells. Could it be that they had finally found the mistake in the urine testing and he was calling to offer his apologies? Or would it be like Bill Belichick's call to tell me that the team was putting me on yet another list? It started much the same way as Belichick's call with some small talk like "Hey, pal, how you doing?

Blah, blah, blah . . . ," and then I got "I need you back!" What? You need me back? Apparently Parcells thought losing George Martin and me at the same time was a bit too much of a loss of leadership for the team to overcome. I know that George had been talked out of retiring a couple of times by the team and by Parcells. This was definitely a new experience for me, and I almost couldn't fathom it. I could understand Bill's position because he did rely on his veterans quite a bit to manage the team internally and exert leadership in the locker room, especially with younger players. Bill told me that he could go to Tim Mara to make the deal happen dollar-wise. As much as I then hated the Giants for the pissing-in-the-bottle thing, they were the only team that I would even consider coming out of retirement to play for. But once again, I had to think long and hard about that decision. I also knew that I had to talk the situation over with my wife. Parcells was willing to wait, but I knew he was not going to wait for long.

When I broached the subject with Shari, she was floored! That I would even entertain the thought of playing for Parcells and the Giants again was insulting to her. When I told her of the offer, she immediately and without any hesitation said, "Fuck Parcells! Fuck the Giants!" (Wow, tell me how you really feel!) I'd felt a little weak and thought about caving in when Parcells called, but in no fucking way was she going to back me on this. She was the only person who knew of the indignity I went through my final year as a New York Giants player.

When I eventually spoke again with Bill, I told him that I appreciated the offer but I was going to stay retired. I knew my teammates and wondered why Bill felt there would be a leadership void. I knew Carl Banks was capable of being a strong leader for the defense, as well as Pepper Johnson. While they were younger players, I knew George and I left the team in a good place and had mentored these guys to take up the batons that we'd left behind. I didn't want to come back and usurp Pepper's or Carl's leadership role. At times in my past I was impulsive and acted before thoroughly thinking a situation through. This was not one of those times. I'd thought long and hard about turning the page on football. I knew my time had passed and I accepted it. There was no reason to wonder what it would be like going back. Even though the carrot was dangled, I didn't bite. My football career was officially a wrap!

I did not know any other player who would not have jumped at the opportunity to go back to his old team to play, especially if the team asked as Parcells had. All players think they can play forever, but for those who get that knock at the door and are told, "The coach wants to see you and bring your playbook," the decision is generally made for them. The game is taken from them. But to get a call to return to what is any football player's comfort zone and then to know that the head coach would intercede with the owner to make things right financially was tempting.

Most players leave well before they are ready and are unprepared when the door hits them in the ass on the way out. I had seen so many guys leave football only to wonder what they would do next with their life. I also saw some of those same guys go from having the nicest cars or wearing the best clothing to downsizing their lifestyle considerably when their money ran out only a year or two after football. I considered myself luckier than most professional players leaving the game. I had two things going for me. Craig and I at least had the foresight when I signed my last contract to defer a portion of my contract to be paid out after my retirement from football. Each year after 1983, $100,000 to $150,000 was being "deferred without interest by the team to be paid on the first day of April following receipt by the club of my notice of retirement as a professional football player." After building up a nest egg of about $900,000 that I could take at almost any time from the Giants, I was under no pressure to have to do anything once I left the game. The other thing I had going for me was name recognition with Giants fans in New York. I had worked hard to stay out of controversy and to maintain a good reputation.

The team was about to open their season, and I was ready to make a transition to broadcasting on several different levels. I accepted two opportunities as one of the fresh former players looking to do television. Each year the networks look for just-out-of-the-game guys to offer their opinions of what they experienced on the field. The first assignment was on Cable News Network's *Pro Football Preview,* and the other was with the Madison Square Garden

Network *Sports Desk*. With the CNN gig I provided pregame analysis on Sunday morning prior to all 1:00 p.m. games. My MSG responsibilities were to offer postgame commentary on both the Giants and the Jets games played that day. Since the Giants and Jets games never went head-to-head on television, I had to watch both teams from 1:00 to 7:00 p.m. in back-to-back games on Sundays. With the CNN commitment I did the show out of the CNN News Bureau studio in Manhattan. I interacted with the host of the show, who was in Atlanta. The bad parts of doing that show were not being physically right next to someone to bounce a comment off and at times experiencing technical problems such as feedback in my ear as I tried to comment. The show was shown around the world since it was on CNN, but I couldn't think about that while I was on the air. If I had, it might have freaked me out knowing that the queen of England or Saddam Hussein could have been watching me talk about football.

At Madison Square Garden I remember meeting with the two top guys, Bob Gutkowski, the president of MSG, and Pete Silverman, the VP of broadcasting. They knew I was raw and didn't have a lot of broadcasting experience, but both urged me to just be myself and have fun providing commentary on the NFL. You couldn't do much better than that. The one problem was nobody told the host of *Sports Desk,* Bob Page, that I wasn't a veteran sports guy. We would have production meetings prior to the live telecast to go over what we needed to discuss about the day's Jets and Giants games to be certain that the telecast would flow smoothly. While I was prepared for those points of interest, on the air Bob would occasionally ask me something that was so far out in left field that I knew absolutely nothing about it. That was not a good thing, especially when you are on live television. Bob considered me a rookie and called me a "neophyte" during a broadcast. Initially I took a slight offense to the reference, but he was right! I often found myself bracing for those left-field questions from Bob and thus found it difficult to be totally relaxed on the air with him. Those questions didn't come every week. Some weeks I got them, while other weeks he played it straight and stuck with the program. Bob Page was an excellent sports anchor who was not shy about sharing his opinion about the local teams and their athletes. From Bob I learned that when you are talking sports to New York fans, you cannot straddle the fence; you not only have to have an opinion, but a strong one that you can back up with facts. I often felt that Bob resented that Gutkowski and Silverman made him work with a former Giants player to draw in viewers. If that was the case, then he was probably right.

This was my first postfootball job, and that first year out of the game was an adjustment and somewhat frustrating. I had more than my share of ups and downs in the real world that made me understand that playing the game was more familiar to me than anything else. As a football player I knew what I was supposed to do on the field, and when I did it, I was pretty damn good. When the team won, we won together, and when we lost, we lost together. Whatever we did, we did it together. One of the more difficult things for any former player, especially when he's just left the game, is to go back into the mode of being an individual. For twenty-one years it had been instilled in me to conform to the group. Once away from the game, I had to learn that when I lost or failed, I did so all by myself, and when I did well or won, it was all on me. Winning is always sweet, but when you fail and you have no teammates to share that loss with, it's tough!

My second year became a continuation of the first, except that the CNN partnership ended. I had no problem with that as it was not as much fun as I thought it would be, though it was good to get national and international exposure. I was attending a Giants game at the beginning of that next season when I bumped into Jon Bon Jovi. Bon Jovi was a rock star from New Jersey who was a huge Giants fan and season-ticket holder. He told me that he enjoyed seeing me on CNN as I was the only link he had to keep up with the team while he and his band toured in other parts of the world. Jon was one of the few people who told me they saw the show since the network was geared more for news than sports coverage.

I was then offered a job as a sideline reporter with the Big East Network, covering college football. I had never given college football much thought. The main part of football coverage is to provide the color and the play-by-play, whether it is high school, college, or professional football. Sideline reporting is a little different, but how hard could it be? A couple of injury reports during the game, interviewing the head coaches at halftime to get their feel for the game—it was that simple! Right? Well, I found my own ways to make what could have been a lightweight job difficult. As I prepared for each game, I developed various points of interest to discuss during the game. But each time the telecasts began, I felt as I did when I was a player: my heart began to race and I got anxious, as if I were going to go out on the field and hit someone. At least when I played football, once I got that first bit of contact out of the way, I would settle down and play relaxed. But now I felt anxious knowing that I was going to be on center stage early in the telecast. I hadn't thought I would have a problem with it since I had stood before so many cameras and microphones as a football player in the New York sports market.

My on-the-air presence was less than spectacular. I always felt nervous, self-conscious, and thought I looked uncomfortable. When I watched replays of the telecasts, oh my God, it was painful for me to watch myself. I did my preparation and research for the games, but once a game started, I would seem to fall apart. I would lose my train of thought while making a point or would be thrown off because the marching band was playing right behind me. I would also be thrown off whenever the producer talked to me through my earpiece while I was trying to make my points.

The worst example could have been when I covered a game at the Carrier Dome between Syracuse and Virginia Tech. I was interviewing the head coach of Syracuse, Paul Pasqualoni, and forgot or mispronounced his name on the air. Early the next week I received a call from Mike Tranghese, the commissioner of the Big East Conference. Tranghese was very professional in telling me that the network was going to go with someone else as sideline reporter. He did not say it out loud, but in essence I was fired!!! Wow! I had never been dismissed from any project before. As I was a competitor, my pride was wounded. It's one thing to work a job in anonymity and get canned by your boss; it's another thing to be a former captain of the New York football Giants and a Super Bowl champion and to get fired from sideline reporting on college football games.

I was disappointed and embarrassed by my own performance, but I had no one to blame except myself. I had entered an arena in which I had not fully understood the challenges. I didn't always understand that when asked a question by the color commentator or the play-by-play analyst, sometimes I only had four or five seconds to answer that question before throwing it back to the booth. I've always been a bit too long-winded for my own good. Through my broadcast experience I gained a greater respect for newsmen who provide information to the public while listening to the constant talk of directors and producers in their ear. I could not emulate off the field what I was able to do on the field: be an all-star performer.

I still had my job with Madison Square Garden Network covering the Giants and the Jets for *Sports Desk*. While that position was not quite as structured as what I did for the Big East, I at least had more time to make my points whenever I was on air with Bob Page. He was the "ringmaster" who asked the questions, and while I wore an earpiece, he got the directions from our producer, Joe Townley, in the control room. The format was more relaxed and conducive to my adding some substance to the telecast.

One incident while covering the Jets that year stands out in my mind. The Jets and the Indianapolis Colts had been playing good football that season. During the telecast, I intended to say that the two teams were on track to perhaps make people forget about the great Super Bowl game in 1969 that the Jets played against the Baltimore Colts when Joe Namath predicted a win for his team over the class of the National Football Conference. The telecast was about to head into a commercial break, so I was trying to make my point quickly, and apparently I referred to Baltimore as Buffalo. In my mind, I knew I said "Baltimore." When we ended the segment and I was about to leave the set, someone told me I said "Buffalo," which would have made absolutely no sense. I thought the guy was wrong and I played it off. At home after the show, I mentioned it to my wife, and she said, "You did say 'Buffalo.'" I could not believe it, but she showed me the tape of the show. My presentation, energy, projection—everything was good except that mention that the Jets played against Buffalo instead of Baltimore. I was beginning to feel good about what I was bringing to the show, then this slipup came out of left field.

CHAPTER 15

Harry, Now We Really Have a Problem!

As the 1990 football season was winding down, I scheduled my yearly physical as usual with my personal physician, Dr. Lester Levine. Since leaving football, I wanted to be certain to maintain my health and stay on top of managing my body. For the thirteen years I played professional football, getting a physical once or twice a year by not just one but a team of doctors was a given. I was a commodity, a product, that if found to be defective would not be able to play and produce as part of the team.

My relationship with Dr. Levine began purely by accident. A couple of summers earlier I was experiencing flu-like symptoms and needed a doctor to see me quickly and prescribe medication. I was referred to Dr. Levine by my next-door neighbor and found him to be not only competent but also caring and compassionate. When the drug-use allegation occurred in my final year and I needed to make sure I didn't just rely on the NFL testing procedure, I turned to Dr. Levine to have my urine analyzed. I felt confident and comfortable with him and trusted him with my most valuable possession, me! With Dr. Levine I had no apprehensions, even at age thirty-seven, of dropping my pants, bending over, and spreading them to get my prostate examined as well as my heart, hearing, and vision.

At the conclusion of my physical he asked me a series of questions to update my family's health history. Dr. Levine said I was in excellent shape, then asked, "Is there anything else going on with you that I need to know?" I quickly replied, "Nope, I'm fine!" Then he asked, "Are you sure?" That follow-up "Are you sure?" triggered something, and I responded, "Well, I have been having some occasional headaches and blurred vision." Then I thought of other things that came and went without my paying much attention to them. For much of my life I was a football player, so little aches and pains were a given that I had to live with. Other things were not necessarily physical abnormalities, but things a bit deeper that were more difficult for me to put my finger on and describe. I'd always had better-than-average vision, but sometimes my vision would become blurred or I would see spots for no apparent reason. Those symptoms never lasted long, perhaps a few minutes or a couple of hours max, but I noticed. Sometimes when I was talking with someone, my speech would slur. Or I would feel faint when I would stand after sitting for a while.

Dr. Levine noted everything I said, then suggested I be examined by a neuropsychologist, Dr. Ken Kutner. Dr. Levine had his office set up an appointment for a week later. After seeing Dr. Levine, I thought I could perhaps adjust to these problems and that maybe I was making a mountain out of a molehill. Physically I felt fine, and I thought there was no reason to go any further with this. The day of my appointment I started to call to cancel it, but I didn't. I trusted Dr. Levine, and if he thought I should do this, then I would.

When I met Dr. Kutner, I had absolutely no expectations of what my issues were. He had been briefed by Dr. Levine and knew that I was a former player with the Giants. When I told him about the symptoms I was experiencing, I realized that now was not the time to be a macho man and play down what I felt. Instead, I should be candid. To this point, I'd kept to myself everything I felt or experienced. I tried to remember everything I sensed about myself, no matter how insignificant it might have been. I told him that I dealt with either a severe migraine or bout of depression every other month or so. Occasionally I had a difficult time concentrating or finishing a task. Sometimes I felt as if my head were in the clouds and everything was fuzzy. Now and then I experienced involuntary muscle twitches in my arms, hands, and legs. He asked if lights and noise bothered me. It dawned on me that when I attended events where the room was dimly lit and someone wanted to take my picture, the flash of the camera often triggered a headache. The same thing happened if I spent time in a noisy room or on a plane with a baby screaming. Talking with Dr. Kutner, I was able to focus on some of the triggers for my pounding headaches that I had been having for years.

Dr. Kutner and I spent two days together, and I went through a barrage of examinations to determine how my brain responded to certain stimuli. Initially the testing was similar to what I experienced with Dr. Ladata when I first came to the Giants, but these exams were much more in-depth and probing. The early tests were simple, but I began to get frustrated as they became increasingly difficult. I had trouble doing the tasks and even finishing them. I was a college graduate, had done graduate studies, and considered myself a smart man, but I was stymied by some of the tests. One of the tests was to read a short, simple story, then complete another examination dealing with numbers, then go back to the short story and recount as much as I could remember about it. Other tests had me identify objects and colors. The exams seemed geared more for a child, but I had problems completing the tasks.

At the end of the two days of testing, my brain felt exhausted, as if I'd taken three SATs at once to get into college. When Dr. Kutner told me that we were finally finished, I felt relieved. I knew what it felt like to complete a grueling two-a-day practice and what it felt like going through rehabilitation on a surgically repaired knee, but this was different; this wasn't about my physical body, this was all about my brain! He told me to get some rest and that he wanted to see me in two days to go over the results.

When I returned to get the diagnosis, I had no clue what it would be. Dr. Kutner went over how I did on various parts of the examination and explained what each area meant. I listened intensely but some of the terminology went right over my head. He finished, "Mr. Carson, you have a mild postconcussion syndrome, and based on the fact that it has been more than two years since you last hit or got hit by someone on the football field, the condition is most likely permanent." Postconcussion syndrome? I had never heard of that. My only question was "Okay! But am I going to live?" Dr. Kutner looked at me as if I'd asked a silly question, but I was deadly serious: "Am I going to live?" He said, "Yes, you are going to live!" My biggest concern was that I had a brain tumor like Doug Kotar. I'd played in the Meadowlands just like Doug; we both knew that the Meadowlands complex was built on a dump in an area with a high concentration of cancer. I was recently retired just like Doug Kotar, and if I was having symptoms like Doug's, who was to say that I couldn't have the same condition he had? Postconcussion syndrome? If I could live with it, I wasn't going to give it a lot of thought. I was indifferent to the diagnosis, but I knew it could have been worse. I thanked Dr. Kutner, paid the $975, and left feeling pretty good that at least I didn't have cancer. As far as I was concerned, I was good to go!

When I was with Dr. Kutner, I only heard what I wanted to hear, that I would live, but then I realized that I didn't fully hear the remainder of what he said about the diagnosis. If I had been fully in tune with him, I would have heard that I needed to learn how to manage postconcussion syndrome. I had the diagnosis but knew absolutely nothing about the condition. The many years I'd played football and the many dings or concussions I'd sustained while playing were the main contributors to the condition. In Dr. Kutner's 1990 conclusion to his neurological evaluation, he stated, "Evaluation of neurological test results indicates evidence of a mild post-concussional syndrome. Mild neuropsychological problems were evident in several areas. Mr. Carson's post-concussional syndrome is seen to be related to pro football. It is likely the concussion or concussions which resulted in this syndrome occurred more than two years ago. Therefore, his cognitive sequelae are likely to be permanent in nature." I began to understand that some of the things I went through in the early eighties were probably a direct result of the concussions I sustained. I either played through those issues or made adjustments to deal with my inability to communicate effectively, my mood swings, and my depression.

I continued my work with Madison Square Garden Network and started to settle into my role on *Sports Desk*. I began doing more remote features, which were taped during the week and were usually aired on Sunday nights. When I did my features, it was challenging remembering my script at times. It didn't matter a lot because if I screwed up my lines, we could always stop tape and start over. What was even better was the crew I was paired with. I had a great cameraman, Scott St. John, who always tried to put me in the best situation as the "talent." If I started a segment and Scott felt that I could do it better, he would stop tape on his own and tell me flat out, "Harry, I know you've got better stuff than that!" Initially I resented his comments, but then I realized that Scott had been in television much longer than me and he was right and was only looking out for me. Each week I had several different sound guys, but the other constant was the producer Scott and I worked with.

Anthony Fucilli or "Fooch" was an up-and-coming producer who did great research and a good job of putting me in the best position to shine when I was doing features. When we all got together, we talked about all kinds of stuff, from playing the game and different players to women they were seeing. On one remote shoot we were discussing several quarterbacks being knocked out of games that week due to concussions. I casually told Fooch that I was diagnosed with postconcussion syndrome and how these high-profile players might experience the same things that I experienced once they retired. Anthony and Scott were surprised that I was so open about talking about my condition. Most athletes shy away from certain topics. Talk about athletes being gay or homosexuality was touchy, as was any suggestion that someone might be mentally unstable.

Athletes are very, very proud individuals who place great stock in their physical abilities, but even more in their ability to think quickly. Most athletes have been in the company of someone with some kind of physical or mental challenge, whether it's young people in the Special Olympics or someone who has lost a limb. Most athletes feel blessed that they have the mind and the body to do whatever they want to do and are good doing it. Unfortunately, I have been around a lot of people who view people with physical disabilities differently from those who deal with mental disabilities. They may not say it aloud, but they would much rather have a physical challenge to contend with than a mental challenge. Obviously much stigma was still attached to being a mentally injured or mentally challenged person.

Apparently, Anthony mentioned our conversation to a producer friend at ESPN. ESPN was covering a story on concussions in sports and needed someone who was familiar with the issue and willing to discuss it. Anthony told me that he hoped I didn't mind that he'd shared my story with his friend, and that this guy went nuts with the prospect of getting a high-profile former player to talk openly about concussions and postconcussion syndrome. Anthony wanted to know if I would be interested in being interviewed on the subject. I told him I had no problem talking about it. Sure, why not?

I invited the ESPN cameras into my home, where I shared my story. I talked primarily about the concussions I sustained during my career and about being diagnosed with postconcussion syndrome. I was as open and as honest as I could be during the interview. When the feature aired, I got a lot of feedback from people who saw it and said they were sorry and that they didn't know I was dealing with this condition. Well, they didn't have to feel sorry for me, and I didn't know either until it was brought to my attention. Afterward, I realized that while I talked about the condition, I didn't really know what PCS was all about. I generally kept a busy schedule, and I had to stop to make time to educate myself about what I was experiencing. Dr. Kutner was a good doctor who pulled a lot of information out of me that I didn't think much about until I was pressed. Unfortunately, I didn't press him back and ask him the important questions I should have about my condition. I had a name but little else. I began to read all kinds of books as well as information on the Internet to see what post-concussion syndrome was about.

The interview I gave to ESPN was seen by quite a few people around the country. I knew that many current and former players saw it, but various non-sports-related groups saw it as well. One of the first of those groups to contact me was the Brain Injury Association. Headquartered in Washington, D.C., the BIA has chapters around the country. Shortly after the interview aired, the BIA asked if I would be willing to address several chapters around the country. Several other groups, including the Congress of Neurological Surgeons, invited me to speak to their members about my experiences. I eventually agreed to take part in various panel discussions with other athletes and doctors to talk about traumatic brain injury.

I realized that I was entering a world that I'd never given much thought to. Taking part in discussions around the country, I heard firsthand what doctors who specialized in traumatic brain injury had to say about head injuries and concussions. I was no doctor, but audiences wanted to hear what I had to say about living with the condition. They could not care less about my winning games or the roar of the crowds; they wanted to know how I dealt with my circumstances. Many of these people were not even football fans but just regular people affected by traumatic brain injury. They had been in traffic accidents or were the parents or caregivers of young people who'd suffered a head injury participating in gymnastics, soccer, hockey, or football. These people were just minding their own business when an accident or a situation changed their world.

One speech I gave stood out more than any other. I accepted an invitation to speak before the Brain Injury Association's national conference in Charlotte, North Carolina. Originally, sports agent Leigh Steinberg was to deliver the keynote address, but he was unable to make it and I was asked to fill in. I did so without much preparation and spoke to the group from my heart. I shared that I silently went through bouts of depression when I played and had thoughts of suicide. At times I'd felt down emotionally, even though as a successful professional athlete I had no major problems or concerns. I spoke on several other concussion-related issues, but the suicide comment got the most attention, and I think many in the room could relate to it. At the end of the luncheon, many people came up to me and thanked me for sharing my message. They gave me information on their programs or types of therapy they were promoting. Not wanting to be rude, I took everyone's brochures.

After the Charlotte conference I returned to New Jersey, still experiencing the occasional headaches and vision, mood, muscular, and sometimes memory issues. I had a better understanding of what my issues were and how to deal with them. At times my wife, Shari, might say, "Do you remember me asking you to do that?" I would say, "No! I don't remember!" and she might respond, "See, you don't listen to me!" I felt bad because I always listened, but maybe I just didn't hear. With most people I could get away with not remembering a request, a birthday, or a special occasion. That was hard to do with my wife, who could be insulted when I failed to remember something. I was learning to adjust to and accept these things. Just as my body adjusted to mangled fingers or a shoulder without a working deltoid muscle, it was learning to adjust to this condition. Interacting with others caused me the greatest concern because it was still difficult for me to explain what I thought, felt, and why I did something the way I did it. Sometimes my thought processes or the way I would perform a task were completely different from the way most other people would do things. I went back to my early days playing football with the Giants: it didn't matter how I got to the point I needed to get to, as long as I got there!

I was a little different from most people and I accepted that. I might make plans to do something, then back out at the last minute because I didn't feel comfortable, my mood changed, or I just wasn't feeling it. Being a little unpredictable began to become me. It was almost useless for me to try to explain my ways of doing things to people who didn't know me. I knew they would not understand nor would they buy it, especially since most people looked at me as a still-strong man who appeared to be smart.

In cleaning around my office, I ran across a lot of things I had picked up along the way: old letters and cards from friends, business cards that people had given me, and a wide assortment of brochures. As I threw things out, I browsed through everything to make sure it was okay to get rid of. One booklet I vaguely remembered picking up when I was in Charlotte for the Brain Injury Association conference. As I thumbed through it, the words reached out and grabbed me, largely because the book was not written by a doctor in jargon but by brain-injury survivors. *From the Ashes*, written by Constance Miller and Kay Campbell, was a book that I couldn't put down. While I purchased many books, rarely would I sit and read a book from cover to cover. Few books could hold my attention for an extended time, but this book did just that. Since being diagnosed by Dr. Kutner with post-concussion syndrome, I had picked up bits of information on the lingering effects of concussions. This was the first source of information that was in layman's terms that I could fully understand. The book had been sitting on my shelf for several months collecting dust. While I scoured the Internet looking for information, I had the absolute best source right in my office.

From the Ashes hit me like a ton of bricks because it opened my eyes and my mind to exactly what I was experiencing and needed to share with the people I cared most about. People looking at me could see that I looked pretty good physically! But they could not see my invisible brain injuries that I never knew I had. *From the Ashes* provided insight into brain injury from the perspective of the survivor of brain injury. In the coming weeks, months, and years, this book became my bible. I relied on it to educate me in what I needed to share with others. At times I thought I was going out of my mind. By reading the book I realized that I was okay physically and mentally, but brain injuries took me places neurologically that I had no awareness of.

Dr. Kutner's diagnosis was that my condition was permanent. It was hard for me to accept that, but according to the book, studies indicated that brain damage is irreversible. Most head injuries occur in traffic accidents when the head slams against the windshield, roof, or other hard object. A head injury could also occur without direct impact, by way of a whiplash motion. An injury can come from falling and hitting the head or from being battered with a fist or a hard object. In the case of babies, shaking them violently can cause brain injury. My head injuries came as a result of blows to and jarring of my head while I played football, and these dings or concussions did not always result in a loss of consciousness. I had heard a lot about concussions and learned that they were lesions or bruises on the brain. I thought the impact of a concussion was immediate and then faded away, but I learned that the effects could come quickly or after many months. With each page, I gained more insight and felt that someone had finally gotten inside me to help me feel everything I was experiencing but could not always verbally explain.

I took biological sciences (biology, anatomy, physiology, and kinesiology) while in college and knew just how complicated the human brain was; it controls everything. We all know that the brain controls the five senses of smell, touch, taste, sight, and hearing. Other areas we often take for granted. Whether it's the ability to organize thoughts, to communicate effectively, or experience various emotions, everything involves the brain. Everything we know about ourselves and our experiences is shaped and molded by the brain. It carries out all functions of receiving, processing, and storing information. The brain determines the way in which we communicate with the outside world. It controls many functions and sensations such as breathing, blood pressure, temperature, sleep, sexual activity, hunger, thirst, and body coordination. The brain is also responsible for creative and analytical thoughts, emotions, and memory. It made sense that if I lost a certain amount of speed or mobility each time I had a knee injury, losses would occur when I bruised my brain by hitting people on the football field. While doctors could examine my knees or ankles to determine the extent of an injury, nobody examined my head. But then again, I never complained about my head until now!

CHAPTER 16

Living with PCS

The more I read, the more I learned, and the more I began to understand what I had become. Football taught me many valuable life lessons, of which the greatest could have been to know what my strengths and weaknesses are. Over the years, I realized that the Harry Carson who was smart, confident, and articulate had been lost somewhere along the way. People looked at me and saw me as they always had, but they didn't know what I had become inside. Long before Dr. Kutner diagnosed my condition, I knew something was wrong. I knew it was unusual for me to feel deeply depressed for no apparent reason. Most people who were close to me knew that while I could be a very serious person, I was also a fun guy who usually had a sunny attitude even if I didn't always wear a smile. The speech problems and the inability to adequately express myself in the early eighties should have been a wake-up call for me, but I worked my way through them. The anxiousness I felt while I was on the air, as well as the inability at times to recall the correct words to express myself, added to my frustration. I always took pride that my high school English-literature teacher Paul Skoko taught his students how to use words effectively not only to express their points of view but to impress others with the proper usage of complex words. My neurological symptoms were subtle, but the physical indicators—the blurred vision (even though my vision was twenty-twenty or even better), the occasional numbness or tremors in my extremities, and the dizziness I felt when I stood up after sitting for a while— were easier to recognize.

What I was going through was not always consistent. Some days I felt great, my wit was superb, and everything was good, but then other days I knew I was off. When I had those "Hyde" days, my short-term memory was poor, my attention span was bad, and finding the right words to express what I had to say was tough. I knew these things, but I was hesitant to share them with other people. Why should I? I knew people would not understand or be able to relate. But it was also about my personal pride: I knew that people expected me to be the same successful person I was on the football field. I finally "got it" through my efforts of educating myself. Postconcussion syndrome was becoming clearer for me, but for a time I thought I was going insane.

Since post-concussion syndrome was not going to kill me, I had to learn to live with it. With my fuller understanding of the condition, I felt a need to share with my immediate family members and close, trusted friends what I was experiencing. I knew that some people would be skeptical. I developed a list of family members—my sisters and brothers, my nephews, my children—and my close friends such as my old Giants teammate George Martin. I considered all of these people to be my base and my foundation. Those were the people who I knew loved me unconditionally! After compiling the list, I took *From the Ashes* to Staples and made copies of all the pages with underlined sections that I thought pertained to my condition. After making the copies and stapling the information together, I sent each person his or her own letter with a personal note telling them that it was information I felt I needed to share. The information would give them a more definitive understanding of who I was, what I was experiencing, and why.

After several days I began to get feedback from some of those closest to me. The general response was "Thank you for sharing" and "Oh my God, I didn't know!" My oldest sister, Ruth, probably took the letter and information more solemnly than anyone else. Ruth was like a mother figure to all of my family members, so whatever was happening to any of the family, she was likely going to take it harder than anyone else. I was not looking for anything from anyone, especially sympathy. I just wanted those closest to me to know what I was dealing with and to understand that at times I might not be that happy-go-lucky brother, father, or friend they had known.

On every level of football that I played, I learned to adjust. Whether the adjustment was to the speed of the game, a new defensive system, a new coach, playing in a new stadium, or adverse weather on game day, I found ways to keep moving forward. I found my ways to adjust to physical changes in my body as well. For as long as I live, my right shoulder will always be flat as a result of nerve damage I sustained in the 1980 scrimmage. I adjusted to that injury and still made several Pro Bowls afterward. I have no cartilage remaining in my right knee as a result of three knee operations, so whenever I run, walk too much, or even dance, I experience bone-against-bone pain. I will never be able to straighten out several fingers, which were dislocated. With those physical changes I made adjustments to continue doing whatever I wanted or needed to do.

I have never mourned the loss of those parts of my body, nor have I spent time thinking about my loss of mobility or function. But in moving forward with postconcussion I had to confront and deal with the not-so-obvious things that were in my head. I had to learn to be more in tune with everything I did neurologically. Most people don't think twice about what they do or say in their daily lives. I had to think about almost everything I did or said every minute. I had to be aware of my environment to control my tendencies to get headaches. Noise, even screams from babies, bright lights, or odors could trigger migraines. I had to be vigilant to guard against depression. In short, I had to learn how to better manage my life to be aware of me. I had to work harder to remember names, people, occasions, etc. Working harder meant that when I'd meet someone new, I'd have to pay extra attention to his or her name or title and repeat it in my head several times to give myself a chance to remember relevant details. Working harder meant making a list throughout the day so I'd stay focused on what I wanted to do. It meant that when I answered a question, I'd have to take my time to analyze what was being asked and what the appropriate response should be. And working harder was visualizing every word I wanted to say in my mind before allowing it to leave my lips.

Perhaps I should have sought professional help in dealing with my issues, but I've never looked for someone to help me in almost anything. Sure, I could meet with doctors or counselors, but my strange mind-set was that unless someone had been where I was neurologically and could understand exactly what I had been experiencing, then he or she could say nothing that would help me. Listen, I've played golf for years and my game has always sucked! Many people I've played with over the years have tried to give me advice on my game. I hear what they say and I see what they're showing me, but it does not register in my brain, so whenever I play, I have to play my game and make adjustments to my game as I go along. Sometimes I play well and sometimes I stink up the place, but I have to rely on my gut feeling on each shot and live with the consequences of each shot. That was how I was while dealing with PCS.

While I continued working for Madison Square Garden Network, my preference was to do taped features in which I could take my time talking or making my points. I learned to not say a lot while doing that type of media. It was better for me to keep my comments as brief as possible. Otherwise, I got too wordy in making points and went places where I shouldn't. Working harder meant making one or perhaps two valid points and then shutting my mouth. When I did that, I looked better, instead of like a jock whom people felt sorry for because I was not able to make my points concisely.

Some might categorize me as a control freak. I have to plead guilty to that accusation. I was educated to be an educator and trained to be an athlete. Hold it, not just an athlete, but a world-class professional athlete! I very much have an athlete's mentality, and that is to strive to be the best in whatever I do. On the field, that mentality meant competing against other men to secure a position on the team or to win a game. In that environment it was about strength, power, will, and heart. Off the field, being in control was about taking full responsibility for me. Perhaps it stems back to my youth when my mother told me to learn how to take care of myself and not be dependent on others. Perhaps it comes from playing the game and having the mind-set that nobody could do my job better than me even if I was hurt. Or it could have come from knowing that when I've put my fate or my life in the hands of others, I've been hurt or disappointed in some way. What may have been ultra-important to me might not have had the same importance to others.

The educator side of me knew that I could be the best or the absolute worst student depending on my commitment and motivation. Working harder and taking care of me was not about anyone else; it had to be an inside job and the focus had to be me! Throughout my life and during my football career I had been in so many situations where I knew people cheered for and loved me as an athlete, but at the end of the day could give jack shit about me as a person. In taking full responsibility for me, I knew that I had to let go of my past and adopt a newer version of me. I had years earlier accepted the fact that I no longer knew what "normal" felt like with my own body physically. I had to come to the same resolution mentally or neurologically of what "normal" was for me.

As I was going through this time of self-reawareness and reeducating myself, I was dealing with issues with my wife. We went through a rough and rocky period of several months where some of the issues I was dealing with about myself became major issues in our marital lives. We both allowed issues from our past to enter our lives, but my forgetfulness led to a separation for us. I provided my wife and her family with the same information as my family and close friends. While my wife could sense that some things were more complicated, she felt she needed some time away. She was aware of my occasional mood swings as well as other symptoms. But bottom line, I think she felt that whatever I was sharing with her was designed to get sympathy.

That was a difficult time in my life because I felt vulnerable when I shared my issues with my loved ones. Those people I bared my weaknesses to thought my foundation was strong and unshakable. In most situations, my loved ones looked to me for strength and guidance, but now the shoe was on the other foot. I needed as much support and understanding as I could get, especially from the people who knew and loved me. Unfortunately, at that time I felt abandoned by the one person whom I thought would always be there for me and who would, as promised, always have my back!

My football experience taught me what commitment was all about. If you are going to play the game and achieve success, you must be committed to hard work. I took that same attitude into my personal life. I was committed to my marriage, but I also knew that neurological issues played a role in where we were. Several weeks after our separation, we both felt that it was best to move on, and Shari formally filed for divorce.

Since my retirement from the Giants, I had gone through failure after failure in my transition from football and in my personal life. The divorce rate among players leaving the game or recently retired was high. I thought that statistic was for other people, not for me. But there I was, about to be added to that stat with another failed marriage. Since ninth grade, I've never liked the taste of failing at anything. The failures at CNN and the Big East Network were disappointing, but they were small compared to the failure of my marriage.

Some former NFL players who were aware of my neurological problems urged me to file for disability with the NFL. I had done so a couple of years earlier in regard to my back, which occasionally gave me some serious problems. I was denied by the NFL. Players who've played in the NFL and file for disability have to prove that the injury was sustained while playing in the league and that they are disabled and unable to earn an income. That was completely different from what I was adjusting to. A former player applying for disability from the NFL has to be examined by a "neutral physician," selected by the league; so much for neutrality. I applied and was referred to a doctor in New Jersey.

On the morning of the appointment, I drove about forty miles for the examination. When the doctor and I met, he asked me several questions about my family health history, several health-related questions, and then several questions about the symptoms I experienced. He then put me through some exams that took all of ten minutes. I spent twenty minutes with the doctor maximum; that was it! Twenty minutes! When he asked me about my job as a broadcaster with Madison Square Garden Network, I knew where we were headed. Several days later I received a letter from the NFL Disability Board with another rejection of disability, which was what I was expecting. I couldn't understand it. I spent two days with a doctor who put me through a rigorous, comprehensive battery of examinations to determine that my post-concussion syndrome was a permanent disability. I only spent twenty minutes with this doctor and I was denied. It didn't make sense, but I knew, like most other former NFL players, that you either have to be on a cart with a wheel and no legs or on life support with someone almost ready to pull the plug to get disability from the Disability Board. It wasn't so much that I wanted to be taken care of by someone; I wanted what I was experiencing to be documented and acknowledged for future reference.

I had conflicting diagnoses of my condition, but what could I do with them? I put much more stock in what Dr. Kutner said than what this other guy had to report. Regardless of what the Disability Board's doctor reported, I knew what I was dealing with and I knew beyond a shadow of a doubt it was real. I knew that if I had this condition, then many other former football players were probably experiencing the same issues. In talks with players at various events around the country, some guys were very open in asking me questions about my condition, while others would pull me aside and ask me questions in private. I found that former players or even players who were playing at that time misunderstood what a concussion is. When I asked guys if they had ever sustained a concussion, they usually replied, "No." Then I would ask if they'd ever seen stars or their vision had faded to black when they got hit or hit someone either in a game or in practice. The answer would invariably be a firm "Oh, that. Hell yeah!" That is a concussion! These players were usually surprised. Most were under the impression that a concussion only occurs when someone is knocked out on the football field as a result of a violent collision. They considered themselves immune to my condition because they were never knocked out like some of the players we saw on television getting the shit knocked out of them. They didn't know that those hits made while making a block or a tackle that left them feeling a little woozy after they came off the field could be just as bad as a wide receiver's being coldcocked by a safety running across the middle of a zone defense or a quarterback being blindsided by a Lawrence Taylor–type linebacker on an all-out blitz.

I was still close to the game, but yet I was far enough away from it that whatever happened with the teams, especially the Giants, did not affect me. I began to notice that some players leaving the game were having a difficult time transitioning to real life. Many of these guys reminded me of me in that they were intelligent guys who got sidetracked upon leaving the game. Neither the teams nor the league had any kind of transition programs or counseling set up, so when players left, they were basically on their own without any kind of emotional or psychological support. But given the mind-set of professional athletes, especially football players, if programs were available, would they take advantage of them? I would hope so, but I also knew how much pride players have and how they tend to keep their weaknesses to themselves. I know I did until I realized that living in silence with the effects of concussions could be deadly.

About this time I quite unexpectedly received an invitation to become part owner of a newly formed arena football team. A New Jersey entrepreneur, Burke Ross, wanted to establish an indoor football team in the Meadowlands to play games in the Continental Airlines Arena. Two of my former teammates, Carl Banks and Joe Morris, were also invited to become partners in the start-up team that became known as the New Jersey Red Dogs. Arena football is played indoors as opposed to regular football, which is played outdoors. The surface is usually the floor of a basketball arena that is covered by an artificial surface, much like an outdoor field. The games are fast-paced since the playing area is smaller and there are fewer players. Also, the passing game is featured over a running attack. One part of this game that scared me was the barriers set up to separate the playing area from the fans. There was no sideline, so if a receiver was running at full speed and caught a pass near the barrier, he would hit it at full speed.

For a year I was conflicted; I liked the idea of being a partner in the ball club, but as I watched game after game, I knew that some of these players were going to have the same issues I had with concussions. The Red Dogs and the Arena Football League created jobs for many guys who wanted to play in the NFL but were not quite good enough. Probably the best example of this was quarterback Kurt Warner, who went from the Arena League to the NFL's

St. Louis Rams and took that team to the Super Bowl. Playing arena ball at least gave players an opportunity to improve their skills until they got a shot at making a team in the NFL. For others who would never get to that level, it was a chance to extend their playing days and make some cash. Indoor football was good in that the weather was not a factor in the games. Anyone could watch the game from the comfort of a seventy-degree arena and not be concerned with snow, ice, or rain. One of the things that drew my interest was that it produced entertainment for many of those football fans who could not go to a Giants game. The tickets were cheap and the game was tremendously fan-friendly.

The irony for me was I was able to understand how Wellington Mara felt as an owner of a football franchise. As much as I enjoyed being able to see myself as an owner, I was conflicted because I knew what was happening to the players who either hit the side barriers full speed or got clocked by a safety as they were running crossing patterns. To be able to say to someone I was one of the owners of the Red Dogs was ego-gratifying, but to know that players were getting hurt in satisfying that ego was difficult to justify in my heart.

After a nice little two-year run my participation with the Red Dogs fizzled out. It stopped being fun to go to the games and seeing these guys almost knock their brains out. The team had a difficult time attracting fans, as a lot of sports teams do in the Meadowlands, so the ownership group sold the team. The Red Dogs became the Gladiators and were moved to Las Vegas.

Things happen for a reason. Sometimes the strangest opportunities are presented to me and I wonder, "Why would I even entertain the thought of doing this?" From my experience with the Red Dogs I could clearly see how an owner's focus could be solely on winning or on the profit-and-loss statements. I got a clearer understanding of how the players look like interchangeable parts of a larger purpose.

CHAPTER 17

HOF—#231

The moment I stepped off the football field for the last time, I realized that I would forever be linked to the game of football, regardless of whatever else I did in life. I had played twenty-one years of the sport—twenty-one years of training, twenty-one years of running sprints, twenty-one years of opening-day jitters, and twenty-one years of opening-day training camps, smelling that scent of grass. I was good at football and knew it better than anything else.

About five or six years after I left the Giants, I was nominated for the highest honor a football player can receive, the Pro Football Hall of Fame. When I was still a player, I remember Bill Parcells saying in interviews that I was good enough to be a Hall of Fame player. While I was actively playing, I never thought about the Hall of Fame. I had that athlete's mentality of dealing only with what was in the present. Me? A Hall of Famer? That was so remote in my thinking that it just went over my head. Once removed from the game, I could passively begin to entertain the thought, but I was trained not to "go there" by my own experiences. I figured I should tend to what I was in control of and not allow myself to be swallowed up by what others thought or did. It was the best way for me to handle this situation.

I fought thinking about it, but I was flattered to even be mentioned as a possible Hall of Fame candidate. After five to six years I was well removed from the game, but I felt good knowing that what I did meant something to others. I had not given much thought to any of the accolades I'd received as a player, the many trophies and plaques from my days of playing college football and my thirteen years with the Giants. Those items mostly just collected dust. This was different! Many thousands of players had played professionally, but how many of them are mentioned for such a prestigious honor?

I didn't follow the coverage and I didn't hear anything else about the Hall of Fame after I had been nominated. The next year and the year after that, I went through the same process: I was nominated, then I heard nothing. I didn't know anything about advancing to the next stage.

Five years after that first nomination, I was contacted by the Pro Football Hall of Fame and was told that I was a finalist for consideration. Wow!!! In the first year that I was nominated, I was in a group of more than 125 former players up for consideration. After five years, my name had made its way to the top 25 list and then to the top 15 finalists. I took this in stride, but apparently it was a big deal to the media. They went nuts and wanted to get my thoughts on being a finalist on the ballot. I still didn't know a thing about the selection of Hall of Fame members. I felt that if it was going to happen, it would happen! If it didn't, oh, well!

The day before the Super Bowl in 2001, the inductees into the Hall of Fame were announced. I didn't make it! My girlfriend, Maribel, and I had been invited guests of Gatorade for the game between the Giants and the Baltimore Ravens. I was also a participant in the NFL Charities golf tournament, playing with other former and current players at the site of the Super Bowl game. I was on the golf course when the announcement was made, and I didn't have a clue until my foursome returned to the clubhouse and someone mentioned the players who were elected to the Hall. For a fraction of a second, I was a little disappointed after all of the attention placed on my becoming a finalist, but I could not let any disappointment show. I had to be gracious even in defeat. I wasn't running for anything and I had no control over the outcome. I just was not chosen.

When I returned to my hotel room, it was a different story. Maribel had been watching the coverage live on ESPN the entire time while I was on the golf course. She was bitterly disappointed because she felt that I deserved the honor. I tried to calm her down and explain to her that those who were elected really deserved to be elected and honored. I felt strange trying to soothe her about something that was supposed to be more about my career. Shortly after the announcement, I began to get calls from family members and friends offering their regrets that I was not elected. I didn't know if I was missing something or not, but I didn't see it as a big deal.

To help make Maribel feel better, I told her I would take her out for a romantic dinner, just the two of us! That brought a little smile to her face because she knew then that I was okay. Maribel and I had been dating for a while after my divorce. When we began dating, I warned her of the tractor-trailer-load of issues I carried from my past. While she didn't know me when I played for the Giants, she'd learned enough about me as a player and as a person to feel that I should be honored. She merely wanted the best for me and was unhappy because she thought I was disappointed. I told her that if it was meant to be, it would happen. Regardless of whether I made it, I was content with what I had accomplished as an athlete.

The New York Giants and Harry Carson suffered the same fate that weekend, as both the team and I lost big ones. The Giants lost to the Ravens 34–7. The only good thing about the weekend was that I was leaving Tampa and heading to Hawaii, where the Pro Bowl was being played, to participate in another golf tournament for NFL Charities. The golf tournaments became opportunities to get away with other guys I played with and against while in the league. Some of the guys were former teammates such as Brad Van Pelt, Brian Kelley, and even Lawrence Taylor. Some of the other men were Hall of Fame members who would pull me aside and say, "Don't worry, Harry, you'll get there! You deserve it!" It made me feel good to know that those guys had confidence in me and respected my play that much.

Maribel and I began to look forward to traveling to the Super Bowl venue and then on to Hawaii every year. Even when I played, I never cared a lot about attending Super Bowl games. To me, the Super Bowl is reserved primarily for corporate clients of the NFL. Unless the Giants were actually playing or

I had something to do surrounding the game, I had no interest in being there. Our annual plan was to head to the town where the game was being played, I'd do whatever I needed to do either as a golfer or in an appearance, and then we'd leave the morning of the game and fly to Hawaii to watch the Super Bowl.

The next year was a lot like 2001. The FedEx envelope arrived in mid-January from the Pro Football Hall of Fame congratulating me on being a finalist for consideration. Requests for interviews came after that. We traveled to New Orleans for golf and then to Paradise for golf once again. The following year was a carbon copy of the previous two: the staff at the Hall needed to know where I would be when the announcement was made as well as where I would be flying from if selected, to get to Hawaii where the newly elected Hall of Fame members would be formally introduced to the media during Pro Bowl week. When I received that letter again, I became a bit excited about being considered yet again. And just as the first two times, the media was all over it. I received and opened the letter, which came at 10:00 a.m., and started receiving calls from sports-talk radio stations and reporters by noon, wanting to get my thoughts and reaction to being named a finalist once again. One beat reporter on the Giants, Gary Myers, wanted my thoughts, and I told him to just use the same comments I gave him the previous two years. Nothing had changed: "I am humbled to be considered for the honor and I am going to manage my expectations!" Was I a little disappointed that I had not made it the first couple of times? Yes, a little! Was I optimistic this time? Yes! But just as I knew from the first time I was nominated, I could do nothing about the process. All of the nominated players, including some who were finalists with me the previous year, had great careers and deserved to be in the Pro Football Hall of Fame.

The hoopla surrounding the "finalist announcement" was not quite as intense as it had been the previous years with me. Reporters were calling from the local area and from around the country because they needed to get some kind of comment from me to put in their news articles. After the second or third interview it began to get old quickly, talking about the same situation again. Ever since my playing days I had always had a friendly relationship with most reporters, but in minutes I was beginning to grow tired of the attention. One interview, maybe two, was okay, but to do a stream of interviews answering the same questions over and over got tired. But I felt an obligation to continue to be gracious and considerate of the media just as I had as captain with the Giants.

As was the case in previous years, Maribel and I traveled to that year's Super Bowl venue in San Diego for charity golf. On the day of the selection I played in a tournament with several Hall of Fame members. They all wished me good luck before we headed out to the course. While I was on the course, I received a call on my cell phone from a radio station in Atlanta. A guy identified himself as the producer of a local sports show and asked if he could get a comment. I asked, "A comment on what?" He said, "You were just elected to the Pro Football Hall of Fame!" When I heard that, I felt a chill run down my spine, but then something from deep within my gut told me, "Don't say a word!" I told him that I would be happy to give him a comment but I needed to get something officially from the Hall before doing so. We hung up and I continued to play golf, not saying one word to the fellows in my group. My heart felt as if it were going to burst as I kept my cell close to me to make sure I didn't miss the call. Two minutes went by, then five, ten, twenty, and still no call from the Hall of Fame. I then got another phone call from the radio station in Atlanta and the producer said, "Mr. Carson, I am so sorry. I was mistaken when I called you!" I was crushed! I had almost expected it when I never heard anything from the Hall.

In my life I had done some really dumb things, but I was so grateful for having the wisdom and foresight to say nothing that day! If I had taken the word of that producer and commented, I would have been the dumbest dope ever. I would have been the butt of jokes on every morning radio show in the country. It would have been an honest mistake, but it could have been devastating to my psyche. I had endured my own beatdowns or periods of being supercritical of myself for not being the same person I was earlier in my life.

I frequently questioned many of the actions or statements I made in everyday interactions with other people. Through no will of my own, I had been thrust back into the spotlight years after my last tackle. In some ways I welcomed the attention, but in so many other ways I dreaded it. I was so far removed from playing football. Before this renewed attention, many people who were not football fans had no clue of who I was nor cared. I had transitioned from the game and was becoming accustomed to what most former players become once their careers end, invisible and irrelevant. I knew most die-hard Giants fans remembered me, especially those who saw me play in the seventies and early eighties before the team won its first Super Bowl title in '87. The Hall of Fame nominations dragged me back into the focus of fans and the media, who sometimes debated whether I or other former players should be in the Hall.

Guys in the Giants public relations department brought to my attention the fact that when the new inductees for the Hall of Fame were announced, Giants owner Wellington Mara voiced his disappointment that I was not selected. Others in the football community, fans, and members of the media also voiced their disappointment over what they were starting to consider a snub by the selection voters. A part of me felt good knowing that I at least had the support of those who followed the process, but having the support of Mr. Mara, who was also a member of the Pro Football Hall of Fame, really made me feel better. He had been a true judge of talent and had been a part of the National Football League all of his life. Mr. Mara had been around long enough to have seen many Hall of Fame players who either played for or against the Giants.

Maribel and I had already made plans to travel from Southern California to Hawaii the next morning with hopes of arriving in Honolulu in time to watch the Super Bowl at our favorite spots at the Hilton Hawaiian Village hotel. As we boarded our flight, Maribel asked if anything was wrong. She noticed I was more subdued than usual. I told her I was fine! I was just thinking about some things I had on my mind. I've always tended to internalize things that bothered me, so I thought it was best to keep the call from the radio station to myself. Unfortunately, during our flight when my guard was down, I opened up and shared with her what had happened. I didn't do anything to bring this on myself, but for some reason I felt embarrassed. I knew Maribel well enough by that time to know that she would be highly pissed and she was, but not quite as upset about my not being selected as she was in years before. She was getting used to what was becoming the norm for us.

For the next couple of years I felt that I was caught up in the never-ending saga of when or if Harry Carson would ever get into the Pro Football Hall of

Fame. I was told by some people that I needed to start a campaign to make the voters aware of my contributions as a Giant. These people felt I needed to inundate the voters with an ad campaign providing accurate information on my career that the voters might not be aware of. I was told by others that I needed to establish my own reputation because the voters felt that my career and stats rode on the coattails of Lawrence Taylor. I was then told by someone that many of the voters had an "anti–New York bias" when it came to sports. Regardless of what the issues were, the debate on whether I should be in the Hall of Fame started to drain me. I was stuck in limbo over an argument about whether what I did as a player was good enough to earn me entry into a place that I never had on my list of things to do anyway.

Few other people had to deal with this situation. I was never a "political" person and didn't know how to play the games people thought it took to get into the Hall. I just knew that on the field I played football passionately and with dignity! Even when I was injured, I played and never complained. I considered myself a strong leader for my guys, and in spite of anything anyone thinks, I was loyal to the Giants organization and left the game when I wanted to leave and on my own terms. I could have played longer if I wanted to, but I had nothing more to prove or to play for.

With my name being considered for the Hall, my career was revisited years later and was scrutinized by people who had never even put on a fucking football helmet or knew what stopping a running back in his tracks and not giving up an inch in crunch time was about. The voters had no clue of what going through tough two-a-day practices in ninety-eight-degree weather was all about. Those who were sitting in judgment on my career didn't know shit about me or what it took to be a player on the highest level. My coaches, from Coach Jeffries at South Carolina State to Marty Schottenheimer to Bill Parcells and Bill Belichick and all the others who coached me while I was with the Giants, knew what I was made of. All of my teammates knew the person and the player I was, and the players I played against certainly knew that I was a competitor. Their respect was the most important thing I could wish for.

Year after year it was discussed whether I was worthy of being elected to the Pro Football Hall of Fame. Year after year I had grown tired of going to fund-raising dinners in New York City and being introduced to the audience as "He was the captain of the Giants, a nine-time Pro Bowler, and should be in the Pro Football Hall of Fame, Harry Carson!" I was sick of walking the streets of New York or some other town around the country and being told by strangers, "I'm rooting for you to make it into the Hall!" I always tried to take the comments in stride, but at times I didn't want to have to discuss it and could feel my stress level rising, which would often trigger mini-migraines. When I grew more familiar with my postconcussion condition, I recognized that I needed to manage myself and my surroundings to make sure to avoid triggers like that. Unfortunately, some strangers may have felt bruised by my abruptness in changing the subject when they brought up the Hall of Fame in conversation.

Handling my own stress was one thing, but I couldn't handle what others thought. A good example was when I worked out in my gym. The people I encountered daily in my gym avoided me after the Hall of Fame voting because they didn't know what to say to me after yet another year of rejection. You would have thought someone close to me had died. People just didn't know what to say after saying, "I'm sorry, better luck next year," so many times. It seemed that my name and my very being were controlled by my not making it into the Hall. I began to feel much like Susan Lucci, who was a soap opera actress who was forever being nominated for a daytime Emmy and not winning. While she has been an outstanding actress, to some she became the butt of jokes simply because she was forever losing out to others for the award. I was beginning to feel as if I had become the football equivalent to Miss Lucci. No matter how far removed from the game I was, I always had pride within myself. That pride has always been in my DNA and was how I was built by those black teachers who taught me and so many others in our early years.

Pride aside, at one point I wanted to approach the Giants to arrange a sweetheart deal whereby I could sign a contract with them to come out of retirement. The ceremonial signing for $1 would rule me ineligible for the Hall of Fame since I had to be out of football for five years to be considered. I figured that was the least the organization could do for me to help make this situation go away. But knowing where I stood with the team in my last year made me think differently about approaching the Giants for assistance like that. I had to press on and seek other ways to deal with this issue that I didn't want to deal with any longer.

The fifth time I was named a finalist, I knew everything about the process. I knew the exact day the FedEx truck was coming with the envelope, and I knew when the reporters were going to be calling to get a comment. The day the Hall publicly announced the finalists I did a couple of radio and newspaper interviews, as I had grown accustomed to doing. But one interview stood out with me. Steve Serby of the *New York Post* called to get a few comments and asked sympathetically, "Harry, don't you think you should be in the Hall of Fame?" I interpreted that question as one I should stay away from, so I paused and then responded, "Don't ask me that question; ask the people I played against. They are the best judges to determine whether I should be there or not. I will abide by any response they give you." While I was only answering the question to get the reporter off my back, he did just that. Serby went out and interviewed some of those guys, as well as coaches who coached against me. When I read his article, I found that the players and the coaches he interviewed felt unanimously that I should be in the Hall. As I read their comments, peacefulness came over me. It was just as when my mother would say, "Give me my flowers while I can smell them!" In that article my peers gave me the best gift I could have gotten: their respect! At that point, being considered for the Pro Football Hall of Fame became irrelevant to me!

After being named a finalist so many times, I took notice of the other players who were also finalists but didn't make it. I felt that all of the guys deserved to be considered for that honor. The difference between them and me was that they probably always had dreams since childhood of being in the Hall of Fame and actually wanted to be there. I, on the other hand, did not care! I had been in almost every other Hall of Fame you could imagine, but with those honors they were just that, nice honors. My life never changed in any way because of accolades, and I didn't think it would change even if I had this one.

I became more proactive in my approach to "my situation." My family was the most important thing to me, and I felt this enormous desire to take everyone to Hawaii on what I considered a family vacation. I had taken my family on a destination vacation to Hilton Head, South Carolina, before but this was different. Going to Hilton Head was as simple as renting two homes big enough for forty to fifty people and having everyone drive to that location from South Carolina, Alabama, Georgia, and New Jersey. In going to Hawaii, I had to be financially responsible to make sure everyone got there. It had been a dream of mine to get my brothers, sisters, kids, and some of Maribel's family members to a location that I loved so much. Hawaii was exotic yet so peaceful for spending time together as a family.

It took a lot of planning, but we got everyone there. Upon arrival, we provided leis to all of the women. For the men, we provided Hawaiian shirts that looked festive. Once everyone was situated in their rooms, we all got together and went to dinner. When I had everyone in one location, I told them that I had decided to have my name removed from consideration for the Hall of Fame. My family had always been my biggest supporters on every level of my life. I felt they needed to understand where I was coming from live and in person, not over the phone or in a letter. Sharing my decision with them was not the primary reason for the vacation, but it was a good time to break the news. Everyone was disappointed but could understand why I was doing it. They all were heartbroken and felt bad for me year after year; they all wanted the recognition so much for me. Because of my athletic experience I had a different kind of strength from most of my family members. I could deal with the Hall rejection, but I felt bad because I knew how disappointed family members and friends were every year. Once they digested the information, they all accepted it and we went on to enjoy ourselves while we were together.

My older brother Sonny had arrived from Chicago with some medical issues the rest of the family was unaware of. He had been diagnosed with diabetes a couple of months before. On the morning we were all to return home, Sonny had a medical crisis. My son, Donald, came to my room and told me that Uncle Sonny was not breathing. As I made my way to his room that he shared with my brother Ronnie, I braced myself for what I would find, but then calmed myself because I knew he had already passed. When I walked into his room, the paramedics had already done all they could to revive him but he was gone.

My brother was the spiritual leader and patriarch of our family. He and

Ruth provided the rest of the family with the links we all needed to glimpse our past. He was an ordained minister and had lived in Chicago for years, but he had never married nor had children. As shocked and saddened as I was by his sudden passing, I thought that it was appropriate that he had passed away with all of his family with him in such an exotic location. He'd spent his final days in the warmth of Hawaii as opposed to the frigid cold of February in Chicago. I asked all of the family to gather around him. As we held hands, we each said prayers in his memory. After his body was removed by the medical examiner's office, we all went to the North Shore to feel the water and the sand on our feet and for each person to reflect on the life of my brother. I knew that, like my mother's and father's, his spirit would always be with me.

By the end of that day, the rest of my family had departed for the mainland. Maribel and I were the last ones on the island by design to make sure everyone got away without a problem. I remember sitting on the plane the next day waiting to begin my journey back to New Jersey. While I felt at peace with my brother's passing, I didn't want to leave his body in Hawaii all alone. I felt that since I'd convinced him to come here, I should be the one to take him home. Unfortunately, his body had to be shipped by the mortician in Hawaii to the mortician in South Carolina where he was going to be buried, so I had to trust that everything would be okay. As I sat on that plane, my brother was the most important thing to me, not the Hall of Fame stuff I had been dealing with.

After the funeral service and handling the final arrangements necessitated by my brother's passing, I got back to my issues. I felt adamant yet comfortable with my decision to have my name removed from consideration for the Hall. At the beginning of March I sat down and wrote a letter that simply said, "With all due respect to the institution which is the Professional Football Hall of Fame, I respectfully request that my name be removed from present and future consideration for induction." I dated the letter March 15 just in case I changed my mind, as I had in the past made some impulsive decisions regarding my football career. After writing the letter I didn't give my decision much thought as I went about my day-to-day life. That letter sat on my desk for two weeks, and I did not have a change of heart. On March 15 I went to the post office and dropped that letter in the mail. I knew I had sealed my own fate. When the letter left my hand, I had one of the best feelings I have ever experienced. It felt good because I was taking back the control and power over me! As long as I allowed my name to be used and other people felt that they could examine every facet of my career, I was going to be stuck in their little box to play their game. In this way I could tell the Hall, the media, and the sports world to go fuck itself!

I did not give the process any thought after that. I assumed that my request would be respected and my name would be dropped. Several months later a friend told me that I had been included among the top twenty-five finalists again. When I found that out, I was royally pissed! It takes a lot to get me upset, but knowing that my request was ignored made me angry. I had hoped that the whole process would be a memory. I thought I was clear about wanting to be left alone. I sat down and wrote another letter to the Hall of Fame, but in this letter I practically begged them to respect my wishes to be removed from consideration. No one from the Hall of Fame acknowledged my request so I didn't know what was going on. Then it dawned on me that with all of the rules and bylaws that the selection committee had to follow, they probably did not have any mechanism in place to remove someone's name from consideration. I'm sure some people before had verbally asked to be removed, but this was probably the first time anyone had formally requested it in writing. It is an honor and every person associated with football would want to be considered. I felt that I was stuck in a place that no one could understand except me! I felt angry and disappointed regarding the whole situation. I felt I was being dragged back into the same situation that I'd left when I retired in 1988 when I had no control over me and had to piss in the cup, or else. I had to live with me every second of every day. I knew what I had gone through as a player and as a person. I knew that my dignity had been dealt several severe blows without my being the cause of them. You can call it one of the misfortunes of living your life. It was simply the way it was. I made up my mind that I was not going to play along, not anymore!

The game had taught me the discipline to move forward and separate myself from unwanted situations. Whether it was a buddy being cut from the team and me having to move on, I had to do it. My ex-wife and I had separated earlier; it had taken me exactly one month to emotionally divorce myself from that situation. I was going to do the same with this issue. Regardless of what the Hall of Fame wanted to do, I was divorcing myself from it. I found it so ironic and yet so hypocritical that if I had done something illegal, the same people who would not let me off the list could have found cause to remove me. Those in the position to make the decisions might have thought I should have felt honored to be considered for the Hall of Fame. How dare I snub them and have the audacity to ask to be removed from the list? I thought it was ironic that Pete Rose wanted to be reinstated in baseball to be elected to the Baseball Hall of Fame, but he was denied because of his gambling. Then I thought about how O. J. Simpson is in the Hall of Fame but many would like to have him thrown out because of his legal problems off the field.

I considered myself divorced from the Hall and didn't want to get into any more discussions about it. When news of my actions surfaced in the media, I was not totally prepared for the response. What I had hoped would be a quiet acquiescence by officials in Canton turned into a topic of discussion by fans who either liked me as a player or a person or never cared for me at all. Some sports talk show hosts put their own spin on it and said that I was acting like a spoiled baby because I was not elected. Their listeners either agreed or could not understand why I would ask to be removed. On Internet blogs, people anonymously left their comments. I didn't ask for people's opinions but I was getting them. I found it amazing that some people felt insulted that I would turn my back on the honor. Those people obviously didn't know me, and I couldn't care less about them. Those were the same people who would look at a player as nothing but an object to be traded to get something better or felt he should be canned if he was "injury-prone." I played for a long time with a lot of players. I had never played with a player who went out on the field hoping to get hurt! These people never even played the game but they thought that by simply watching it on television they became instant experts. They felt that they could just pick up a phone, call a radio station, and voice their opinions for the entire world to hear. If those people knew what it took for an athlete to even get to the pro level, I'm sure they would have a newfound respect for most athletes. If they knew the training, the sacrifices, the commitment, and the dedication to play the game, then perhaps they would see the athlete in a different light. These fans want the athlete to be who and what they want him or her to be. As I listened to the various comments about me, it was apparent these people didn't know much about me, and for all I cared, they could go to hell!

When the middle of January rolled around, like clockwork I knew when that damn FedEx truck was coming and what it was bringing: my annual gift from the Pro Football Hall of Fame. When the carrier handed me the envelope, I took it and thanked him, then put it on the shelf with all of the other envelopes I had collected over the years. I didn't need to open it because I knew exactly what was in it. Same information but a different year; I knew the routine.

This year Maribel and I decided that we were going to do things differently. The Super Bowl was being played in Jacksonville, but I had no desire to go there. To me, going to Jacksonville, Florida, was like going to the lower part of South Carolina. I was from South Carolina so I knew what that was all about. It was not the same as going to Miami or San Diego for the Super Bowl where the weather is generally mild in late January or the beginning of February. If I was going to play golf that year, I didn't want to play in those northern-Florida temperatures that could be in the forties and fifties, so Maribel and I decided to blow off golf and leave for Hawaii earlier than we normally did with a twist to our plans. Instead of going directly to Honolulu, we decided to spend a couple of days in Maui. Before we arrived in Maui, Maribel issued a communication blackout rule. She did not want us to activate our cell phones, check e-mail, watch television, or listen to the radio while we were in Maui. While many of our family members knew that we were going to Hawaii, no one knew we would be in Maui. I agreed to honor Maribel's request and felt good about our time alone together. It felt great to carry on with my life and not think about what was happening in sports, especially in regard to the "situation."

On Sunday, the day of the Super Bowl, we had a nice brunch, sat on the beach looking for whales, then settled down to watch the game in our room. When I turned on the television to watch the pregame show, I saw a message across the bottom of the screen saying that Steve Young, Dan Marino, Benny Friedman, and Fritz Pollard had been elected to the Pro Football Hall of Fame.

I was happy for all of them, but I didn't really want to know. When the communication blackout ended I turned on my cell phone and found that my voice mail was full. Most were messages from radio stations or reporters I didn't know. Some were from people sending their "condolences" that I did not make it again. Two things struck me about those voice mails. One, I wished people would stop feeling sorry for me, and two, I felt badly for Vinny DiTrani. Vinny was the reporter covering the Giants whose job was to be my advocate. He had to get up year after year to explain to the committee why I should be elected. I knew he was frustrated, and I felt bad that he had to continue to speak on my behalf. Each time I was not chosen, he felt that he had failed me again, but by that time I didn't care about the voting.

I had another voice mail from Peter King, a columnist from *Sports Illustrated* magazine. My relationship with Peter went back many years to when he was a beat reporter covering the Giants. Peter was a voter for the Hall of Fame, and he wanted me to call him whenever I had a minute. When I returned his call, Peter wanted to know how I was doing. I told him that I was good and that I was on vacation. He shared some of his thoughts regarding the voting and said that he thought I was close. He also said that one or two writers may have voted against me because of my letter to the Hall of Fame. As much as I admired and respected Peter personally and as a journalist, I did not care about the situation. I had divorced myself and was hopeful that something could be done to eliminate my name from consideration. No one could begin to understand how strongly I felt about this. As much as I enjoyed supporting various causes by attending fund-raising dinners and events, I began to stop going because I did not want to have to answer questions or talk to anyone about the Hall. At times, just talking about it made my head hurt. It had gotten that bad! Most people could have seen the situation as a blessing. I saw it as a burden, a burden that I didn't want to deal with any longer.

That year, the New York Giants family suffered two devastating losses with the deaths of both owners Bob Tisch and Wellington Mara. I got to know Mr. Tisch (who purchased Tim Mara's 50 percent of the team in the early nineties) mainly for his philanthropy as his foundation restored athletic fields for kids in inner-city communities. I never had the opportunity to play for him as I had with Mr. Mara. All indications were that he was a good owner and a good person to be associated with.

Wellington Mara, on the other hand, had been around the Giants organization all his life. He was a decent family man who loved his religion, his family, his team, and the National Football League. I thought he was a great owner and I highly admired and respected him. He was probably my strongest supporter, and he seemed more disappointed than anyone else when I was voted down time after time for the Hall. I knew he always respected me as a player and a leader, but in his passing I found out again how he felt about me. When I went to Mr. Mara's wake, I saw one of his daughters and she said, "Harry, thanks for coming. You were one of my dad's favorites!" Then I said hello to another of Mr. Mara's daughters, and she said, "You were one of my father's favorite players!" Then I saw Ann Mara, Mr. Mara's widow, who said, "You know, you were one of his favorite players!" It was as if they were all on the same page. I had been a Giant for thirteen years, and while I could have gone to other teams after my career ended there, I wanted to have whatever legacy I had to be as a New York Giant. At times I had my differences with the team over my contract, but I always took pride in being a Giant. From my early days with the team, my one objective was to play and carry myself in such a manner that I would be mentioned in the same breath as some of the greats such as Sam Huff, Rosey Brown, Emlen Tunnell, Y. A. Tittle, Frank Gifford, and Andy Robustelli. That was my ultimate goal as a Giant. That goal was eventually realized when I was inducted into the New York Giants Ring of Honor in October of 2010.

Some other things that shook up my life were mainly about my son, Donald, and daughter, Aja. Donald was just graduating with his biology degree from Savannah State University. On the day of his graduation, I gave him a luncheon for our family and his friends to celebrate his accomplishment. I was as proud as I could be of my son and his accomplishment. It had been a long road for him, being born out of wedlock in 1983 to his mother, Patricia, with us working as a team coparenting him every step of the way to make sure he had both a mother and a father in his life. At the luncheon Donald was having a great time socializing with his family and friends, but he wore sunglasses for most of the day. When he took the glasses off, both Pat and I noticed that the whites of his eyes were yellow. He said he didn't know why, but he felt fine. Pat told him to get it checked out by a doctor. A couple of days later I received a call from Pat that Donald had been admitted to a hospital in Savannah. I immediately left New Jersey for Savannah, and when I arrived, I was told that Donald had severe aplastic anemia. In aplastic anemia, the bone marrow stops making the blood supply necessary for the body. The trigger is some form of hepatitis. Donald's bone marrow was only producing at 5 percent of his needs. Donald's illness came totally out of the blue, with no history of the condition in either Pat's family or mine. But I knew that people died from complications of aplastic anemia.

Donald and I both knew that he was facing some serious adversity that was not going to determine the outcome of a game, but whether he lived. Donald was an athlete who starred in both football and basketball, so he knew what adversity was all about and the commitment it took to work your way out of difficult circumstances. As my son lay in bed with intravenous tubes in his arms, hands, and neck, I told him that we were going to go through this situation together and that I was going to be his "wingman." As football players, we were going to tighten up our chin straps and face the situation head-on. We were not going to wallow in self-pity or question God, "Why us?"

Meanwhile, my daughter, Aja, was expecting her second child (the first was stillborn a year or two earlier) a week or two after Donald's graduation. Aja had been diagnosed with a form of cancer a couple of months earlier. That news was hard to take, but she told me that the cancer was in its early stages and there was nothing to be overly worried about. Cancer was not a part of my family history either, so just knowing that my child had some form of cancer caused me great concern. While I was with Donald in a Savannah hospital, my first grandchild, Jamison, was born in my hometown of Florence, South Carolina, on December 20. Savannah is about three hours away from Florence, but I could not travel late at night without some rest. I was torn as I knew my son needed me with him, but my daughter also needed her father with her at such an important and joyous time in her life.

Meanwhile, I had to travel back to New Jersey to tape a show with the Giants to be aired that weekend. So I left Donald at about three thirty in the morning and drove to Florence to see Aja and little Miss Jamison for the first time. When I arrived at Aja's hospital, it was early, but I was able to see her and she took me to see Jamison. It was a special feeling to see my first grandchild for the first time, but what was even more special was Aja's concern for her brother. Aja and Donald are half brother and sister and did not grow up in the same household, but they loved each other tremendously, unconditionally. Prior to delivery, Aja decided to harvest and freeze cells from her umbilical cord in the hope that they might help Donald if a stem-cell transplant was needed down the road. My daughter and I have always been close, even though we had some pains as she was growing up, but I was so proud of her for being so thoughtful. I was extremely happy to see that Jamison was healthy and looked every bit like her mother when she was born. I made my way back to New Jersey to take care of business, then headed back to Georgia to be with Donald for the Christmas holidays.

Donald spent several weeks in the hospital in Savannah, then was accepted into a research program at the National Institutes of Health in Bethesda, Maryland. He was getting good attention in Savannah, but at NIH he would receive some of the best care in the world by experts who knew aplastic anemia well. I spent many days in the hospital with Donald as he received blood and platelet transfusions. Day after day I wished that I could take the place of my son, but I could only show my support and be strong for him.

When Donald played basketball during his senior year, his team did not win one game. After his last game I told him that I loved him, was proud of him, and that he would learn so much from that season that he would carry with him for the rest of his life. In his football season, it was the same. His team did not win one game. After his last football game, I joined him on the sideline, where I told him that I loved him, was proud of him, and he would learn so much from that trying situation. When I told him those things, I drew off my own early experiences as an athlete with the Giants, and how those experiences made me stronger and wiser. Little did we realize how quickly Donald was going to have to learn from his adversities to help him to cope with his challenges.

After treatment at NIH, Donald's immune system was basically at zero, meaning he had to take extraspecial care to stay away from any kind of infection. If he got an infection where his temperature rose, he had about a six-hour window to get to a hospital to get intravenous medication to bring the fever down. We had a couple of close calls, but we got a grip on dealing with aplastic anemia. After his treatment Donald was relatively okay. He just needed to make sure that he was aware of his environment and stayed germ-free.

Maribel and I wondered if we should even look at traveling that year with Donald in such a delicate condition. Unselfishly, Donald said that he would be okay and that we should go ahead and travel, so we began to plan our trip back to Hawaii. We would not be going to Detroit, where the Super Bowl was to take place that year. If we didn't go to Jacksonville, I sure as hell wasn't going to be going to frigid Detroit, Michigan. We decided to leave the Saturday before the Super Bowl and fly directly to Honolulu. During that week I heard various sportscasters comment on who would make it into the Hall, so I knew it was time for me to hit the road. Once again, we would impose a communications blackout for the trip, but I alerted my family on how I could be reached while my phone was turned off.

Continental Airlines had the only nonstop flight from Newark, New Jersey, to Honolulu, so that was the best way to get there. I knew that the best rest I could get would be the ten hours of peace and solitude at thirty-seven thousand feet headed westbound. The flight left at 1:20 p.m. and I could not wait to take off. Once we were airborne, I felt a sense of peace and comfort I had not felt in some time. I had a lot on my plate, but the health of my kids took precedence over everything else. I had grown accustomed to sleeping in chairs or on couches in the hospital as I supported my son. I was at peace knowing that Aja's pregnancy was successful this time around. For once I just wanted some time to leave everything that was on my mind in New Jersey. During the ten hours of that flight the only things that reminded me of football were the people traveling to Hawaii with their children to participate in Pro Bowl activities. I tried to be as cordial as I could to those Giants fans on the flight who wanted to talk football. I honestly didn't care about talking football; I was looking forward to some tropical weather wherein I could rest and perhaps play a round of golf.

Upon our arrival in Hawaii, we made our way from the gate to a corridor that took us outside, where I felt the warm air hit my skin. It felt great to be back in a place that I had grown to love and enjoy. We had to go through another set of doors to take us back inside the main terminal. As we were heading down the escalators to the baggage claim, my main concern was whether I wanted to pay three bucks for a luggage cart or if I just wanted to lug our stuff over to the car. As I got off the escalator, I saw a young man sitting on a bench near the luggage carousel. He was familiar with the current and former players arriving for the beginning of Pro Bowl week and was waiting to get autographs. As I was about to walk by him, he said, "Hello, Mr. Carson." I said, "Hello." He then said, "Congratulations!" I responded with "For what?" He said, "For making the Hall of Fame!" I automatically said, "Thanks!" Maribel heard what the guy said but didn't comment.

As I stood at the carousel waiting for my bags, other people approached me and asked for autographs and congratulated me. As I signed a few items, I saw two guys whom I had grown accustomed to seeing in the baggage claim area when I traveled to Hawaii around Super Bowl and Pro Bowl time. They were always nice and courteous, so we struck up a conversation. They said I was finally elected, along with John Madden, Reggie White, Troy Aikman, Warren Moon, and Rayfield Wright. As I signed the items, they wanted me to put an *HOF 06* inscription behind my signature. I obliged them with my autograph but refused to add the inscription. I had been set up before by the Atlanta radio station, and I was not going to be set up again. I made some conversation, then headed over to the car rental area, and Maribel turned her phone on to see what was up. She had several messages from friends and family members who told her that I was elected. I then turned on my cell phone, and my voice mail was full. I called my son, Donald, to let him know that we'd arrived safely, and he said it was true, I had been elected to the Pro Football Hall of Fame.

We had left Newark, New Jersey, on Continental flight #15 at 1:20 p.m., and the announcement of newly elected members was made in Detroit at 2:00 p.m., so for almost nine hours everyone except us knew what had happened. As we made our way to the hotel, we drove with little conversation (which was not unusual). Then we stopped at Longs Drug Store at Ala Moana mall to get some needed items, and Maribel said, "Stop, Harry Carson! Tell me what you're thinking!"

I said, "We need to get our items and get to the hotel!"

"No, tell me what you're thinking about this situation."

"That's nice!"

The reality was, I felt nothing! What could have been a special time for me meant nothing. I fell on my sword by my own choosing and wanted no part of this situation. We eventually arrived at the hotel. Several messages were waiting for us when we checked in and on the phone in our room. What started as time to get away and relax was turning into something I did not particularly want. It had been a long trip and I didn't rest the way I thought I would during the flight. I was actually exhausted from the travel and just wanted to get some rest with the five-hour time difference. I remember that before going to bed I felt pissed off that I was in this situation. It seemed that the Hall of Fame and my football past had a grip on me and I could not break free of it, no matter what I wanted.

Many things came back to me that night as I tried to fall asleep. The first was the battles with George Young to determine my worth as a player in my contracts. From the first contract I signed, I had to fight for everything I got! Then there was the indignity of being accused of taking drugs and having to piss in a cup to prove my innocence. Further, I was placed on injured reserve by Parcells after my surgery my last season, and then the HOF didn't take into account my wish to be removed from consideration. Those things made me angry, but I also grew angry at the thought of laying my body on the line as a player and walking away from the game with aches and pains that I would have to deal with for the rest of my life. The bad shoulder, my back, my knees, and most important the injuries my brain sustained would be with me forever. To some people I should have been "honored" and considered it "a privilege to have had an opportunity to play professional football in the National Football League." Bullshit! Professional football should have been honored to have had me and others like me foolish enough to lay our bodies on the line as players to put what Wellington Mara once referred to as "a good product" on the field.

I wished that I had known at the beginning of my professional career what I came to know about the business and the sport of football. I wish someone had told me when I was signing my first contract that it was not solely about the talent I brought to the table as an athlete, but that I was also "leasing" out my body to the team and the league. My body was like a fine, well-tuned car upon entering professional football, and after thirteen years it had so many dents, scrapes, and scratches and so many miles on it that its value would have been almost nothing upon turning it in at the end of the lease period. Those dents would have been the most obvious damage, seen on the exterior. Opening the hood and checking the engine and the computer system of the car would have told a different story, and the damage might have been even more severe. When I played, I wondered why, if there was a warning on the side of a pack of cigarettes about the dangers of smoking, there wasn't a label on the back of every football helmet warning of the hazards of playing football. Playing football was hazardous not only to the body but also to the brain. The new contract of a professional athlete is oftentimes glorified in the media and by many spectators of the game. The judgment of an athlete's value is almost always based on his talent; no value is ever based on the injuries almost every player leaves the game with. One thing I wish I could have included in my contract was an "anticipatory clause," which would pay me and others for injuries we would have to live with for the rest of our lives from playing the game.

As I thought more and more about this situation, my anger grew. No one, not even Maribel, could begin to understand why I felt as I did. I had always been pretty easygoing, but that night I had a lot of hurt, disappointment, anger, and pain suppressed somewhere deep within my soul. I felt that I was either fucked or unappreciated in situation after situation with the Giants and with football in general. I don't know if I would have felt the same way if I had been a "regular" role player on the team. I think each situation could have been magnified because I was "the captain." As I fell asleep, the only thing I felt like saying was "Fuck *it* all!"

I didn't sleep well even though I was tired. When I woke up the next morning, my biological clock was still set for East Coast time. It was still dark outside, but my body was telling me that it was 10:00 a.m. even though it was

5:00 a.m. in Hawaii. I had received a call from the Giants public relations department that needed to be returned, but before I did so, Maribel and I had a talk. She told me that in spite of how I felt, I needed to express humility at being elected and not hold on to the hard line that I had adopted. She asked me to be gracious and at least accept the selection for my kids, even if I didn't care. To an extent she was right; I didn't care about the honor, but I agreed with her. I thought that I should remove any of my personal feelings and focus on those who wanted it for me. I could not care less, but I began to realize that I had to accept the honor for many family, friends, and teammates who'd helped and supported me throughout my football-playing years. I especially felt a need to accept the honor because of Mr. Mara's very public support over the years.

When I finally connected with the Giants, they set up a conference call with members of the New York media. I kept thinking to myself that no matter what I felt, I could not reject the recognition because Wellington Mara had wanted it for me. If I had rejected it, it would have been disrespectful of his wishes. When I finally did the conference call with the New York media, most of the reporters were in Detroit for the Super Bowl that day. For me it was early morning, I was tired, and I didn't feel like talking to anyone, but I tried to put the best possible spin on the situation and at least sound as if I were grateful to receive the honor.

I realized that the folks at the Hall of Fame were petrified that I was going to stiff them by not accepting the recognition. When they could not reach me on Saturday prior to the announcement, some thought I was deliberately not answering the phone. They were wrong, I was not ignoring their calls, but they certainly weren't on my mind. I had become a creature of what I had been taught to be as a football player. Marty Schottenheimer instilled in me, over and over, "Don't clutter your mind with unimportant things!" You have to find ways to adjust; getting away to Hawaii became my MO to unclutter my mind and handle the issues I needed to deal with.

For a couple of days Maribel continued to try to get me to verbalize what I was feeling, and I continued to not be "feeling" the Hall of Fame. Sunday and then Monday went by, and on the third day we were lying in bed when I began to share with her my thoughts. (It seems for all of my life I've only spoken when I am ready to speak, not because someone wants me to.) I told her that I couldn't care less about the honor, but I wanted to use it to help others. I had been monitoring the various e-mails of former players who were disgruntled and disappointed with their pensions and benefits. I felt that I needed to use the honor to highlight those issues. I had read a couple of magazine articles in which former players said they felt as if they were thrown away after their careers ended and it seemed that nobody gave a fuck about them. I have always tried to be a peacemaker and resolve differences, but I can be quite vocal and very much a militant if I need to be. Over the years I had seen many former players who played before me or during my era struggle with physical ailments, and it seemed as if nobody gave a shit about them!

The more I thought about the honor, the more I felt that things happen for a reason, and perhaps this honor could be used to call attention to issues I knew a lot about. I knew how I felt about the guys I played with, and they knew that I would always look out for them. My former teammates Phil McConkey and Jim Burt call me their "captain for life"! I have always been honored by that title and cherish the respect I continue to get from "my guys." The Hall honor was also an opportunity to help many former players I played against. I had been following the blogs of players who were bitter about their circumstances, and I'd also read various articles by players who'd fought the NFL system to get disability and lost. Some of those same people were already in the Pro Football Hall of Fame—players such as Johnny Unitas. He and others were denied disability when their bodies started to break down just because they did not file within a certain time limit. It made no sense. My body also had aches and pains that would come and go. When those pains came, it could be the absolute worst pain in the world to deal with. I admired those older players from afar for how they played the game in the fifties, sixties, and seventies, but now I was one of them.

I admired Earl Campbell so much as a player. I'd watched him when he played at Texas and then when he came to the NFL. I was a hard-nosed middle linebacker who had no problems taking on the toughest blockers and running backs, but I did not want any part of Earl Campbell. Like many others, I saw what he did to linebacker Isiah Robertson when he basically walked up Isiah's chest in a game when the Houston Oilers played against the Rams. When I went against Earl in games, I had much respect for him, but as a team we knew we had to gang-tackle him and not rely on one player to take him down. To this day when people ask, "Who was the hardest running back to bring down?" I acknowledge that at the NFL level everybody is tough, but Earl and Walter Payton top my list. Now when I see him, my heart aches for Earl as I see the pain and the suffering he has to go through. If I could use this Hall honor as a spotlight to shed attention on the plight of former players and the pain and hardship that many have to endure, then it would be worth it. As I talked to Maribel about the honor, I felt emotions that I normally shut down when I talk about the game. So many players came to mind as I began thinking about men I knew who left pieces of themselves out on the field when they played.

Maribel could probably not understand why I was getting emotional as I talked about this. Probably few people who never played football could understand. You had to have gone through what a player goes through to play for the love of the game and, more important, for your teammates. One player who immediately came to mind was Pittsburgh Steelers center Mike Webster. Mike was the epitome of a prideful player on the football field. Whenever the Giants played against the Steelers, I knew that I was going to have to work my ass off all day against someone who would never give up on the field. Considered by many to be the strongest man in the NFL, Mike wasn't a big guy in stature, but he made up for it in grit and determination. When I think of Mike Webster, I remember watching the Steelers breaking the offensive huddle and seeing Mike not walking but sprinting to the line of scrimmage with his arms bared even in the coldest weather, exposing his muscular biceps and triceps shining with a coat of Vaseline.

When Mike was on the field, I knew I was going to have to load up and bring it on every play. *Bringing it* simply means that it was going to be physical: power against power! Mike was not a cut blocker; he attacked the body of a defender. I knew he was going to try to get into my body to block me out of plays. Getting into my torso also gave him an opportunity to hold me. To keep him away from me, I had to attack him with as much power as I could, use my forearm flipper to the face and head to stun and neutralize him, then use my hands to quickly throw him away from where he was trying to block me. If he was coming right at me, I would have to attack him with my full force, hitting him with my forearm with as much power as possible from my lower body, and practically lift him with the upward force of what we called the flipper or shiver. I was exceptionally good at delivering a forearm to offensive linemen to get them off my body. The key was not just in getting the forearm in another guy's face, but to get the power from my lower body to accompany the shot. Parcells always indicated he liked guys from the South as defensive players because we had big asses with huge thighs. If you want power and thrust, we had it. We big-ass guys might not look that great in a uniform, but we delivered powerful blows on the football field.

All game long on running plays, if Webster was going to block me, I was going to be certain to get that forearm into his face to ward him off. We had some classic battles in which at times he got the best of me and I in turn got the best of him. Mike went on to have a Hall of Fame career with the Pittsburgh Steelers and then the Kansas City Chiefs, playing for seventeen years. When he retired, he went back to Pittsburgh, where he encountered many different problems off the field. It seemed that he could not get his life in order. Reportedly he was homeless and arrested for buying prescribed medication. From what I heard, I thought he had probably been dealing with some serious neurological issues. I knew that to play football you have to display intelligence and discipline. When abnormal things such as what happened to Mike occur after a career ends, there has to be a reason why.

Mike Webster passed away on September 24, 2002, at the age of fifty, and when he did, I had my suspicions. I had so much respect for Mike as a player and as a person. I felt the need to personally pay my respects and condolences to his family by attending his funeral service. While I was in Pennsylvania for his service, I met Garrett, Mike's son, who said his father had some "issues" before he passed away. I found out Mike had traumatic brain injuries, which caused his unusual actions.

As I joined former Pittsburgh Steelers players at the service, I prayed for Mike Webster and ached for his family. I felt partly responsible for the injuries he sustained. His downward spiral after football was a result of the pounding to the face and head he took from guys like me. Knowing the way Mike played, he would probably say, "Harry, that is the way the game was supposed to be played!" I would agree, but I still feel that I contributed to his condition and his demise. Nobody can begin to understand that except another player.

As I talked to Maribel, I could feel the streams of tears flowing down my cheeks. It was a good thing the lights were off because I might otherwise have been a little embarrassed. I was a proud guy who tried to suppress my emotions, but when I thought of those things they made me even more emotional. I think she may have understood better when I shared with her the observation I made from watching the Hall of Fame induction ceremonies over the years. I told her how, over several years, I watched the health of those great players who were touted as the "best of the NFL" and "those who made the NFL what it is today" decline quickly. Several years earlier, the former players were able to walk across the stage, but then their conditions deteriorated so quickly that they either limped or were wheeled across the stage and then eventually passed away. These HOF guys, such as Unitas, Campbell, and Webster, were no different from me. They started playing football when they were young, they didn't have the best equipment, nor did they have state-of-the-art facilities, but most knew what grass smelled like. Most of them were broken like me, if not physically, then neurologically. If I didn't say anything while I had a chance, I knew nobody was going to speak up on my behalf if anything happened to me down the road. At that point, both Maribel and I got it!

During that week in Hawaii we had to start thinking about who would present me for induction. I considered several choices. Coach Jeffries was my mentor and was like a surrogate father to me. I trusted him and he was a strong choice. I considered my daughter, Aja, my firstborn. We had a close and unique father/daughter bond. In speaking with Maribel, we decided that my son, Donald, was the best choice to handle that duty. We both felt it would give Donald the incentive to maintain his focus on getting better through his treatments. I called him while on the beach and asked him if he was up for the challenge of introducing me for induction. He was thrilled and said, "Hey, man, I live for the spotlight!" Surely it was his way of answering one of the more important calls from his dad.

As my induction date in Canton approached, I had no clue as to what I was going to say. At home, as I mowed the grass in my yard, I would practice in my head what I felt I needed to say. Much can be written about the Hall of Fame experience. Some people say it's a once-in-a-lifetime experience! I beg to differ; experiences like that do not occur in most people's lifetime at all. To that point, only 229 men out of the many thousands who had played and contributed to professional football had earned the honor of being inducted into the Pro Football Hall of Fame.

Maribel and I chose to drive to Canton instead of flying like most people, simply to enjoy the ride and take in the scenery. Taking our time and driving through picturesque areas of Pennsylvania gave me an opportunity to reflect on so many things, people, and memories. When we arrived in Canton, my focus was to make sure our families were situated and taken care of. More than anything else I wanted them to enjoy every minute of the experience. I had to take part in all of the activities that were on the schedule for the enshrinees. The highlight of the weekend was the induction ceremony. I had already received the golden Hall of Fame blazer the evening before at the enshrinement dinner, but at the actual induction the bust would be unveiled. I worked directly with the sculptor, Tuck Langland; when he completed my bust, he assured me that it would be around for at least forty thousand years. Hearing him say that made me understand that this was not just another trophy or plaque, of which I had acquired more than my share over my football career. This would outlive all of my relatives many times over. I felt like a dinosaur with my bones being discovered far off somewhere in the future.

I was so proud of Donald when he introduced me, especially since he had just undergone a second round of treatment for his condition at the National Institutes of Health in Maryland. He was strong and thoughtful in his presentation. I almost lost it emotionally when he finished. When we unveiled the bust, I gave him a big hug and prepared to say my piece. I didn't write a speech as I had an idea of what I wanted to say and I wasn't going to be long in making my point. I had ten minutes to say whatever I wanted to, so I started by challenging the NFL and the NFL Players Association to do a better job of taking care of "those who made the league what it is." Over the months leading up to the Hall of Fame inductions, I tried to talk with various media outlets about the issues of former players. When I did the interviews, most of the outlets opted not to air any criticisms I made of the NFL. Having the platform with millions watching on live television and standing in front of thousands of fans witnessing the inductions, I said what I felt I needed to say about the plight of retired players. Then I thanked various people for helping or inspiring me as a player. I felt humbled standing before my family, my friends, and former teammates on all levels of football. I realized that whatever honor I was receiving was not solely for me; whatever came to me had to be shared with every player I ever played with. They were the ones who challenged and inspired me every day on the football field.

I found the Hall of Fame weekend was interesting, not because of the honor, but primarily because everyone who supported me over the years, before, during, and after my football career, was in Canton to support me. Planning the invitation list was like coordinating a combination of a wedding and a head-of-state funeral. It was going to be such a joyous occasion that I did not want to omit anyone that I knew, but the event had a sense of finality. Out of the six enshrinees, I had more guests attending than anyone else, which surprised me a little. I thought Troy Aikman, John Madden, or Warren Moon would have more guests than me. Some of my guests who attended and I reconnected with I had not seen in thirty to forty years. While it was great to see most of these people, only an occasion such as this could get people from my past to travel to Canton, Ohio, in the middle of summer with temperatures bordering on a hundred degrees. Unfortunately, some of those people who attended the ceremonies that I had not seen in such a long time I knew I would never see again. If they did come anywhere to see me again, I would be in a casket and wouldn't know anyway.

I've never been much of a party person, but I enjoyed the experience for the sake of my family. When everything was over and everyone made it back to their homes, I felt relief. The party was over and I was happy to get back to living my life. But there was one thing I kept thinking about and it resonated deep in my soul as we were driving back through Pennsylvania. Regardless of how I felt about the Hall of Fame recognition, it was mind-blowing to be that one person in my family to reach such a level of accomplishment. I've never traced my roots back to my slave ancestors arriving on ships to this country, but it is humbling, out of all the many men and women for generations and generations, to be the one to reach that level of accomplishment. If the Hall of Fame honor was ever going to mean something to me, this was it! I realized I represented more than I could ever imagine. My granddaughter, Jamison, who was about eight months old at the time of the induction, was sitting in the first row on the lap of my daughter, Aja. I thought to myself that she, her daughter, and her daughter's daughter had something to shoot for. Anytime they have doubts about their ability to do something special or be the best at what they want to do, all they have to do is come to see their papa in Canton.

I was always cognizant that I represented more than Harry Carson when I played football. Actually, whether I played football or not, I'd always felt that I represented more than myself. Because of the exposure I got from football, I felt I had to hold myself up more and try to be an example of something good and positive as opposed to some of the negative stuff athletes, especially black athletes, are tagged with by the general public. Coming out of South Carolina State, I knew when I went to the Giants that if I had fucked up in any way, those folks I left at State would never forgive me. The same was true of all the black folks in Florence. Nobody told me per se, but I automatically knew it. I had my own life, but a part of me belonged to so many other people whom I represented.

My family, my coaches, my ministers, my teachers, my friends, people from Florence, people from South Carolina, or black people in general, I knew what they wanted. I had been around enough people of each group to know how they felt when someone did something despicable: they all hoped that whoever it was was not their race or color, from their city, state, or school. Each group did not want to be identified with some criminal who raped and killed some woman or child. When I used to hear folks say, "I hope they are not black" when something bad happened, I clearly knew as an athlete that the unspoken expectation was that I be a good role model to make those groups I represented proud. I did not totally belong to me. I belonged to so many other groups that I never thought about. I think back on many instances, such as meeting the old black gentleman in Harlem who told me that I made him proud to be a black man when he saw me on television, or how my hometown had a Harry Carson Day after the Giants won Super Bowl XXI. So many people, young and old, black and white, came out to honor and celebrate me. Attending SC State and my early years at Holmes School taught me to always be humble and carry myself with dignity, pride, and respect. Had I not gotten the "memo" from my black educational experiences, perhaps I would have had a different mind-set, but what had been ingrained in me from so many sources has worked to make me the person I am.

Some people that I had hoped to be able to acknowledge at the Hall of Fame I was unable to. Those were the football players I played with in high school, college, and the Giants. When I stood back and assessed my career, I knew that no matter how good I may have been, I could not have done it by myself. For every Jim Brown or Barry Sanders, there has to be a teammate who threw the block and opened the hole to help him be the success he was. If I was going to be recognized, I had to thank all of those guys whom I played with and who inspired me. I had already sent autographed Hall of Fame helmets to all of my head football coaches, but I wanted to thank every player as well.

When I returned to New Jersey, I invited all of my Giants teammates, regardless of when they played, to a dinner at the Assembly Steak House in Englewood Cliffs, New Jersey, to thank them for their support and inspiration. Those guys were the ones who pushed me to be their captain and leader. After that dinner in New Jersey, I put together a similar dinner during my college homecoming that fall. This gave me an opportunity to reconnect with guys I played with when I was at South Carolina State. I got so much from my college experience that whatever I did in the NFL had to be shared with those guys I played with in Orangeburg. As I stood in front of them, I shared with them the humility I felt to have been able to represent them all both on the field and off it. After that, I arranged a small dinner at a steak house in my hometown of Florence with as many guys as I could find that I played high school football with. I was able to connect with eight to ten guys, but being with them took me back to a time that I had been so far removed from. In both the high school and college groups there were guys I had not spoken to for years and years and years. To those guys I was not Harry Carson Hall of Famer; to them I was either Carson, the name I was called in high school, or Big Dog, the name I was called in college. Of the many guys I played with in high school and college, I wondered why I was the one to do what I did as an athlete. With each group I felt a special bond. In some ways it seemed that I was supposed to be the one to handle the mission that was to be completed.

If I had regrets regarding the Hall of Fame, it would be that my departed loved ones could not be there with the rest of my family. Sharing this special time with my family was the best gift I could ever have gotten them. Dedicating this experience to them could well have made my life's journey complete. I've always maintained that I am not a religious person, but I am a spiritual person. My family members who were on the other side were not there in body, but I'm sure they were all there in spirit. I would bet all of my relatives got together in heaven, along with Troy Archer, Doug Kotar, Rosey Brown, Emlen Tunnell, John Dziegel, and Wellington Mara, to celebrate the occasion. And I know that if my mama had anything to do with the occasion, everybody there would have been eating her fried chicken, potato salad, and macaroni and cheese—my favorite meal.

The most important thing I did in my fifteen seconds of fame may have been imploring the National Football League and National Football League Players Association to do better by past players who gave parts of their lives to football. It didn't take me long playing the game to understand that any player who plays the game, especially on the NFL level, leaves something on the field that he will never get back. I was aware of my own sacrificial offerings: my knees, shoulder, and brain matter. But I also knew many guys whom I played with and against who had multiple knee operations, sometimes to replace the knee joint, or hip-replacement surgery. Those knees and hips will eventually heal. What concerns me most about myself and all the other guys who played are the concussions and the long-term effects they will have.

Whenever former players get together, we all talk about different guys having to have knees or hips replaced or back surgeries after leaving the game. But few players talk about the head injuries they sustained. Ironically, a couple of players I played against have shared with me stories of when we competed against each other and how hard I hit them. In an earlier chapter I spoke of the comments O. J. Simpson made to me back in the day. But several other former players, such as fullback Robert Newhouse of the Dallas Cowboys and fullback Theotis Brown of the St. Louis Cardinals, felt comfortable enough to share with me the news that I gave them concussions when we played. Information like that never comes up while players are still active, but once they are out of the game some truths can be spoken aloud. While today we can sometimes joke about it in passing, I know how serious those concussions may have been when they were sustained. Newhouse told me that while he was trying to block me low on a running play, my knee caught him in the head. Theotis told me that I caught him in the head on a play when he was trying to convert a third-down run into a first down, and I knocked the crap out of him. As a result, he lost a good five hours of his life and he does not have any recollection of it. I've heard all kinds of stories like that from players I've played against. At times I wish I'd had that information when I played, but it's good to know now in retirement.

I've never had any apprehension about sharing my neurological issues with another player or his family, which gives them insight about what they or their loved ones might be experiencing. By sharing and listening to others, I know most players don't have a clue that the dings or concussions they have sustained can have serious long-term effects. I didn't know what was going on with me until I was tested and diagnosed several years after I left professional football. Many others could have the same neurological issues without even knowing it.

I have never viewed making the Pro Football Hall of Fame as being about me. When I watch today's football players make big plays, they thump their chest and point at themselves as if to say, "It's all about me!" Making a play or two sometimes in a meaningless game is one thing. But if there's one time to beam with pride and get a big head, it's getting a golden blazer and a bust in Canton. Fortunately, I never felt I needed that validation and I was perfectly happy to just live my life as a former player in obscurity. But the recognition gave me a voice. My knowledge of my own concussions and what it took to play the game on the highest level give me insight and an understanding that is priceless. I am acutely aware that I am not the first former football player to be where I am now. But now that I am so far removed from playing the game, I can clearly see where I came from. With the passage of time, I am not the same gung ho guy as I was as an active player. Over time I have developed broad concerns for younger players and how they play the game now. They are bigger, faster, and stronger than ever. That is what football has become on every level.

I can see the road ahead might not be as clear or as smooth as I would want it to be. I have spent so much time around football and football players in almost everything I've done. In looking ahead and getting to know those who played before me and some I played against when I was younger, I am astonished by the number who are dealing with dementia, Alzheimer's disease, or some other neurological impairment. The number of these former players, many who were not high-profile players, is staggering. Playing on a team such as the New York Giants, Wellington Mara always emphasized, "Once a Giant, always a Giant." The Giants organization has always been pretty good about being involved with its alumni players. But to hear that player after player from those great Giants teams are being diagnosed with dementia is amazing. When I learned of other well-known cases such as Mike Webster and John Mackey, it opened my eyes to something that was very real and could be a possibility for me down the line.

Those years it took to be elected to the Hall gave me an opportunity to even see several Hall of Famers battling those conditions before passing on. John Mackey had been an outstanding tight end for the Baltimore Colts back in the sixties and early seventies. After my career ended, I dealt with John on business. He was a smart and astute businessperson whom all players greatly admired. To discover that John was no longer the John Mackey I remembered was a blow to me, but also to so many others associated with the game. How could dementia get a grip on such an athletically and intellectually strong person as John Mackey?

Nobody wants to talk about dementia and football players. Why? Probably because the condition is normally attributed to aged people who are confined in a nursing home somewhere. It does not happen to big, strong former football players. When I first heard that John Mackey was a victim of dementia, I had no clue as to what the condition was, but once I learned about it, I could not believe it. My heart went out to his wife, Sylvia, who is such a sweetheart. She had to step up to become John's caregiver after he was diagnosed. Sylvia has great courage and strength, and she advocated and lobbied the then commissioner, Paul Tagliabue, and the NFL on behalf of John and other players and their families in the same position for assistance. Because of Sylvia's efforts the league created the 88 Plan to help players and their families stricken with dementia. Mackey's jersey number was 88, so the plan was created in his honor. Former players who are cared for at home by family members receive $50,000 a year for their care. Those who have to be institutionalized receive $88,000 yearly for their care from the National Football League. The use of John Mackey's fame and celebrity by his wife helped to shine a light on a condition that many NFL families dealt with primarily in private. The money to help a player and his family can never be enough. How can you put a price tag on being a shell of yourself? But, it is better than nothing!

Knowing about my own condition and sensing a need to share as much as possible with others, I have become an advocate for my pro football brethren. I've taken part in various neurological testing programs to see what can be done to help former players. Because of my willingness to share information, several players I've played with and against have felt comfortable enough to seek my help with the neurological issues they have experienced. As their captain for life, my guys know that I would do almost anything I can to help them. Some who are having head issues fear sharing what they are experiencing with their wives or significant others, but they trust me to assist them with getting neurologically evaluated.

Usually when the players won't reach out for help it's because of tremendous pride or being in denial. Fortunately, some wives have noticed changes in their husbands' demeanors and have reached out for assistance. I am always available to help, but the disturbing trend that I am now seeing is that most of the former players who are having neurological issues are younger than me. Not only are they younger than me, but some of those players had told me that they had never sustained a concussion. Now I hear things like "Harry, I'm having problems trying to stay focused" or "I feel like I'm going crazy" or "I can't remember some things that I should." Some have been experiencing seizures even while driving, or they have been battling bouts of depression. Some wives have taken car keys from their husbands for fear that they will get lost in their own neighborhood. Some of these guys I know about are still somewhat physically active or may more recently have been diagnosed with dementia, while others have slowed down and are housebound because their condition has significantly progressed. I always think of how proud those guys were as players and how they sometimes now live without the dignity they should be experiencing as former players. Whether it's not being able to remember family members, to recall the name of a friend, or to control their bodily functions, it's hard to see or even know that a former player is in that position and that nothing can be done for him.

I feel a contradiction in the whole issue of fame. As a Hall of Famer, I walk a line that most people cannot identify with. I am cheered and adorned with praise by fans for what I did on the football field. But most people don't know who I am or care. I was a good player, not a great player, and as I walk that line, I always have to keep myself in check to understand that whatever I did as a football player is of no relevance to anyone, including me. When I reflect back on my journey to get to the Hall, I now feel that God knew exactly what he was doing with me in that process. I was put in situation after situation to understand what really matters. Having the courage and a voice to speak up for all retired players opened the ears and the eyes of many, including the National Football League. It opened the eyes of the media and the eyes of the general public, who thought former football players had it made once they retired from the game.

Several months after my Hall of Fame induction, I was invited by Commissioner Roger Goodell to the National Football League headquarters at 280 Park Avenue in New York to discuss the issues of retired NFL players. Before that meeting, I felt like so many other former players that nobody gave a fuck about after they left the game, especially all those guys who played well before big contracts or did not have a recognizable name. My meeting with Roger Goodell set the stage for dialogues with other groups, such as the National Football League Players Association, NFL Alumni Association, the Pro Football

Hall of Fame, and retired players, to create the NFL Alliance. The Alliance's purpose is to create programs that help former players with injuries and issues that stemmed from playing in the NFL. With the creation of that alliance, I feel that league officials have at least made a good-faith effort to begin programs to assist retired players. One of these plans is a joint-replacement program for former players who do not have the financial means to have a knee, hip, or shoulder replaced. The league has also developed a relationship with assisted-living facilities around the country for former players who need that kind of long-term care. These are only a couple of programs, but they are at least the start of a dialogue to help make things better for former players.

I've spoken to many former players I played with and against who have thanked me for standing up for them. Many told me that when I made the Hall of Fame, they felt that they made the Hall of Fame. That in itself makes me happy and proud!

CHAPTER 18

Quack . . . Quack!

As I move forward with my life, I will readily admit that I have never experienced a helluva lot of things. I've never run the New York City or Boston Marathons, nor have I ever climbed mountains that look like a challenge to conquer. Some Harry Carson fans know I've always semisecretly yearned to be a pilot. I was lucky enough to fly in the backseat of an F-4 Phantom jet. The flight took place just prior to my last season as a player and was one of the thrills of my lifetime. After strafing a few targets with cannon fire and dropping a couple of dummy bombs at a firing range in southern New Jersey, the pilot and I headed back to McGuire Air Force Base in New Jersey and shared some small talk. I told him that I thought it was so damn cool that he could fly jets every day for a living, but he thought my job playing football was the coolest. To play before so many fans on Sunday afternoons appealed to him. I never doubted his knowledge in flying a multimillion-dollar military aircraft, but he didn't know all that it took to play so many seasons of professional football; I did. I knew firsthand all of the variables or obstacles it took just to get from those playing fields of Florence, South Carolina, to the National Football League, not to mention being able to stay there for as long as I had.

To have even made the transition from lineman to linebacker took more intelligence and determination than I ever thought I had. To play the average four-year NFL career took great skill and talent for most players, but for me to play (at that point) twelve years took luck, will, discipline, talent, but also a lot of skill, adjustments, and determination. I could not say all of that from the backseat as we were descending for our landing. Most people don't want to hear about the trivial things such as labor pains in giving birth; they just want to see the baby. I didn't know the journey he took to be able to sit in the front seat and command such a powerful machine. I didn't want to bog him down with my journey to wear a Giants uniform, but there was much I could have told him.

While I have never experienced many things, the things that I have experienced and the things that I know, I know for pretty damn sure! Here are just a few no-brainer "for sure" things that I am willing to share. I know that for every beginning, there has to be an end. As a player I saw that almost every week when another player was either released, retired, or traded from the Giants. I know that if you have a secret that you want to remain a secret, keep it to yourself. I know that not all truths are to be spoken at all times. And I definitely know that all that you have can be taken in the blink of an eye!

Football was a fantastic platform for me to learn many valuable lessons, some of which I've shared in writing this book. Some lessons are learned quickly, such as if you don't have the toughness to play a sport such as football, it's better to stay in the stands and be a spectator than to attempt to play. I know for damn sure that football is not a game for timid or soft people.

I've always been intrigued by hotshot athletes who look at their talent and automatically think that it will last forever. We often take for granted the speed, the quickness, the agility, and the strength of athletes, but one hit, one snap of the Achilles tendon, or one wrong twist of the knee, ankle, or turn of the back can adversely affect an athlete's ability to perform. Year after year I saw players come into the league with so much talent, then fall by the wayside because of one hit or one wrong turn. With that one hit or misstep, a career or a dream was over. *Over* can mean the end of a career, but *over* can also mean the loss of the ability to live one's life as it had been before.

When I think of all that can be taken in the blink of an eye, I immediately think of my good friend Marc Buoniconti, who played for the Citadel. On one play in 1985, while making a tackle, he severed his spinal cord. In one instant, Marc lost his ability to walk or use his arms. In one blink of an eye, Marc went from being a big, strong athlete like his Pro Football Hall of Fame linebacker father, Nick Buoniconti, to a quadriplegic confined to a wheelchair. Whether it's the talent of an athlete being stripped instantaneously, or breaking a leg and not being able to run, or losing a loved one, in the blink of an eye all can be gone. Football taught me to never take what I have for granted because in that blink of an eye everything can be taken, *just like that*!

I know for damn sure that even though I played football at the highest level, I was never built to be a real football player. I played because I wanted to belong and be a part of something. I was influenced by many people or situations as I was growing up. Whether it was the pretty girls (who when around the practice field or at a game made me and my teammates stand up straight with our stomachs in, chests out, and shoulders back like a platoon of marines) or the uniform, I wanted to be a part of what I saw on the field.

One reporter who covered me while I played with the Giants hit the proverbial nail on the head when he wrote an article on concussions and interviewed me for the piece. Bob Drury of *Men's Health* magazine wrote, "I began my career in journalism as a sportswriter, covering [Harry] Carson and the NY Giants. Of the hundreds of athletes I've observed and conversed with, I found Carson to be the most sensitive, introspective and soft-spoken—an anomaly, given the manic violence he brought to the football field."

Drury was one of the few writers, teammates, coaches, or even fans who got the essence of who I was as a player. My mind-set was never like that of "real" linebackers such as Dick Butkus, Ray Nitschke, Willie Lanier, or Jack Lambert. Those players wanted to rip a running back's head off and took pride in doing so. I played and enjoyed the game, but I never wanted to hurt anyone. I've always been a big old mama's boy, and while I grew into being a rather big and physically imposing man, I was always gentle and was taught from an early age to be caring and compassionate. Those football players who projected themselves as being glass-eating wild dogs were the antithesis of who I was as a player and as a person. I cared about those I played with and even those I played against. Most important, I cared about myself and my own well-being. Early in my football journey, once I understood what I had to do to be my best both on and off the field, I did it. I learned early on that cutting corners to achieve a goal or making excuses for failures was unacceptable. For so many years as a football player I heard coaches tell players that to be the best player or to be the best team you had to be willing to "pay the price." While I heard that phrase a thousand times, nobody ever told me what price I was paying when I was competing.

In playing the game I was always cognizant of my own physical nature and my method of processing information intellectually. From the moment I stepped on a football field I had to learn positions and schemes. I also had to think about how I thought and solved problems. To most people, football is just about guys running around on the field knocking the shit out of one another. To me, it was remembering everything that had been drilled into me, from the basic fundamentals I was taught at the very beginning to more complicated goal-line defenses or blitz packages. I had to implement what was covered in practice in a game, even with so much adrenaline in my system that I could hardly feel my legs supporting my body. When I played, I had to be cerebral to achieve success. The same gathering and storing of information became a part of my off-the-field life.

As I live my life after the game, I also know for sure that the effects of injuries I sustained as a football player are with me every minute of every day. My links to the NFL and football in general are there forever. My lingering injuries are part of the price I paid to play and to be one of the best at what I did. I'm aware of the physical pain, but even more of the brain injuries that I gave to others and sustained myself on the field. The physical and neurological damage many players suffer in games is not the main topic people want to discuss when they sit down to watch their favorite football teams play one another.

I know for sure that the issue is real, and for as long as players play football I know for damn sure that it will not be going away. I've done much in educating myself on concussion-related issues, and I've been actively involved with traumatic-brain-injury causes. I've sat on and taken part in medical panel discussions with some of the country's most renowned neurologists and individuals who specialize in concussion and brain-injury studies. I've shared the stage with Dr. Joseph Maroon, Dr. Mark Lovell, Dr. Robert Cantu, and Dr. Julian Bailes, four of the foremost authorities on the condition, and I've learned much from all of them. I've spoken before numerous medical groups looking for information on reducing concussions. Since playing football I've been a member of many commissions, advisory boards, and committees. Everyone is looking for ways to reduce the number of concussions players sustain while playing football.

Concussions are an issue not only for professional football, but for other sports such as youth soccer, boxing, wrestling, hockey, horseback riding, lacrosse, and even auto racing. Since I've personally seen the effects of concussions, I have no problem advising parents who seek my opinion regarding their children. Often they are looking for guidance with a son who has had several concussions as a ninth, tenth, and eleventh grader but still wants to play football or wrestle as a senior because he needs to earn an athletic scholarship to attend college. I've counseled and given encouragement to young women who have sustained concussions after hitting soccer balls with their head or have fallen off horses, hitting their head. The case of hockey's Pat LaFontaine, formerly of the New York Rangers, is well documented, but so many other hockey players, such as brothers Brett and Eric Lindros, have had to sit because of the effects of concussions they sustained. The cases of my fellow Hall of Famers quarterbacks Steve Young and Troy Aikman are also well documented. We all know about these athletes, but most fans know nothing about other athletes. Few know that Dale Earnhardt Jr. sustained a concussion several years ago in a track accident. He did not want to acknowledge it because he witnessed the scrutiny his fellow racer Steve Park was subjected to and feared how his sponsors would react. I see the effects of concussions on athletes from other sports, but most of my attention is focused on incidences in football.

Some people in the media wonder what my position is regarding concussions, especially when former players such as Wayne Chrebet and Al Toon of the New York Jets, or even Tim Tebow as a college player, have been affected by a big hit in a game. They want to know because I've been vocal about head injuries since the mid-1990s and I've been willing to talk about the issue with almost anyone. Most people who have never played a down of football fail to realize that players sustaining a ding (even multiple dings) or light concussions during a game or practice never report them to the team's medical staff. Most athletes know, whether the sport is football, hockey, or NASCAR, that "competing through injuries is expected!" That quote didn't come from me; it came from former racer Dale Jarrett. Usually, unless a player is unable to continue in practice or a game, not much is made of it. Only when big hits are highlighted on ESPN's *SportsCenter* or when high-profile players such as quarterbacks Aikman and Young, wide receivers such as Chrebet and Toon, or running backs such as Clinton Portis and Brian Westbrook are affected is attention given to head injuries.

I know the love and the passion you need to play football on the highest level. I appreciate even more the many valuable life lessons that can be acquired as a result of playing the game. But I can say emphatically and without hesitation that the human body was not built to play football, especially professional football. If I were a huge football fan and loved the game like so many people, I would probably say, "That Carson doesn't know what the hell he's talking about!" Unless you've played the game as I have and have the same experiences as I have, "stay the fuck in your lane." I know what I'm talking about, for sure!

From the beginning of my football experience to the end, I knew what it took to play the game; I know the good and I know the bad. In my journey through professional football, all who have followed the game with some degree of knowledge will have to admit that I had some of the absolute best defensive coaches to prepare me to play. With coaches such as Bill Arnsparger, Marty Schottenheimer, Bill Parcells, and Bill Belichick to learn from, I was good enough to earn many awards, make nine trips to the Pro Bowl, and ultimately make the Pro Football Hall of Fame. With the outstanding coaching I received mixed with my athletic talent and leadership qualities, I was a good player. I was trained to pay attention to minor details as well as to have an understanding of the cause and effect of situations on and off the field.

In the first pages of this book I noted that out of the many millions of young men ever to play football, no two players have had the same experiences getting to the top. My experiences are mine and cannot be disputed by anyone, but especially not by anyone who has never played the game. When I am in the company of other former players, or when I read some of their stories, I often hear them automatically say with passion, "I loved the game, I wouldn't change a thing, and I'd do it all over again in a heartbeat!" At some point I fell in line and said the same thing. Perhaps I was trying to be politically correct or something like that. In doing so, I was not being my authentic self. For most of my life I never went along with anyone else's program to be politically correct. Over time I realized that as a man who played at the highest level and eventually achieved the sport's highest honor, I needed to say as openly and honestly as I possibly could, "Not me!" I enjoyed playing the game, but I never really loved it like so many others. Playing football was something I fell into; it was never ever who I was!

One of God's true blessings is the ability to exercise hindsight, to be retrospective. I can remember being a football fan like so many other people. While I watched football games on television, I can't remember those New York Giants teams that played in the Polo Grounds or Yankee Stadium. But in my everyday travels I encounter so many football fans (especially Giants fans) who speak of their team loyalty that goes back to those venues. Those fans want me to know just how die-hard they are in support of their team. I can only remember a few Washington Redskins, Baltimore Colts, and maybe Philadelphia Eagles games here and there being shown in my little area of South Carolina as a kid in the 1960s. I do remember those early Super Bowls with teams such as the Kansas City Chiefs, the Baltimore Colts, and even the Steelers teams of the midseventies. When I think of stars from those teams, players such as Otis Taylor, John Mackey, and Mike Webster are standouts that come to mind. Unfortunately, I see players who preceded me in the game and what the effects of blows to their heads and concussions have done to them. Many of those former players from that era are now experiencing symptoms of dementia and Alzheimer's or may have passed away as a result of complications from those illnesses. I played the game just like those great players and countless others like them. To know that

I might be heading in the same direction as they've gone, it would be insane, idiotic, and asinine for me to say, "I'd do it all over again!"

We all played football of our own free will. Nobody put a gun to our heads and forced us to play. We were gladiators on the football field who were compensated for the talent we displayed. But for all of us gladiators who leased out our bodies to make the plays that fans cheered for, where do we go to be compensated for the pain and discomfort we now deal with? Our knees and hips may have been surgically replaced, our ankle, shoulder, and back pains may have subsided, but where do we go when our brains begin to fail us as a result of hits to the head? Because I know what I know for sure, I cannot passively sit back, bite my tongue, and go along with the program like many former players who were just "happy" to play the game.

Saying nothing and keeping my mouth shut is the easiest and safest thing to do for a former player such as me. Most would say, "Carson, you played. You are a Hall of Famer. Keep your mouth shut. Don't create any waves and just live your life." That was not the way I was built as a human being or as a man. When my family members get together and reminisce about the past, they always remind me that I didn't begin to talk until I was four years old. Most relatives who truly know me say, "Don Don [my family nickname] was always pretty quiet unless he really had something to say." Ironically, that was also the case when I was captain of the Giants. When I had something to say, I had no problem saying it and standing by it, such as with my out-of-the-box requests to Parcells for "live entertainment" for our players or even with my stance with the Pro Football Hall of Fame. The problem most close friends know I have is that when I do speak, I am sometimes not as tactful or politically correct as I should be and sometimes hurt people's feelings while trying to make my point clear.

Many things I learned long ago continue to echo in my head. Marty Schottenheimer's instructions "When the center blocks back, step up" and "Don't clutter your mind with unimportant things!" have always resonated in my head. I could not care less for unnecessary bullshit such as the reality programs and awards programs that we are now bombarded with on television, and I have no time for simple-minded, bigoted people in real life. As Bob Drury indicated, I've always been introspective and more serious-minded than most athletes, and I've always gravitated to people and causes that were important to me, even at the risk of alienating others from me.

I know for sure that playing professional football was a diversion in my life, yet it was the best "temp job" I could have had. While I played the game, I had fun and I took my job seriously. But, in retrospect, the toll on my body and my brain to play the game was not worth the glory, fame, or the money. If someone had told me a long time ago that by playing football I would risk permanent physical pain long after my last play, I might have weighed the risks and still played. In the first football game I saw in person, at the age of seven or eight, I was fascinated by the play on the field, but I also saw injured players being helped off that field. I knew players got hurt, but I could not comprehend what pain and injury were at that time. Now I can say to anyone who is even thinking about playing football that he has to keep his eyes wide-open to the possibility that he will get seriously hurt.

If someone had told me that I risked permanent brain damage long after my last play on the football field, I would have said, "Oh, hell no!" All players are aware of the physical risks of playing, and they still play. But few players understand the long-term neurological risks. They see the injured knee by way of an X-ray, they see the hip damage via MRI, but they don't see the bruise on the brain after a blow to the head. They don't realize that a concussion they sustain today can impact their lives forever.

Many of my coaches and teammates could have told me almost everything I needed to know to be the best on the football field. Unfortunately, none of them ever told me of the neurological risks I was assuming in playing. They couldn't tell me because they didn't know themselves. They didn't know because no one told them! For generations, no one knew the long-term neurological risks of playing football. The players didn't know, their coaches didn't know, and the doctors who treated them probably didn't know the long-term effects of the dings, getting your bell rung, or whatever other name you want to give a concussion. No one knew because no one talked about it or people just didn't understand the long-term effects of head trauma.

I have always tried to be a keen observer of my own life, and while at times I didn't want to see certain things about myself, I had to be concerned about my well-being because if I wasn't, no one else would be. The sometimes minor lapses of memory, the anxiety, the headaches, the sensitivity to bright lights and noise, and the bouts of depression were symptoms I noticed long before anyone else. I lived with those things in silence for the longest time. It was more convenient to leave things alone and hope that everything went away than to try to explain myself to others. I was clearly in denial, hoping the symptoms would go away, but those symptoms usually came back. When I began to focus on my condition, I thought I was going crazy until I was tested and eventually diagnosed with postconcussion syndrome. I knew these things were happening while I played, but I was trained from the first time I stepped on the football field to man up, ignore pain, be tough, and press on. Over the years I've spoken with countless players who have had the same symptoms I've had, and although they have not officially been diagnosed by a medical professional, I know full well they are dealing with the lingering effects of concussions.

What was not publicly discussed or even acknowledged, especially by macho football players, years ago is now receiving prime-time attention by the media, by government officials, and by fans of football. People are finally talking about how concussions in football players lead to dementia, Alzheimer's, and ALS (Lou Gehrig's disease). Medical professionals have conducted and will continue to conduct study after study on former players to see the correlations between concussions and neurological disorders. A growing number of current and former professional players have gone so far as to say they will donate their brains after their death for research to determine the links between the concussions they sustained on the playing fields and debilitating neurological conditions later in life. The NFL has conducted its own studies on the correlation between concussions and long-term neurological conditions. After years of having medical professionals (hired by the league) deny a connection between dings and players' neurological issues later in life, the league has done an about-face and is now warning players of the possible problems.

I appreciate the National Football League stepping forward to answer questions on possible correlations. After years of league doctors' proclaiming that there was "no evidence of a connection," I was shocked to see the NFL acknowledge what many former players already knew. After years of hearing the same refrain, I had grown pessimistic and thought the league would never come to any "definitive conclusion" linking concussions in football to neurological abnormalities in later years. I had grown to believe the NFL was going to be just like the U.S. military when it denied any correlation between soldiers' exposure to the defoliant Agent Orange during the Vietnam War and the illnesses they experienced years later. Those soldiers who gallantly fought in Vietnam, Cambodia, or Thailand were almost in the same situation as former pro football players. Those football players did not put their lives on the line like those soldiers, but they did, unbeknownst to them, put their brains at risk to entertain. A father who knows what war is all about and who perhaps suffers from an illness as a result of fighting as a loyal soldier, and who is then screwed around by his government over benefits, will teach his son not to be as blindly trusting as he was. That brings me to my next sure thing that I know.

Ironically, while I had a good football career, I know for damn sure that I never wanted my sons to follow in my footsteps. Many former players had sons who were talented enough to follow them into the National Football League. I applaud them! My sons loved that I had been a respected professional football player. I know deep inside that they would have loved to have played the same as I did. Fortunately, their father knows something that most parents don't know, and I am not willing to put them at risk. The physical and, more important, the neurological risks are not worth it for them to show me or anyone else that they might be just as good as I was as a football player. *My family* is the absolute most important thing to me. They are what I feel most passionate about, and they are the only ones in the world I would lay my life on the line for. I know for sure that I value the health and well-being of my sons enough to steer them away from football. I never ever wanted them to play professionally for the fame or the money, only to have to deal with resulting neurological issues.

When I was an active player with the New York Giants we played against Andre Waters, a defensive back who played for the Philadelphia Eagles and Arizona Cardinals. Waters developed a reputation as one of the hardest hitters in the NFL. Many offensive players who played against him also knew him for not being the cleanest player on the field. Once Waters retired, he apparently wrestled with some serious neurological issues, which eventually led him to commit suicide by shooting himself in the head. According to the *New York Times,* "Brain damage by way of successive concussions may have led to Waters's depression and ultimate suicide." Andre Waters died at only forty-four years of age, but the forensic pathologist who studied his brain tissue believed that "if Waters had lived another ten to fifteen years he would have been fully incapacitated." When something like that happens to an Andre Waters or Terry Long or Justin Strzelczyk or Mike Webster and now Dave Duerson, all retired players sit up and take notice. I know each occurrence got my attention. I was at the same place as Waters and Duerson sometime earlier in my own life when I had depression that came out of nowhere. When a current or former player dies, especially one that is so young, or by his own hands, all former players feel the pain of losing one of our own.

Losing one of our own from the NFL is one thing, but losing one as a young person who will never get the opportunity to play again is just as tough. That was the case of Ryne Dougherty, a junior at Montclair High School in New Jersey who in a junior varsity game against Don Bosco Prep sustained a concussion and eventually died as a result of the head trauma. Every year, many young people around the country, with one hit, sustain a concussion and die. Those are usually local stories that seldom get national attention. As each football season rolls around, players die as a result of various causes, but it seems that more and more are dying from head trauma.

Once upon a time, I enjoyed watching all levels of football, from little kids playing Pee Wee to the pros showing their stuff. I even provided commentary on television on college and pro games. But I now look at football from a much different perspective. Even as an old defensive player who could blindside a quarterback or lay out a running back trying to get a first down, I now cringe when I see violent hits and then hear the applause of fans who approve. My eyes are so well trained that I can almost tell instantly when a player is concussed on a play. But I also know that even though that player is injured, he's going to do his best to get back into the game; competing is what he's been trained to do!

The dangers of playing football are greater than most people realize. What few people take notice of are all the former players who are diagnosed with dementia or Alzheimer's and eventually pass away with little news coverage. Usually, only members of the person's immediate family and close friends know the pain of losing a loved one who was full of life and pride as an athlete but was lost due to traumatic brain injuries.

While I never wanted my sons to follow in my footsteps, almost every day I meet parents who with great pride tell me that they hope their infant or toddler son grows up to play professional football like me, Lawrence Taylor, or some other football great. Those parents are usually taken aback when I say, "I hope your kid opts for a good medical school instead of playing football." Generally people think I am kidding because I usually say it with a smile on my face, but I mean it. I hope parents promote education to the hilt and eventually focus on a good law, medical, or graduate school for their child to attend rather than hope their kid plays for some professional football team. One mother told me she "prays" for the day when her young son is standing next to the NFL commissioner on the stage at Radio City Music Hall. She says that because only the top picks in each year's NFL draft are introduced and get to stand next to and take pictures with the commissioner that day. I'm sure that mother loves her son, but I'm also certain that she has no clue that she would be leasing her son's body to be used for sport and entertainment, not fully understanding the ramifications of injuries her son might sustain and how they might affect him long after his football career is over. As I spoke with her, I could sense that her focus was totally on the dollars her son could generate as a top-round draft choice. Thoughts of a new home and new cars are usually on the minds of those who stand behind a young man and cheer him on. I know they mean well, but unfortunately they just don't know the risks in playing football.

When I was drafted, I only got one phone call letting me know that I had been selected by the New York Giants. There was no live television coverage or huge production made for players being drafted. The contract was decent for that time, especially for a kid coming right out of college. My draft day was so many years ago. Over the years, tremendous changes have taken place in promoting professional football to what it is now. Many fans and critics see today's

National Football League as being more about business and entertainment than sport. The league does a great job of marketing its brand and products through extensive coverage of the NFL draft on ESPN and the NFL Network. One of the more effective things that endear fans to the draft is that they show a player waiting with his family cheering him on backstage as he is about to be introduced to the football world. That can be a real feel-good story, especially when the player highlighted has battled his way through some type of adversity. The case of offensive lineman Michael Oher, a pick by the Baltimore Ravens, is a good example. Cameras can show a player's family's sheer excitement at his being selected, with their hopes of multimillion-dollar contracts to support family and friends. But those people won't ever see two things through all of the joy and excitement. The first is, after the player's being signed and brought in with much fanfare, when the career is over, no matter how long or how brief, the family never sees the player leaving the locker room with all his shit in garbage bags when he is shown the door. The second is, the family might be aware of a knee or a back injury that might cut a player's career short, but they may never know the neurological issues their loved one may experience as a result of the hits and thrills he provided on the football field.

To use a slang expression of one of my sons, "I'm not looking to knock anybody's hustle!" People are going to do what they want to do. But knowing what I know for sure, I want every parent who is considering signing a consent form for their son to play football, or any young man who is contemplating playing football, to be fully informed of the physical and especially the neurological risks they take when they play the game. Some might think that I have a bitter attitude toward the game. On the contrary, I harbor no bitterness toward the game, and I certainly don't harbor any bitterness toward anyone associated with the game. I have good relationships with many NFL owners, high school, college, and NFL coaches, the commissioner of the National Football League, Roger Goodell, and others within those circles.

When it comes to the hazards of football, no one is to blame! The nature of the sport is simply physical and violent. For years, football players played the way they were taught to play, hard and aggressively. Once their careers ended, whether it was high school, college, or professional, most transitioned to life after football not knowing that the hits they gave and took would affect them long after their last snap. I've done many media interviews sharing with viewers, listeners, and readers my thoughts on sports-related concussions. What has amazed me in sharing my feelings is the number of e-mails and letters I've gotten from men in their thirties, forties, and fifties who played football in high school and college and now sense something is wrong with them neurologically.

Most football fans look at football as it is now, not fully aware of the history and the brutality of the game, which came to a head in 1905 with nineteen fatalities nationwide. Today's fans don't know that President Theodore Roosevelt threatened to shut the game down if drastic changes were not taken to make it safer. While the game is much more sophisticated now and safer than in 1905, football is violent. In the early 1900s the concern was for the physical safety of the players; today the emphasis is on the neurological impact the game will have on players, especially younger players.

I can see the game from a much different perspective today than when I played. Years ago the prevailing concern was how the game could be made safer. The challenge is the same today, but people wonder, given the speed and the power of the game, how it can be made safer in regard to concussions. Concussions have always been a part of football regardless of the equipment used. Unless the game is reduced to half-speed and two-hand touch, players will continue to sustain head trauma.

I came to that conclusion long before I started to receive e-mails from parents of young men who, after suffering three or four concussions, still wanted to play with their friends. I came to that conclusion long before watching current college and professional players get concussions and seeing in high definition that dazed look in their eyes of not fully understanding what happened on that last play. And I came to the conclusion that football will always be violent and can have long-term effects when I recently visited one of my high school coaches in my hometown.

Several years earlier, Coach Stephen Brunson and I were inducted into the Florence, South Carolina, Athletic Hall of Fame together. Coach Brunson was honored as an outstanding athlete, having excelled in football in Florence and at the University of Georgia. While I have fond memories of Coach "Lukie" Brunson on the football field, later in life he was diagnosed with dementia and was moved to a nursing home. His wife visits him every day at the facility and feels that his condition is a result of the concussions he sustained long ago as a football player.

The glitz and pageantry of a prominent college bowl game or Super Bowl will always take precedence over the long-term effects of the collisions sustained by players trying to be the best in their sport. I remember that I was attracted to and influenced by what I saw as a youth. Little did I know that those players I wanted to be like were knocking themselves silly to win at all costs or just to be a part of their group. What they did was done with the best of intentions; they had no way of knowing that the injuries sustained in practice and in games would resurface weeks, months, or even many years down the line when their careers were long over.

Over the years I've encountered many young men who watched me play, including some who eventually made it to the NFL. Some, such as linebacker Zack Thomas, formerly of the Miami Dolphins, told me that he had a Harry Carson poster in his bedroom as a young athlete. He and others tried to pattern their play after what they saw me do on the field. While I may have influenced those men, they went on to influence even younger players, and on and on. So, as we see, we do. One generation follows in the footsteps of another. That is what I did when I was making my conversion from one position to another: I watched film of other linebackers to see how to play the position. Unfortunately, I could not see film or video on the unforeseen head issues they've since had to cope with over the years.

As long as what I call the "front side" of the game is glorified and emphasized with commercials, entertaining pregame shows, snazzy graphics, cheerleaders, and sound tracks, no one will ever begin to understand the "back side," where there are no spotlights, fanfare, or commercials. The back side will not be sponsored by Budweiser, Nike, Gatorade, or any other sponsor that wants to get its logo in front of the cameras for the world to see. The back side is now what is becoming more evident with former players being diagnosed with neurological disorders most likely precipitated by the blows to the head they sustained as players.

What I know for sure is all the players who are now having neurological issues never gave a thought about this turn in their lives when they were gladiators in the arena, putting their futures on the line playing football. Now, *they* are paying the price! Doctors and medical research groups are conducting study after study to determine the links between football and neurological issues later in life. These groups are making tremendous progress. Unfortunately, most of the players in today's games will long be out of football before they know the damage they've done to themselves and they start to forget simple things such as how to get home from the grocery store.

In advance the results of the years of research being done and yet to be done, I know for damn sure that no study will convince me that head injuries sustained as a player are not a contributing factor to serious neurological impairment in later life. As I continue to associate with former players, I can hear the despair in their voices when they confide in me that they are battling severe depression. I think I know football players well enough to understand that most would never acknowledge that unless they were in distress. I can also see with my own eyes the pain and anxiety in the faces of those who played before me, and the struggles of their family members who must now take care of once strong, talented, and proud men who were the best at playing football.

I'm not a brain surgeon but it doesn't take much for me to understand situations and come to my own conclusions. I subscribe to the duck theory. As simple as it is, if it looks like a duck, waddles like a duck, and quacks like a duck, it's a damn duck. What I know from being a participant and then living my life as best as possible confirms my own findings. I know for sure that I need to be proactive and not wait for my neurological symptoms to lead me to a place of darkness like so many other players who sustained concussions during their football careers.

Hell no! I would not play the game again knowing what I know now. But, if I could turn back the hands of time, I would want to enjoy the absolute best part of football. For me the best part of the game was not about winning and losing, it was not about the rivalries I played in, the plays I made, or the money I made. The best part of football was not about making the Hall of Fame. On the contrary, I've always appreciated that the best part of football was the people I had the opportunity to develop relationships with and to associate with in locker rooms, on buses, or on the fields of competition. On every level those coaches and players were men who inspired me to give the best I had, not just on the football field but also in life. I only wish I could bottle up all the experiences to share with every young person, especially young boys, all the lessons they may never learn while sitting at a desk in school. I wish I could share with young players what I learned from playing the game so that no other young men would feel the need to risk injuring their brains to compete or to learn lessons from the game.

As you read this, please understand that I am not against the sport of football; football has made me to some degree the person that I am today. But having played the sport on every level, I now want to inform those who don't know of the sometimes unforeseen risks of playing the game. First and foremost this book is to educate my own family, especially my children, of not just what the game is about, but what it took for their father to play, and where I am today physically, mentally, and neurologically. It is important for me to let those who know me understand who and what I was while I can still lucidly express myself. I live every day with the understanding that my life as I've known can change at any time.

I wanted to write this book to give other players and their family members an understanding of what some players who gave their all on football fields may be experiencing but are unable to communicate in their own words.

While many think it's cute to see a young boy wearing a football uniform and looking like a family's favorite player, I want every parent to understand the risk on the back side from not just a stellar professional career, but also from college and high school football.

My home is adorned with countless honors, trophies, plaques, recognitions, and awards. At the time of each presentation I had a fuzzy good feeling for being recognized or honored. Hours or a day later, the fuzziness would be gone. I continuously saw that what I did to achieve those honors and the price paid for the recognition did not make sense. Now, I know the risks were certainly not worth the rewards. I don't wish to seem ungrateful for any award I've been given, but the only thing I can say about those honors now is that they take up lots of space.

In light of the potential neurological problems I may be facing in my future, any recognition of what I did in football is long forgotten or means absolutely nothing to me. The past and the trinkets of playing the game are irrelevant now in my life as I move forward, especially as I watch my own heroes of the game age, deteriorate, and eventually pass away. I see my future much as I've seen that of proud men who with great pride and dignity played football the way they were trained to play.

I cannot undo anything that I've already done to my body and my brain. What's done is done! While I may have some regrets, I know for sure that I continue to hold close to my heart the men I led on every level of the game and the great honor of being their captain, not just when we played but even now as an advocate for their needs and concerns and as their captain for life!